Books from *Books Abroad*

The Perpetual Present

The Poetry and Prose of Octavio Paz

Octavio and Marie José Paz. Photograph by Mike Dirham

The Perpetual Present

The Poetry and Prose of Octavio Paz

Edited by Ivar Ivask

UNIVERSITY OF OKLAHOMA PRESS : NORMAN

Library of Congress Cataloging in Publication Data
Ivask, Ivar, 1927–   comp.
    The perpetual present.
    Includes papers originally presented at a Paz conference, sponsored by the De-
partment of Modern Languages of the University of Oklahoma and the Books abroad.
    CONTENTS: Sucre, G. Octavio Paz: poetics of vivacity.—Paz, O. "Paisaje inme-
morial." "Immemorial landscape," translated by T. J. Lewis.—Guibert, R. Paz on
himself and his writing: selections from an interview. [etc.]
    1. Paz, Octavio, 1914–   I. Oklahoma.
University. Department of Modern Languages. II. Title.
PQ7297.P285Z75   868   72–4568
ISBN O–8061–1048–1

Preface

> The spaces move away
> > The present is perpetual
> At the top of the world Shiva and Parvati
> Caress
> > Each caress lasts a century
> For the god and for the man
> > The same kind of time
>
> "Wind from All Directions"

It is common knowledge that Octavio Paz is the leading, exemplary intellectual of Latin America whose pronouncements are awaited with excited anticipation all over the literary world. His essayistic production ranges from literature to anthropology, from art to psychology, from philosophy to science, always aiming at the relevant synthesis for our age. But the incisiveness of his mind alone would not speak to so many if it were not matched by the imagination of a major poet. Since this is the case, poetry and prose, intuition and logic form an inextricable whole which bears the unmistakable imprint of Paz's personality.

It is too early for a definitive scholarly monograph on a writer who does not cease to astonish and surprise friends of literature from one year to the next. Just consider the year 1971 when Paz published *Renga*, a collective chain of quadrilingual poems which he authored together with French, Italian, and English poets; when he edited the first issues of the Mexican cultural and literary monthly *Plural*, inspired by *The New York Review of Books* but quickly surpassing it in both editorial imagination and contemporary layout; and when he began to deliver his Charles Eliot Norton lectures at Harvard, which are to be published soon as "Modern Poetry: A Tradition Against Itself." Also in that year *Las cosas en su sitio* (Things in Their Place) was a polemical exchange of views with Juan Marichal about the achievement of twentieth-century Spanish literature while *Traducción: literatura y literalidad* (Translation: Literature and Literalness) contained translations and interpretations of poems by John Donne, Stéphane Mallarmé, Guillaume Apollinaire, and e. e. cummings, at the same time discussing in depth problems of translation. Then 1972 brought the startling text *Le singe grammairien* (The Monkey Grammarian), which fused poetry and essay into a unique summary of Paz's thoughts on life and art to date. Who knows with what texts he will astound us tomorrow?

An exhaustive study would have to devote chapters to the poet (from the first *Luna silvestre* [1933] to the concrete poems of *Topoemas* [1971]), the far-ranging essayist (from the classic *The Labyrinth of Solitude* [1950] to *The Monkey Grammarian* of 1972), the thinker who represents a confluence of Western and Eastern thought (see for example his latest *Conjunctions and Disjunctions* [1969]), the translator (Bashō,

Fernando Pessoa, *et al*), the editor (*Taller, El hijo pródigo, Plural*), and the diplomat (in Japan and India). But luckily Paz is not even sixty, still exploding creatively, far from polishing and perfecting his collected works of years past. Therefore a many-faceted, refracted critical kaleidoscope of contemporary reactions seems more apt than a solemn academic canonization; criticism in movement suits better the mercurial explorer of the perpetual present of all ages.

This volume grew out of several recent efforts at the University of Oklahoma to gauge the scope and impact of Octavio Paz's achievement. In October, 1971, he gave two public lectures in English there, dealing with "The New Analogy: Poetry and Technology" and André Breton; his graduate seminar, "Poesía hispanoamericana moderna: postmodernismo y vanguardismo" (six lectures), elucidated aspects of Spanish American poetry in its evolution from romanticism to symbolism and on to the present, and the essential differences between Spanish American and Spanish Peninsular literature as well as European literature. His contact with the audience was quite different than that of Borges, who had concentrated on Argentine literature in 1969: while Borges had dwelt on the past, Paz launched us always into the present; while the world of Borges tended to be circularly closed and self-sufficient, the reality of Paz remained porous, open to the universal future; Borges appealed as the slightly ironic, humble bard of mythic memory, while Paz won over with his prophetic fervor, exploring the ever new, yet old as the dew in the morning. The presence of these two living classics made any simplified image of Spanish American letters impossible. This is, of course, precisely the impulse animating the Oklahoma Conferences on Writers of the Hispanic World and is their justification; the center of creative gravity seems to be shifting away from French and English to Spanish.

Sponsored by *Books Abroad* and the Department of Modern Languages, the first Oklahoma Conference was dedicated to the Castilian poet Jorge Guillén (1968), the second to Borges (1969), and the third to Paz. The opening words of President Paul F. Sharp were followed by the papers of Emir Rodríguez Monegal, Ramón Xirau, Ruth Needleman, Manuel Durán, Allen W. Phillips, Tomás Segovia, and Ricardo Gullón. Durán moderated the panel discussion in which Alfredo Roggiano, Rachel Phillips, and Tomás Segovia participated. At the dinner in his honor, Paz responded with the following generous words:

> From the day we arrived in Oklahoma, Marie-José and I have felt surrounded by a lucid cordiality which seemed a kind of spiritual correspondence to the brightness of these autumn days. We encountered here the lively friendship of Astrid and Ivar Ivask, two poets, two names more lunar than solar, two hearts closer to the hearth than to the snow; the broad hospitality of Lowell Dunham—generous as these fields interrupted here and there by graceful hills (one of those hills is named Francis); the warmth of Karen and Tom Lewis, impassioned and idealistic in the moral, not the philosophic sense—as is the North American youth of our day in its admirable rebellion; and among all these proofs of friendship, there is one we hadn't counted on: the exquisite courtesy of a cloudless sky and of radiant air. And all the friends who have gathered here to speak of a person I know and do not know, who has the same name as I but who is not to be confused with me and

who is the author of books that bear my name. Extraordinary, unusual days in whose atmosphere a sensation of strangeness developed—a delicious sensation not without irony and melancholy—which you have created in me when talking about me and my work as a writer. The other day I read that Picasso had said, "I frequently paint false Picassos." Something about that strikes me as curious: an author's works are perhaps not so much portraits of him, although each literary work contains autobiographical elements, as of his reader—his readers. Literary works are mirrors that never reflect the same images; they invent the author who writes them and the reader who recreates them. Thanks, kind friends, for such varied, intelligent and penetrating readings: I do not see myself in what I have written; rather I see you. I see landscapes and words created by you, by your creative sympathy. Thanks also to Dr. Jim Artman who has awarded me the key to this city, a city without walls or doors. Thanks finally, and above all, to President and Mrs. Sharp who have honored us with their presence.

The dinner was followed by a reading from Paz's poetry, during which he commented on each poem and read the Spanish original, while I followed up with a reading of available translations in English. Paz chose for this occasion seventeen poems from the collections *¿Aguila o sol?* and *Ladera este*: 1. "Escribo sobre la mesa," 2. "Jadeo, viscoso aleteo," 3. "Hace años," 4. "Un poeta," 5. "Hacia el poema I, II," 6. "Aquí," 7. "Madrugada," 8. "Juventud," 9. "Pueblo," 10. "Aparición," 11. "Madurai," 12. "México, Olimpiada 1968," 13. "Lectura de John Cage," 14. "Pasaje," 15. "Contigo," 16. "Ejemplo," and 17. "Viento entero."

The autumn 1972 issue of *Books Abroad* published the papers of the Paz Conference. They are reprinted again in the present volume together with several new contributions to round out this first comprehensive critical presentation of Paz's work in English.

Selections from Rita Guibert's revealing interview let the poet speak for himself and make one eager to read some prose fiction by him in the future. An overview of Paz's labyrinthine work is attempted by Guillermo Sucre in his penetrating essay and Ricardo Gullón in his article on "The Universalism of Octavio Paz." The mature poetry is elucidated by Ruth Needleman, Manuel Durán, and Ramón Xirau in their respective analyses. Two aspects of Paz the brilliant essayist are examined by Emir Rodríguez Monegal in his "Borges and Paz: Toward a Dialogue of Critical Texts" and Allen W. Phillips in his "Octavio Paz: Critic of Modern Mexican Poetry." The following articles are of a somewhat more specialized nature: Graciela P. Nemes views Paz within the context of Spanish and Spanish American Poetry; Elsa Dehennin traces the stone and water imagery in the poetry of Paz and at the same time contrasts their use with that of an admired contemporary, Jorge Guillén; Rachel Phillips, author of the first English book on Paz's poetry, explores his poetic treatment of women by comparing one of his poems with one by the French poet Paul Valéry; and Tomás Segovia again analyzes several of Paz's poems in the context of the most recent structuralist criticism and linguistic theories. The bibliography by and on Paz, compiled by Alfredo Roggiano, will prove invaluable to anyone who wants to pursue in depth the study of this intriguing author who has already been widely translated and examined.

In conclusion, special thanks are due to the translators of various articles, Tom J.

Lewis, Wendell McClendon, Nick D. Mills (from the University of Oklahoma), and Esther Whitmarsh Phillips, and to the Center for Inter-American Relations which provided financial assistance to several of these translators. Octavio Paz himself put at our disposal his new poem, and Marie José Paz sought out the rare photographs which illustrate our volume. Without the close collaboration of Professor Lowell Dunham, chairman of the Department of Modern Languages at the University of Oklahoma, neither this nor any of the preceding Oklahoma Conferences on Writers of the Hispanic World could have been so successfully realized. It was through the efforts of Dr. Paul F. Sharp, President of the University of Oklahoma, that financial support for the Paz Conference was made available.

Introducing Octavio Paz, I would like to apply his words about Bashō to himself: his is more than a literary work; it is an invitation to live truly both life and poetry. We learn that "El presente es perpetuo" or, to quote from the Estonian translation by Jaan Kaplinski, which I first read to Paz in Norman, and which he kept repeating as a magic charm, "Alati on olevik." The invitation is clear in whatever translation we may happen to read the message of this universal Mexican.

IVAR IVASK

Norman, Oklahoma
June, 1973

x

Contents

Illustrations

The review *Plural*

Paz's *Discos visuales* (1968)

Paz's *Blanco* (1967)

The Perpetual Present

The Poetry and Prose of Octavio Paz

Octavio Paz: Poetics of Vivacity

By GUILLERMO SUCRE

Conjunction, Disjunction and Reconstruction
of Language, Space and Time

About forty years ago, Octavio Paz, then 19 years old, published his first book of poems, *Luna silvestre* (1933). Over such a long period of time the work of a writer might well be reduced (fall prey) to the laws of inertia: his work may survive through repetition, even though the mark of a certain style and even talent may be recognized in it. One of the greater merits of Paz's work is that, far from declining into monotony with the passing of time, it tends to acquire intensity—a subtle, secret intensity.

It would be a mistake to think that this intensity is just the product of personal talent. Such a view leads inevitably to glorification of vanity. To resort constantly to talent as an explanation of everything (or as a way to cover up everything?) is, we know, one of the fetishes of modern times. That is why André Breton, in his first manifesto, rather arrogantly declared, "We have no talent." In contemporary Latin American literature, it might be said that Pablo Neruda has talent, and he himself calls attention to it explicitly in many of his poems; actually, his work is not very problematical and this is what has allowed him to celebrate everything in poetry. On the other hand, Borges, Lezama Lima and Paz do not have talent. What they do have is lucidity; their work is possible only because it is based on an ethic of writing, not simply on style.

Therefore, I believe that the intensity of Paz's work lies in its lucidity. This lucidity is evident in both the passion and the intelligence of his work which mutually and simultaneously confront and clarify one another. Unlike those whose primary reliance on passion leads them to ultimate blindness and dogmatism, which in turn acquires a pathetic character, Paz achieves passion through clarity. This is, in fact, the predominant characteristic of his work, evident even in its marked philosophical tendency. Though its philosophical content is not simply added but underlies his entire work, it is even less a residual commentary of someone who sets out to spread culture; it is a way of creating culture. In this sense, Paz has been one of the *chefs de file* of contemporary Latin American literature as an essayist and a literary critic as well as a poet. Paz has thus destroyed the stereotyped image of the Latin American poet as a being inspired by exuberance and instinct.

In Paz, furthermore, thought is a kind of wisdom, which, it should be said, goes hand in hand with experience, based not so much on erudition as on a particular stance *vis-à-vis* the world. This wisdom is also a system of relationships following the idea of the universality of all intellectual activity. This point is worth emphasizing. For Paz, the idea of universality does not have a privileged center—not Paris, nor London, nor New York—whose criteria must be followed. Today there are no longer any centers or patterns. We all speak, Paz says, if not the same language, at least the same idiom: an idiom which is no longer lineal but simultaneous. In his work, then, culture is a continual debate, and a confrontation of quite different views.

If one could say that surrealism, with its ascendancy in the XIX century, is the center of his book on poetics *El arco y la lira* (1956), one cannot ignore the fact that ideas from Heideggerian existentialism as well as Oriental philosophy are also combined with it; at the same time, the poetic aspect is formulated within a context which embraces the present-day searches of linguistics, anthropology, and even Marxist philosophy. On the other hand, in *El laberinto de la soledad*, Paz carries out one of the most penetrating studies—a kind of collective psychoanalysis—of the history of Mexico and the Mexican people. Nothing, however, is less nationalistic in the arrogant or narrow sense of the term; on the contrary, what prevails is an open vision which inserts the Mexican and even the Latin American into the problems of the present-day world. In one of his latest books of essays, *Conjunciones y disyunciones* (1969), Paz sees the history of civilizations as a dialectic between the body and the non-body. His approach covers the hidden structure (and the prejudices) of Christianity, Catholic or Protestant, as well as Oriental thought, especially tantrism. It concludes with the analysis of the most recent manifestations of this dialectic: the rebellion of youth and eroticism in the Western world.

Commenting on this book, the French philosopher Henri Lefebvre asked himself and at the same time gave the answer, "How many 'men of thought,' as we say, think on a world scale, on a planetary level? Octavio Paz knows both the Orient and the Western world, the philosophers of India as well as Judaeo-Christianism. He can contrast the ideological and problematic traditions of the capitalist and non-capitalist countries, of the industrialized countries and the lesser developed countries of Asia and Latin America."

This opinion is, of course, applicable to all of Paz's work. His work truly communicates an endless passion for the world: a continuous voyage—like his very life—across time and space. Voyages, relationships, movement. This is the character of his work and of his life. Voyages as distance and participation, as well as pleasure or exile; there is also in this idea something of a spiritual discipline: knowledge which seeks to found itself on experience, the intuition that knowledge of self (of individual and collective persons) is a path which envelops the world. Even that discipline takes on the character of a philosophy *vis-à-vis* destiny. Paz himself in a recent essay says, "The European proverb is false; to travel is not to 'die a little' but to exercise oneself in the art of leavetaking so that, having left part of oneself behind, one is able to learn to receive. Detachment: learning."

Paz's work is therefore a broad system of combinations. It is evident that any literary work is autonomous to the degree that it cannot be reduced to the simple reproduction of reality. That autonomy nevertheless does not imply that the work is strictly an individual creation. It is superfluous to say that; literary work always has a relation to definite contexts, especially literary contexts. In literary works such as Paz's, these contexts must be very diverse, and the author himself has made reference to them in his essays. Paz speaks frequently of the modern tradition as a "tradition of fragmentation," except that the concept of fragmentation should not be understood as negation but rather as an explanation of one's heritage.

His work, thus, adheres above all to the Mexican tradition. When Paz appeared on the scene, poetry in his country seemed to be dominated by two trends: the meditative poetry of José Gorostiza and Xavier Villaurrutia, obsessed by metaphysical questioning and the inevitability of death; and the *physical* poetry, sensory and filled with light, of Carlos Pellicer. Paz combines these two tendencies and transcends them. His metaphysical meditations do not force him to a belief in solipsism, as in Gorostiza and Villaurrutia; further, death is for him an experience inherent in life itself. The expansion of sensitivity is, moreover, in his work, something other than the ecstatic joy of Pellicer, a form of knowledge and even of exploration of the world. In this latter sense, Paz tends to prolong, obviously with a new vision, one of the characteristics of Mexican poetry of the XVII century: poetry as knowledge and a questioning of knowledge such as is found in Sor Juana Inés de la Cruz (*Primero sueño*). But there are two Mexican poets particularly with whom Paz feels more affinity, Lopez Velarde and José Juan Tablada, both schooled in the aesthetics of Hispano-American modernism. Lopez Velarde, with his erotic-religious drama and critical and ironical expression, is an example for Paz of the uprooted contemporary conscience. Perhaps Tablada is even more important for Paz because he is the first to introduce the *haiku* into Hispanic poetry and one of the first to practice ideographic poetry; in these terms, he is among those who pave the way for a kind of *spatial writing* which will later characterize the most recent works of Octavio Paz, although it is true that the authentic Latin American precedent of this style of writing is found in the Chilean Vicente Huidobro, with whom Paz has many affinities.

In the context of contemporary Spanish—not to speak of Quevedo or Góngora—Paz's early interests seem to be more closely related to the poetry of Juan Ramón Jiménez but without sharing its excessive spiritual character, and to the work of Antonio Machado, whose poetic principles (the idea, for example, of *otherness*) are clearly visible in Paz's own conception. Nevertheless, with the passing of the years, Paz has felt more closely identified with two other poets, Jorge Guillén and Luis Cernuda. He identifies with Guillén through a new way of experiencing poetry as an intelligible sensitivity to the world and as a *presence* in which successive time is abolished. In Cernuda's work he is attracted by what he himself calls the "rediscovery of the tragic conscience, i.e., an acceptance of the human condition which discounts any world after death either in time or space"; the debate as well between the force of desire and the inhibitions imposed by society.

His contexts are broadened first in the direction of France. Frequently—and this is still true—Paz is considered a surrealist. In the 1940's, after his experience in the Spanish Civil War, Paz not only becomes thoroughly familiar with the poetics of this movement but also becomes one of its members. Thus, he participates in some of its expositions and is included in its anthologies. But, in contrast to the younger generation of surrealists (especially in Latin America), Paz is not tempted by simple technical formulas and less by automatic writing which becomes nothing more than verbal mechanism. In the French tradition, I think, there are two poets who left their mark on Paz's writing: Mallarmé and his strivings for open work and spatial text, and Apollinaire with his calligraphic poems and the simultaneousness of poetic discourse. On the other hand, Paz is faithful to the surrealistic spirit: the exaltation of eroticism, the search for the alliance between imagination (or dream) and reality, and the need to break away from the set forms of language. It is not surprising, therefore, that the surrealist experience brought him closer to, rather than alienating him from, most recent French structuralism. For Roland Barthes it is possible to speak of a structuralist activity just as it was possible to speak of a surrealist activity. What is more, he comes to recognize that surrealism "produces the first experience in structural literature." In this respect, it would be sufficient to recall that, just as they devoted themselves to the investigation of dreams, the surrealists devoted themselves also to the investigation of language: the multiple meanings of words, its ambiguity, and the subconscious threads of which it is made; the plays on words were, in addition, a way of rediscovering and liberating the energy of words themselves.

Another context which throws light on Paz's work is his experience in the Orient where he lived at different times (Japan and India) and his study of various aspects of their cultures while there. Far from the practice of a new kind of exoticism, this experience is, for Paz, a field of confrontation in which the Western world seeks to complement itself and, even, its secret affinities. That experience not only appears in a conceptual way in his books of essays but also and perhaps more profoundly in his poetry. In 1956, in collaboration with Eikichi Hayashiya, Paz publishes what is perhaps the first version in a Western language of Matsuo Bashō's book, *Oku no Hosomichi*.[1] The clairvoyance of the human condition in this book—fulfillment and at the same time frailty—as well as its laconism and compactness of language—especially in its haikus—were doubtless an enlightening example for Paz. His brief composition of poems entitled "Las piedras sueltas" (1955) is the first time he uses the technique of haiku in his work, the constructive simplicity of which corresponds, also in Paz, to a kind of elementary cosmic force: the existence of the world is its presence, man is vital and mortal communion with the universe. In his latest book of poems, *Ladera este* (1969), this vision acquires broader implications. In 1969, when

6

he came back from India, Paz carried out a singular poetic experiment; in Paris he joined three other poets of different languages (the Frenchman Jacques Roubaud, the Italian Edoardo Sanguineti, and the Englishman Charles Tomlinson) and together they wrote each in his own language, a book which they called *Renga*,[2] a type of Japanese poem written by several poets in collaboration. In a significant way, Paz thus succeeded in bringing together two traditions: the Oriental and the surrealist whose poets, as we know, practiced both automatic and collective writing. This *Renga* was also an application of the principle Lautréamont had already proposed: "Poetry should be made by everybody."

Paz's work also touches other contexts. I think I have pointed out the ones that seem to me to be important. I ought to make one final observation in this respect. In a true writer, contexts do not serve as an example but as stimuli: they awaken creative imagination and, especially, they open the possibility of new combinations. It is in this latter sense that one must see their function in Paz's work so that more than simplicity being justified by the contexts which surround it, the work itself justifies them: it demonstrates their validity and the power they still contain. The creative adventure is for Paz the recovery and a modification of what precedes it. This will be the nature of future art. Paz proposes it in an essay, "The works of the time which is dawning will not be governed by the idea of lineal succession but that of combination: conjunction, dispersion and reconstruction of languages, spaces and times."

The Primary Truth of Life is its Vivacity

In an essay written in 1943 when he was a young man, Paz quoted a phrase from Nietzsche as a summary of his own creative efforts, "Not life eternal but eternal vivacity: that is the most important thing." This philosophical viewpoint is not marginal in his poetic work. Again and again with increasing intensity, it appears throughout his work; it is, in fact, its deepest drive. In a 1948 poem, Paz says, "beyond the boundaries of existence,/ another fuller life calls us"; in another poem in 1958, "I look for a time lively as a bird." In a poem appearing in his latest book (*Ladera este*) it reappears as a culminating and more basic statement:

> Los absolutos las eternidades
> Y sus aledaños
> No son mi tema
> Tengo hambre de vida y también de morir

How does one characterize this vivacity? And further, how is it expressed?

Let us say first what is most obvious: vivacity is intensity, energy. As such it always seems like a challenge which it is impossible to accept. How, in fact, can one always attain that intensity and prolong a moment of life with its original force? Eternity may or may not be an abstraction for those who aspire to it. It demands faith not proof. Vivacity on the other hand can be founded only on the concrete, on a desire which, although fulfilled, never stops being a desire; its true domains are those of the body and of the time at hand which in themselves are ephemeral. If eternity means passion for that which is transcendent, vivacity aspires to be transparency of the immanent and therefore aspires to convert the relative (the *here* and *now*) into an absolute. Therefore, it demands not only proof, it is itself a proof, and certainly not the easiest one to accept.

But further the opposition between vivacity in the world and vivacity in the poem does not exist as far as Paz is concerned. Or if there is an opposition it would not be erroneous to think that he would choose vivacity in the world, except that this option also implies vivacity in the poem. Throughout his work there persists the question which Paz raises in the introduction to *El arco y la lira* (1956): "Wouldn't it be better to turn life into poetry rather than to make poetry from life? And cannot poetry have as its primary objective, rather than the creation of poems, the creation of poetic moments?" It should be pointed out: one should not be led to think that Paz is proposing to make life beautiful; life is neither beautiful nor ugly, noble nor ignoble. It is not a question, therefore, of these two apparently opposite formulae but that of two identical formulae, as we know; neither "artistic life" (the ideal of vague romanticism) nor "vital art" (the ideal of all realism, including the so-called socialist realism). With that question, what Paz is actually formulating is the same utopia as the surrealists; to practice poetry, to have poetry govern man's experience in this world, which would not be possible if the world itself does not recover its original plenitude, i.e., its unity: that extreme point, according to Breton, where all opposing forces strike an agreement.

Vivacity in Paz would be this extreme point of universal reconciliation. But, even as this reconciliation is not assured beforehand, it must be sought and made possible, and so vivacity is also a search; not only of experience which has been lived but an experience to be lived in the poem. That is, lived experience has to be rediscovered in its intensity in words: it is further on this plane where it finally becomes understandable and reveals its true meaning. In some way, then, vivacity is a verbal invention. In the same poem, *Ladera este*, mentioned above, when he attempts to define himself, the author says: "I am a history/ A memory which invents itself" and he adds: "I go in darkness and I plant signs." Thus, it is not a matter of expressing arrogant vitalism or of exalting a purely sensorial plenitude. To choose the instant —instantaneous vivacity—is not to choose pleasure but clarity, Paz warns. Clarity: to become aware of the frailty of all vivacity, of all intensity; on the one hand, threatened by time; on the other, threatened by its own energy—"if it lasted another instant" it would consume us, says Paz in a poem. Clarity, in spite of that double threat, chooses vivacity. From this perspective, it is still the union of opposites; an incandescent experience in which passion and stoicism both participate. As Paz explains in an essay on the poetry of Bashō (1954): "Life's original truth is its vivacity and that vivacity is the consequence of life's being mortal and finite: the fabric of life is death." In that essay, Paz also translates some of Bashō's haikus, one of which might illustrate his own attitude:

> Admirable
> aquel que ante el relámpago
> no dice: la vida huye . . .[3]

For this reason, vivacity is more than just a theme about which Paz writes poetry. Vivacity is in the very structure of this work. One even has the impression that it becomes more intense as the work unfolds. I do not know whether it has anything to do with what the critics (or literary publicists, in this case) usually call "poetic grandeur"; it seems to me indeed that it is related to the idea that man has of youth: a gift of being able to see the world with wonder. A gift also of preserving a certain innocence, although that innocence does not exclude—rather it supposes—wisdom and even intelligence. To be more exact: the gift of wonder not simply the gift of wanting to be original or modern; the gift in turn of innocence, not the gift of a dubious tellurism or primitiveness.

In effect, if Paz's poetry is experimental it is so to the extent that for him all poetic language is exploration of the world; nevertheless, he avoids hermeticism and retains a sense of intelligibility and even of simplicity. On the other hand, Paz rejects anything experimental which he considers merely a zeal for novelty. "The ideas of originality, personality and novelty," he says, "are the clichés of our time."

On the other hand, the telluric concepts in his poetry are somewhat removed from the tellurism found in some Latin American poets from the Argentine Leopoldo Lugones to the Chilean Pablo Neruda: descriptive exuberance, geographic enumerations, an almost interminable list of elements of nature—everything, of course, crowded with metaphors. Nature in Paz is always free from accumulative and picturesque excesses. Only a few elements are necessary to make the presence of Nature felt; those elements, while very material, seem to be very archetypal. Their very clarity transfigures them. Like certain painters (i.e., Braque) who worked for years on the same theme, Paz repeats them continually in his work: the high noon, transparent water, sparkling stones, the sound of the wind, the tree, birds, the dry hot earth. It is a sun-drenched, austere nature. But Paz sees in it especially the spectrum of all human relations. Thus, in his great poems—*Piedra de sol*, "Viento entero," *Blanco*—there is a kind of identity of poetic space with cosmic space: the poem conveys a movement which in turn conveys the movement of the world. More than cosmogony, what Paz strives for, I believe, is cosmology: he seeks the palpable and intelligible order of things. Because of that, there is in his poetry a natural mysticism: he aspires to no transcendency but to rescuing the original body of the world. In a poem in *Ladera este*, he invokes Shiva and Parvati, the couple representative of erotic energy in Hinduism, but he invokes them not as gods but as "images of the divinity of man" and, finally, he asks not for supernatural grace but grace of the world itself:

> Shiva y Parvati:
> > La mujer que es mi mujer
> Y yo,
> > Nada les pedimos, nada
> Que sea cosa del otro mundo:
> > > Sólo
> La luz sobre el mar,
> La luz descalza sobre el mar y la tierra dormidos

Paz's poetry is a search for the original purity of the world, but it does not assume to establish any absolute innocence, much less to place itself in a period prior to the existence of all culture. What he attempts rather is a reconciliation of nature and culture, historic man and original man. Paz would not easily say what Neruda said with so much assurance in one of his *Odas elementales*: "I was not born of a book,/ my poems/ have not comsumed poems,/ they devour/ impassioned events,/ they are nourished by the open air,/ they draw their nourishment/ from the earth and from man." Apart from the fact that Whitman had already said this with more sobriety and more authentic candor (at least without resorting to pathetic and dietary images), a certain conscious or unconscious confusion underlies this attitude. I don't know whether it is completely contained in this context but I think that one of Paz's phrases could be in part (im)pertinent: "There are two types of barbarians: the one who knows he is a barbarian (the vandal, the Aztec) and presumes to assume a civilized life style; and the civilized barbarian who lives the 'end of a civilization' and tries to escape by submerging himself in the waters of savagery. The savage does not know that he is a savage: barbarianism is, then, feeling disgraced because of savagery or feeling nostalgia for savagery. Both are founded on inauthenticity."

Inauthenticity may be explained because beneath this new primitivism there lies the idea that the world preserves its total meaning which, in turn, is expressed in a total work by a unique poet. But seen from Paz's perspective, the meaning of the world (as nature and especially as history) and the notion of literary work, have become problematical. Poetry can speak of the plenitude or the totality of the world only from the point of view of its absence, emptiness and fragmentation. "Perhaps in out time," Paz says, "the artist can no longer call forth presence. The other road, opened by Mallarmé, is left: to manifest absence, to incarnate emptiness." In the same way, a literary work—as a finished and perfect object, as an original creation of its author or as a totalizing image of the world—is an illusion. An illusion, let us say, founded on a false concept of history: the idea of progress and perfection. For Paz, there are no longer works but only fragments of works, scattered signs that search for a meaning. In an essay in 1967, he even foresees: "The epoch which is beginning now will finally put an end to 'works' and contemplation will melt into *action*. Not a new art: a new ritual, a celebration—the invention of a form of passion which will be a repetition of time, space and language."

An Immense and Total Word

According to the meaning which it attempts to express, one could say that Paz's work has its center of irradiation in the book *Semillas para un himno* (1954). The dominant point of view in this book is essentially utopian: the intuition of an original time—a time without time or that is all time—in which man lived in complete harmony with other men and with the universe; a language which was the perfect representation of the universe corresponded to this social and cosmic harmony,[4] and the

10

intuition of that kind of "Golden Age" is what gives depth to the book. Paz condenses it in his poem entitled "Fábula":

> Todo era de todos
> > Todos eran todo
> Sólo había una palabra inmensa y sin revés
> Palabra como un sol
> Un día se rompió en fragmentos diminutos
> Son las palabras del lenguaje que hablamos
> Fragmentos que nunca se unirán
> Espejos rotos donde el mundo se mira destrozado

If then, according to this poem, poetry is condemned to fragmentation, it also seems destined to the evocation of the *original Word*, that "immense and total word." Although inexpressible, it alone makes it possible for the poet to say what he says. The entire book is organized around that Word: not as a presence, certainly, but as an absence. "At dawn the nascent being seeks its name," is the beginning of the first poem. A very significant beginning: dawn is a birth whose existence does not reside so much in material expansion as it does in the identity of the name, i.e., the world must be created through the word. It is yet revealing that the metaphorical system of the book uses elements of the language itself. On the one hand the world has its particular idiom: "The light spreads its fan of names/ There is a beginning of a hymn like a tree." On the other hand, words become objects of the world: "It speaks/ a piragua flows towards the light/ A word moves forward at full sail." Word and world are equivalent or seek their equivalency. That is why he chose for the title of the book *seeds* instead of *words*. In addition, the title indicates that neither the world nor the word are given reality but one which must be sought. Both are signs pointing *to* an absolute or original reality.

This book refers us to one of Paz's much earlier texts *Libertad bajo palabra* (1949). Its title "Libertad bajo palabra" in turn served as the title of a volume in which this text was published and later as the title of the revised and enlarged edition in which Paz collects all his poetic work up to 1958. Then and afterwards it was published as an introduction, a poetic not a conceptual introduction, in which the imagination, not the intellect, speaks.

The predominant word in it is *invent*. The poet does not say that he is going to express a world, not even *his* world, but that he is going to invent it: in all of its spatial or physical, spiritual or moral diversity, and, according to the most disparate signs (obscure or luminous, elevated or lowly). Nevertheless, throughout a long enumeration one perceives that what the poet is doing is naming the world in its minute reality, and even with an acuity which does not exclude the sordid. What is it then that he is inventing? At a certain moment, the text seems to fall into an abyss: it passes from the enumeration of the world to the counterpoint of conscience faced with itself. This conscience is dizzying: it has no center or identity; it is at one and the same time "the judge, the victim, and the witness" and therefore can appeal to nothing; it is divided between solipsism ("there are no doors, there are mirrors": "this clarity does not abandon me") and an effort of communication which, nevertheless, cannot be realized without violence ("I will break the mirrors, I will tear my image to bits"). Alienation is then two-fold: "the solitude of conscience and the conscience of solitude." So that if conscience attempts to project itself towards the world by imagining it, this is because it is isolated from it. From this act there comes "a world dreamed in suffering." *In suffering*, not because it is dreamed but because it is dreamed as real: the dream is not an escape into irreality but a ransoming of reality. The poet does not invent *a* world but *the* world, not *another* world but *this* world. The invention therefore goes back to the search for reality. It is also true that this search goes back to the invention: the dreamed reality is infinitely more fulfilling than its pure contingency; reconciliation of opposites: reality recovers its true meaning and is seen again with "clear eyes." And so the text begins by imposing a distance *vis-à-vis* the world; that is, a dimension where contradictory appearances vanish: "There beyond, where the boundaries (end), the way becomes hazy. Where silence begins. I advance slowly and I populate the night with stars, with words, with the breathing of remote waters which await me where the dawn begins." From night to dawn the distance becomes *presence*: the dream is what makes this transformation possible.

Invention of reality: this is, I believe, what separates Paz's poetry from that of the Chilean Vicente Huidobro, whose intent was to create *another* reality, parallel to the world's reality. It is at the same time what brings Paz closer to surrealism. The wonderful thing about the concept of the marvellous, Breton said, is that there is no longer anything marvellous but rather reality. And because of that, for the surrealists and for Paz, poetry is above all else an *exploration* and at the same time a *practice* in the world.

But Paz's text does not end on this alone. At the end the poet says: "Against the silence and the noise I invent the Word, freedom that creates itself and creates me each day." It is obvious that this phrase emphasizes the reciprocal relationship between the poet and language. But it seems that the predominant feature in this relationship is language. The poet invents it to the extent that he rediscovers it: language speaks through his mouth but it speaks freely. In effect, what is defined as freedom is not so much the poet as language, even the poet has access to freedom through language. That language is free means, as Paz himself recognizes in his most recent essays, that it is a consequence of neither human nor divine power; language constitutes an unconscious system which bases itself on its own laws: that is why it is a "freedom *which* invents itself." Furthermore, language is free because, in its origins, it contains multiple meaning: its many values reproduce the diversity of the world and the relationships of man with the world. Thus when Paz speaks of the *Word* he is referring to the *original Word* where true vivacity resides. And so for him poetry is always "the revelation of our original condition." So that if language invents us, it also reveals us to ourselves. Invention and revelation are equivalent terms in Paz except that this equivalency perhaps should not be understood on a purely semantic level; the equivalency exists because both terms are located in a field of mutual attraction. In this poetry the world is an immanence ("water flowing and pouring out prophecies all night") and the work of the poet consists in making it possible for this immanence finally to be revealed or become, although only for an instant, presence, vivacity. To invent is then to have the clairvoyance of this possibility or to imagine it.

All of these texts we have analyzed represent a true zeal for language. This zeal, nevertheless, is always found in Paz side by side with a sharp critical conscience. Why? All language tends to perish or lose its value because it carries within itself its own contradiction. In effect, language is use, and, as such, is the object of a double threat. On the one hand, languages are mortal; they are condemned to a given situation and a given time. This is not, I think, the greatest threat for them; on the contrary, in some way it reveals something which is essential—the frailty of language—of its nature. The greatest threat, it seems to me, is the degradation to which language is submitted by the deliberately imprecise use which society makes of it: words serve for everything and for everybody, that is, they are of no use for anything or to anyone; far from being a means—and an end—or true dialogue, they become instruments of domination and manipulation. Isn't that one of the evils of present-day society? Don't we even have the impression that there are too many words and yet not enough? We are lacking in words but are unaware of the silence caused by their absence. This silence is regarded as an incapacity or source of embarrassment; it is no longer wisdom or the recognition of a limitation. We live in a frenzy of words which in the present day are a form of propaganda. Everything has now become advertising, i.e., aggressive verbiage. Advertising has discredited silence and, as Paz himself says, "has at the same time discredited language. One is inseparable from the other; the art of speaking was always the art of knowing when to be quiet."

We must then return to language the richness and clarity of its origin. This task does not require that it be subject to any impossible purification. There is no pure poetry (as Juan Ramón Jiménez postulated) nor impure poetry (as Pablo Neruda seemed to respond). Like Jorge Guillén, Paz chooses another more exact formulation: there is no privileged language; poetry is the poem. The effusiveness of the "lyrical poets" and the bitterness of the "social poets," Paz observes, are already anachronistic; poetry today is criticism. And its criticism begins with the criticism of language, which is the most basic form of criticism of the world: the foundation of this world is language and not the opposite. The history of man, according to Paz, could be reduced to the relationship between word and thought. In this sense, like Pound in his book *Guide to Kulchur*, Paz quotes a passage from the *Analects* of Confucius, which may serve as an example. When Confucius was asked what he would do first if put in charge of a government, he answered, "Call people and things by their names, i.e., by their correct denominations, see that terminology is exact." In a more recent book Paz adds, "When a society becomes corrupted, the first thing that deteriorates is its language" (*Posdata*, 1970).

Criticism of language is, then, another one of the dominant perspectives in Paz's work and appears in it almost from the beginning. In one of his poems in the 1940's, appropriately titled "Words," Paz expressed it in an elementary way: "Turn them over,/ catch them by the tail (let the whores scream)"; "make them, poet, swallow all their words." This attitude gradually becomes more extreme and acquires the feeling of an experience which is at the same time violently and intimately solitary with regard to language. On the one hand, the will to destroy language, to put it through a kind of trial of atonement, the purpose of which would be to regain the word (and its richness), we must first make it quiver and transform it. "He who has not felt the temptation to destroy language," said Paz in an essay, "or to create another one is not a poet; neither is he who has not experienced the fascination of non-meaning and the no less terrifying one of inexpressible meaning" (*Corriente alterna,* 1967).

This is the theme of his book *¿Aguila o sol?* (1951). Written in rapid, concise prose, the first part ("Los trabajos del poeta") is an exploration of words in the *physical* world: plays on words, puns, alliterations, abrupt antitheses, destruction of meaning, search for other meaning—which evokes a long tradition beginning with Quevedo's "Los Sueños," through Huidobro's "Altazor" up to the experiments of the surrealists and even those of the French writer Raymond Roussel; at the same time, it seems to be a point of reference, and warning, which has an influence on the new Latin American novelists. That first part revolves around a central question: "Where is the infirmity? Where did th infection begin, in the word or the thing?" Whatever the answer may be, what Paz proposes is not so much an explanation as a search for a language which in itself contains the power of an exterminating and demystifying force. "Today I dream," says the poet, "of a language of knives and picks, acids and flames, a language of whips"; "a language which cuts the breath, rasping, slashing, cutting." That is, he searches for a language capable of affecting reality and changing it. Capable of absorbing history and giving it new meaning. And so, after all the apocalyptic visions, the book ends with a text entitled "Hacia el poema." As is evident, it is again a question of an effort in the direction of poetry and not the poem considered as a result. That is, the poem will be possible only when history is changed. When, as Paz says, history is no longer a nightmare or slavery ("a constellation of blood"). "When history awakens, the image becomes an act, the poem takes form; poetry enters into action." At that moment, poetry becomes identified with life itself and the destiny of man; in some way it disappears as writing and becomes incarnate in the world.

On the other hand, the poem is an immersion in the emptiness of words. "In the middle of a poem I am always overcome with a great feeling of helplessness," says Paz in *La estación violenta* (1958). This is the perspective of a book such as *Salamandra* (1962). In it, words do not say what they say and we must make them say what they do not say. To write is to discover beyond the written (or spoken) word another word which directs it and which, nonetheless, never flowers in the poem. To speak is an ambiguous act which leads to the contradiction or negation of all speech ("What you say can be unsaid/ From silence to shouting/ Unheard"). So, this fact paralyzes language and places the world between parenthesis. "I know that I am alive/ Between two parentheses." The *parenthesis*: Paz uses it repeatedly in this book. It is a technique frequently used by modern poets such as Cummings. But in the poetry of Cummings, this technique has, we might say, a *positive* value: it intensifies meaning, it makes of one text several texts. In Paz, the parenthesis intensifies the non-meaning. In the poem "La palabra escrita," this technique is carried to an extreme: the only thing the poet mentions is a truncated phrase ("The first word is already written") to which he continually superimposes, in parenthesis, the comments of a conscience which intuitively looks for another word but which never manages to be voiced and remains implicit only. Thus, its theme is the parenthesis as an absence of the poem.

Almost all the book is dialectic play in which nothing crystallizes: a *beginning* which repeatedly remains in suspense and unresolved: opposition between discourse and silence. The world and language thus appear to suffer from a sort of neutrality. And what Paz proposes is a return to innocence ("innocence and not science:/ Learn to be silent in order to speak") and the search for the original word, "the burning word of the beginning," the word "before the fall." But, just as in *¿Aguila o sol?*, the book does not end in a complete vacuum. Its last poem "Sólo a dos voces") is developed, as is frequent in this poetry, on two levels: nature and the act of writing a poem. The cosmic moment now, in contrast to the solar orbit, always constant in Paz, is the winter solstice: the lethargy of the earth and the disappearance of the sun. In the same way, the poem is the disappearance of the word, the forgetting of language itself. "Not what you say, what you forget/ Is what you say;/ Today is the winter solstice/ In the world/ Today you are separated/ In the world;/ Today is the world/ A soul in sorrow in the world." But what Paz suggests basically is concealment of the word in order to make way for, like the renewal of the earth, its new presence. This recalls what Breton proposed in the *Second Manifesto*: "I demand true, deep concealment of Surrealism." Both attitudes have, I believe, a ritual meaning: not a disillusioned withdrawal of beautiful souls, but criticism of the abjection and emptiness of contemporary history. In both, what speaks is clarity and not resignation.

Destruction and atonement of the word: a search for its authenticity. Hiding of the word: search for its real presence. This dual critical movement, far from falling into an impasse, creates a feeling of continuous tension which is the poem itself. In the final text of *¿Aguila o sol?* Paz says: "We turn in the animal womb, in the mineral womb, in the temporal womb; find the way: the poem."[5] The poem is the outcome because in it opposites are reconciled and so the original meaning (and therefore the new meaning) of the world comes forth. Because of this, poetry in turn tends to make of itself a destiny, i.e., a true utopia. "Modern poetry is an effort to abolish all meanings because poetry itself is a prophecy of the ultimate meaning of life and man," Paz states.

Reconciliation of opposites, the poem is in itself an erotic force. "The poem prepares an amorous order," Paz says. His great poems tend to create that order; an order which is erotic and cosmic. In effect, they continually propose the identity between woman and nature ("I go through your body as through the world"). Further, the erotic is accomplished as participation in the movement of the world; love is unloosed—and measures itself—just as for the natural elements, the night and the day, the seasons are the temple of their true ritual. Thus, love is above all exultation of the body without falling into any superficial sensualism: the body of woman is the emblem of the world and *vice versa*. In this poetry we perceive in truth that the body is man's unity recovered and the very foundation of the world; in it all of the analogies and transmutations of the universe are realized; through it Paz imagines a secret but immanent order of things. Because passion is itself passion: not the mere instinct but instinct of the imagination. The body, says Paz, is a musical and sacred instrument of depersonalization and participation in an absolute reality. Depersonalization does not mean indiscrimination: love in Paz is always selection and therefore an adventure of the couple; it means a re-encounter with the universe. This eroticism then is a total experience which eliminates moral limits; it is neither moral nor immoral, neither noble nor ignoble. Its value is the intensity with which the couple or the individual commit themselves. What justifies it, if it needs justification, is passion.

Eroticism therefore includes *criticism*. In the first place, it is a criticism of sublimated Occidental love: the body saved (idealized) by the spirit. The movement of Paz's poetry would be the opposite: the spirit saved (incarnate) by the body. It is therefore a criticism of the Western world itself, whose constitutional infirmity, Paz points out, is that it makes a secret of culture, the spirit, and sublimations. Finally, it is a criticism of history. In effect, in his poem *Piedra de sol*, Paz confronts the destructive power of history, which makes of man an abstraction, with conciliating power of the erotic couple; against the abstract, the concrete, the body. In the same way, in another of his great erotic poems, "Viento entero," love becomes a multiple unity; it is a *perpetual present* which crosses diverse times and space. In this poem Paz foresees, as he later says in an essay, *the death or waning of the future*: not only as a reaction against rectilinear and progressive time, but also as criticism of a plenitude which is always postponed. So we see that Paz's utopia is not, in the traditional sense, an absolute which is never achieved and which acts as the perfecting model or archetype; his is *the utopia of now, of the present*: without waiting for the great beyond but creating one here.

Signs of a Fragmented Alphabet

In a poem already quoted, Paz saw the language we speak as a fragmentation of the original language of man. Nevertheless, that fragmentation does not appear immediately in the body of his poetry itself. To a great extent, Paz's poems continue to be structured according to a successive movement although such a movement presents cyclical time—the best example of this would be *Piedra de sol*, a long work in hendecasyllabic verse. Beginning with *Salamandra*, fragmentation invades the structure of the poem. "Signs of a fragmented alphabet," a phrase with which Paz defines in a certain way the contemporary world, could equally well illustrate the very nature of his most recent poetry. The poem is no longer governed so much by certain order as by disorder. The verse ceases to be linear and may be read on different levels, the run-on lines create a continuous "suspense" in the phrase which, although not completely, is generally liberated from a rigorous punctuation; in other words, the poem attempts to sketch the world which it imagines and therefore it becomes progressively spatial: rhythm and even silence are visualized, the *statement* is not completely intelligible if it is not *seen* at the same time it is heard. On the other hand, this material dispersion of the language creates semantic dispersion: the ambivalencies and even the ambiguities are multiplied, the poem becomes more and more a fabric of relationships and, according to these relations, other poems are gradually born within the poem itself.

So, in Paz the concept of the *open work* becomes the structure itself and the theme of his work, which in turn seems to be the formal realization of his idea of poetry as man's revelation to himself of his own condition. In effect, if out of one text there come other texts, this means that the poem is created and born from within itself; in this sense, it becomes an autonomous world independent of the author. In the same way the reading of the poem approaches the experience of revelation: it depends on the choice by which the reader may combine in one way or another the plurality of possible texts. In either case, the poem is an imminence: without ceasing to be what it is, it seems ready to be *something else*. "Each reader is another poet; each poem, another poem," Paz says. It is this intuition which takes form in *Blanco* (1967), perhaps Paz's most dazzling poem in the last several years.

Paz's metaphorical system has also become complex and at the same time more simple. I am not insinuating any paradox. Its complexity has little to do with the hermeticism of a certain type of contemporary Occidental poetry. It resides rather in the possibilities it opens or the relationships it suggests; that system requires furthermore a certain attitude on the part of the reader, both aesthetic and ethical. This system is also simple because it turns wealth into barrenness (and the opposite is equally true); it is not presented as a talent for invention. It gives another meaning to this talent. To invent is to *see* the world. In effect, in the new image of this poetry the limits between the imagined and the real are much more blurred. One must take this image literally: it is not a substitution of the world, it attempts to reveal the world. But no type of "realism" must be implied in this: to reveal the world is to bring it back in all its purity; to make of its appearances *one* (the only) absolute. This effort is not new in Paz, whose poetry has been a continuous rejection of a transcendency, but it is evidently presented now with great intensity.

In a poem from *Ladera este*, a book written almost entirely in the Orient, Paz evokes the atmosphere of Islamic civilization and Sufi mysticism as well as Buddhism:

> Vi al mundo reposar en sí mismo.
> Vi las apariencias.
> Y llamé a esa media hora:
> Perfección de lo Finito

According to the title of this poem ("Felicidad en Herat"), Paz defines that experience as *happiness*. It is, I think, not only in proportion as it implies the enlightened acceptance of the world but also because of its coincidence between contemplating and that which is contemplated. In an essay perhaps written during the same period, when speaking of eroticism and metaphor as experiences peculiar to man, Paz said both are "the model of that moment of almost perfect merging of the symbol with another which we call analogy and the true name of which is happiness." In a significant way, he was defining the metaphor as the alliance between the intelligible and the sensitive. To observe is not then a purely sensory act; it is a kind of wisdom of the senses: to make possible the union with the world, i.e., the revelation of the world through it.

That is why I think the dazzling aspect of Paz's language can be explained less by its lavishness and more and more by its direct and dry tone. Its laconism represents passion and asceticism. Paz does not say *this is like that* nor even *this is that*; he says *this and that* ("Mountains of mica. Black goats"). In this sense, it could be said that his poetry is not "symbolic" although the image may represent and it does represent something else beyond itself, it is above all *image*: a gaze, a vision; it is a presence, and so we arrive at the essence of his metaphoric system.

We have lost the meaning of totality because we have lost the meaning of the relationship among things and, perhaps also, because our prejudices have created hierarchies among them. In order to be able to relate them and abolish those hierarchies, we must first see things as they are, as they appear. Thus, the analogy does not reside so much in particular images as in the total poem. It is scattered and runs through it: the fragments are related not so much because of their previous similarities or contrasts, as by their proximity; they are vague, in the same space they come together or they separate, they disappear or they are prolonged in others; it is through this movement that they gradually become one true piece. The poem does not speak of or enunciate an analogy; it makes it possible through its own structure of dispersion, expansion and concentration.

Similarly, what best defines Paz's language is *clarity*. It is not a matter of that questionable, pragmatic ideal of writing simple poetry—possibly more confusing because of the didactic and ideological intention behind it. Much less the belief in a previously established truth which one only communicates: "With a clear letter the poet writes/ His obscure truths," Paz says. His clarity requires other connotations. It is naturally the clarity of the verbal material itself with which he works, increasingly closer to luminosity and spatial breadth: weightless and dense material; abstract material: the concrete which becomes diaphanous or *limpid* (which is more his own word). It is for this very reason a discipline: the work of clarity on the senses, on any confusion of the senses, or on any excess of mere passion. From this perspective it is perhaps not out of order to say that clarity in Paz is a way of knowledge, and, thus, a function of poetry is equivalent to the function of philosophy as Wittgenstein understood it: not the solution of problems but their disappearance, which is a way of making the error disappear. Thus, clarity "simply means that the philosophical problems should completely disappear (*Philosophical Investigations*, 133).

18

And, therefore, clarity in Paz is especially identified with *transparency*, a key word in his poetry.

What is *transparency*? We have already suggested this in part at the beginning of this article: it is *vivacity* itself, i.e., the revelation of the immanence of the world as a relativity which is also a single (the unique) absolute. In one of Paz's poems, love or woman is in the center of a flaming world and pauses, creates another space in it; so day becomes a "great clear word" and woman herself is a "palpitation of words" who matures under the eyes of the poet; finally, he recognizes, with humility which does not hide the luster, his own identity and that of the world: "I am real/ I see my life and my death/ The world is true/ I see/ I live in a transparent world." A revelation of things as they are and what they are as they appear, transparency also presupposes wisdom: the exact balance between possessing and not possessing or perhaps rather the dialectic relationship between these two terms. In one of the erotic poems from *Blanco*, an exaltation of the body and the union of the bodies, he says at the end: "Transparency is all that remains." In another poem from *Ladera este* when he evokes his experience in India the poet says:

> A esta misma hora
> Delhi y sus piedras rojas,
> Su río oscuro,
> Sus domos blancos,
> Sus siglos en añicos,
> Se transfigura:
> Arquitectura sin peso,
> Cristalizaciones
> Casi mentales,
> Altos vértigos sobre un espejo:
> Espiral
> De transparencias.
> (. . .)
> Los signos se borran: yo miro la claridad.

In both texts, transparency is what is left: a vivid memory which, distant from things, still possesses them through a continuous flow of time; but this possession is not deceiving: it only possesses "almost mental crystallizations." Neither emptiness nor plenitude: *nothingness*, where these terms are identical.

In this sense, transparency incarnates the very nature of the poem. In one of his essays Paz says, "When we read or listen to a poem we do not smell, taste or touch the word. All of these sensations are mental images. In order to feel a poem one must understand it; in order to understand it, hear it, see it, contemplate it, change it into an echo, into shadow, into nothing. Comprehension is a spiritual exercise." Just as the experience of man in the world, the poem is incarnation and distance, plenitude and precariousness at the same time; like the world, the poem draws its life from the dialectic between affirmation and negation. In recent years, Paz proposes a more and more radical *no*: "Take negation to its limit. There contemplation awaits us: the disincarnation of language, transparency."

Thus, transparency leads to silence: that which is true reality is inexpressible. In this way, Paz seems to come to the same conclusion as the Igitur of Mallarmé: "Nothingness having departed, there remains the castle of purity." But will not this purity be the ultimate form in which the word is revealed to us or becomes transparent, i.e., the ultimate form in which the world becomes incarnate and fully real, so real that it cannot be named? This, I believe, is Paz's utopian vision: the appearance of the world—of the world, it is understood, in its complete original state—implies the disappearance of language and of poetry. All that is left is to live poetry: to write the world.

[1] Paz translated it with the title *Sendas de Oku*. The first English translation was by Nobuyuki Yuasa, *The Narrow Road to the Deep North* (London, 1966).

[2] Gallimard, Paris, 1971.

[3] R. H. Blyth (*Haiku*, 1969) translates it as follows:

> How admirable,
> He who thinks not: "Life is fleeting,"
> When he sees the lightning!

[4] Paz believes that Lévi-Strauss may be right when he places a possible golden age in the neolithic age (cf. *Conjunciones y disyunciones*, Mexico, 1969).

[5] With this phrase Norman O. Brown begins Chapter III, "Trinity" of his book *Love's Body* (1966). It should be mentioned that Brown's thought has deep resonance in the work of Paz.

OCTAVIO PAZ

Paisaje Inmemorial

Se mece aérea
                  se desliza
entre ramas troncos postes
revolotea
           perezosa
entre los altos frutos eléctricos
cae
         oblicua
              ya azul
sobre la otra nieve
                     Hecha
de la misma inmateria que la sombra
no arroja sombra alguna
                  La nieve
es nieve pero quema
                   Tiene
la densidad del silencio
                Los faros
perforan súbitos túneles
              al instante
desmoronados
              La noche
acribillada
             crece se adentra
se ennochece
             Pasan
los autos obstinados
               todos
por distintas direcciones
                   hacia
el mismo destino

Un día
en los tallos de hierro
estallarán las lámparas
Un día
el mugido del río de motores
ha de apagarse
Un día
estas casas serán colinas
otra vez
el viento entre las piedras
hablará a solas
Oblicua
entre las sombras
insombra
ha de caer
casi azul
sobre la tierra
La misma ahora
la nieve de hace un millón de años

Cambridge, a 23 de febrero de 1972

Immemorial Landscape

Airily swaying
                    glides
among branches trunks posts
drifts
            lightly
among the tall electric fruit
falls
            oblique
                        now blue
onto other snow
                        Made
of the same immaterial stuff as shadow
casts no shadow at all
                            The snow
is snow but burns
                    Has
the density of silence
                            Headlights
bore sudden tunnels
                        in an instant
eroded
            Pocked
night
            grows unfolding
darkens
            Stubborn
cars go by
            each
in a different direction
                            destined
for the same place

Some day
headlights will burst
from steel stems
Some day
the bellowing of the river of engines
will die
Some day
these houses will be hills
again
the wind among rocks
will talk to itself
Oblique
among shadows
the stuff of non-shadow
will fall
nearly blue
over the earth
The same as now
the snow of one million years ago

Cambridge, 23 February 1972

Translated from the Spanish
By
Tom J. Lewis

Paz on Himself and His Writing: Selections from an Interview

By RITA GUIBERT

*You have gone back to the first century to explain certain contemporary events
. . . could we now move backwards a mere half century, and talk about Octavio
Paz, his boyhood, his life and work?*

I come from a typical Mexican family. My father's family is a very old one, from
Jalisco State. A mestizo family. My paternal grandfather was a Mexican with mark-
edly Indian features. My mother's parents were Andalusians and my mother was born
in Mexico. So that my family is European on one side and Indian on the other. My
paternal grandfather was a well-known journalist and writer. He campaigned against
French intervention and was a supporter of Porfirio Díaz, although at the end of his
life he opposed the old dictator. My father took part in the Mexican Revolution and
represented Zapata in the United States. He was one of the founders of agrarian
reform. I was born in Mexico City, but as a boy I lived in a place called Mixcoac, near
the capital. We lived in a large house with a garden. Our family had been impover-
ished by the revolution and the civil war. Our house, full of antique furniture, books,
and other objects, was gradually crumbling to bits. As rooms collapsed we moved the
furniture into another. I remember that for a long time I lived in a spacious room
with part of one of the walls missing. Some magnificent screens protected me inade-
quately from wind and rain. A creeper invaded my room . . . A premonition of that
surrealist exhibition where there was a bed lying in a swamp.

Your family were Catholic, weren't they?

As in all Mexican houses at that time, at least those of the bourgeoisie and middle
classes, the men of my house weren't very good Catholics, but rather freethinkers,
Masons, or liberals. Whereas the women were devout Catholics. As a boy, because of
my aunt and my mother, I went to a French school kept by Marist fathers, and like
all boys I went through a crisis of religious enthusiasm. I was very anxious to find
out if my grandfather, who wasn't a believer but whom I considered to be one of the
best men in the world, would be saved or not. For him to be condemned to hell seemed
to me atrocious. An incongruity on God's part: to condemn a good man simply be-

cause he didn't believe in Him. And this made me reflect that the pagan philosophers and the heroes we were taught to admire at school had also ended up in hell. I was horrified by all this, but at the same time it fomented my ardor.

Did this conflict make you lose your faith?

No, neither Alexander nor any of the other famous pagans condemned to hell were responsible for that. I went astray out of boredom. It's the devil's most powerful weapon, you know. . . . Going to Mass was compulsory, and Mass was held in a very beautiful chapel—the school was a hacienda of the end of the eighteenth or beginning of the nineteenth century. The Mass was long, the sermons tedious, and my faith began to grow cold. I was bored and that was blasphemy because I realized I was bored. Also I was thinking about girls. The Church became a purveyor of ever more indecent erotic daydreams; and those dreams made me more and more doubtful, and my doubts nourished my anger against God. One fine day, as I left the Church, I realized once more that communion had had no effect on me. I was just as much fallen from God's grace after communion as I had been before it. I spat on the ground as if to get rid of the host, I danced on my spittle, uttered two or three curses and defied God. From that day, although I told no one, I was a belligerent atheist.

When did you first go to Europe?

I went to Spain in 1937 for a congress of antifascist writers. After the congress my colleagues went back to Paris and then to their own countries, but I stayed in Spain about a year. After that I returned to Mexico.

Did you fight in the civil war?

I was at the front, but I didn't really fight. I spent some time at the southern front with a Mexican who afterwards died, Juan B. Gómez. He was colonel of a brigade. I was in Madrid before that and afterwards in Valencia, in different jobs.

Did Spain have a great influence on you?

Spain taught me the meaning of the word "fraternity." There are some things I shall never forget. One Sunday I went with two friends, the poets Manuel Altolaguirre and Arturo Serrano Plaja, to a place near Valencia, and we had to return on foot because we missed the last bus. It was already night, we were walking along the road and suddenly the sky was lit up by anti-aircraft guns. Enemy planes couldn't penetrate over Valencia because of the fire from republican batteries, and they started to unload their bombs in the outskirts of the city, exactly where we were. The next village we came to was lit up by the glare of the explosions. We went through it singing the "Internationale" to keep up our own courage and also to encourage the inhabitants, and then we took shelter in a vegetable garden. The peasants came to look at us and were interested to hear I was a Mexican. Mexico was sending help to the Republicans, and some of those peasants were anarchists. They went back to their houses in the middle of the bombardment to look for food, and brought us a little bread, a melon, cheese and wine. Eating with those peasants during a bombardment . . . that's something I can't forget.

I think you first came in contact with surrealist thought at that time. How did it affect you?

From Spain I went to Paris where I met several of the friends I had made at the congress. Alejo Carpentier among others. He took me to see Robert Desnos and that was my first contact with the surrealists, though Desnos wasn't any longer a member of the group. I didn't really know what surrealism was at that time, though I felt a lot of sympathy for them. My experiences in Spain confirmed my revolutionary ardor, but at the same time made me mistrust revolutionary theories. This brought me closer to the political attitude of the surrealists. And the more I saw of them, the more I realized how much we agreed, not only because all my reading of the German romantics and William Blake had prepared me to accept surrealism, but also because its political attitude was fairly close to mine. But that happened later.

When did you return to Mexico?

In 1938. I worked for the Spanish Republicans. Those were the years of my intensest political activity. I was on the editorial board of *El Popular*, the daily paper of a union of Mexican workers. I wrote a daily article commenting on international politics. When I was a journalist I never wrote about literary subjects. Since before my visit to Spain I had had serious differences of opinion with the communist bureaucracy, especially with the supporters of social realism. When the Munich pact was signed a group of the staff of *El Popular* criticized the bourgeois democracies for capitulating to Hitler, adding that this was the result of the policy of the Third International, and resigned from the paper. However I stayed on, and only left it at the time of the German-Soviet pact. I then almost entirely withdrew from political activity, although for a time I went on collaborating with the revolutionary opposition. I had some Trotskyite friends, among others José Ferrer, editor of *Clave*, the magazine of the Fourth International in Mexico.

Had you given up literature?

By no means. In those years, I founded two magazines with other writers: first, *Taller*, and afterwards *El Hijo Pródigo* (The Prodigal Son). At my suggestion Ferrer translated Rimbaud's *Une saison en enfer*, which was published in *Taller*, and Lautréamont's *Poésies*, which appeared in *El Hijo Pródigo*. They were the first translations of these two texts into Spanish. *Taller* also printed the first anthology of T. S. Eliot in Spanish. It was wartime, and many revolutionary intellectuals and artists had taken refuge in Mexico. I soon got to know Victor Serge, one of the founders of the Third International, who had been persecuted by Stalin. Indeed I owe to Victor Serge my first reading of Henri Michaux, a great poet whom I met some years later and to whom I'm now bound by close friendship. Michaux was a discovery of capital importance for me—his work constitutes a vertiginous verbal and spiritual universe. Another of my friends then (and always) was Benjamin Peret, who also was a refugee in Mexico. Through Peret I got to know the other surrealists living in Mexico, like Paalen and Leonora Carrington—an extraordinary woman, a bewitched enchantress.

And Buñuel?

No, I met Buñuel years later in Paris. I showed *Los olvidados* (The Forgotten) at the Cannes film festival, in spite of opposition from many Mexicans in official positions. They thought it was derogatory to Mexico. The film won a prize, and although this enraged them even more, it made them shut up.

Los olvidados *marked Buñuel's return to world cinema.*

I would say: his return to great art, to his passionate and critical vision. A return to *L'age d'or* (The Golden Age) and *Le chien andalou* (The Andalusian Dog), films which literally opened our eyes to what we really are. All realism is visionary . . . But we were in Mexico during the war years. I had broken with the communists at that time and found myself involved in a great many controversies about what was called "social realism." I got into serious difficulties with a poet I admire—Pablo Neruda. When I think back to those years I wonder how it was possible for so many remarkable minds to suffer the contagion of that moral leprosy, Stalinism. Aberrations of the religious instinct—an instinct that has been much too little studied.

Where were you during the war?

In Mexico first, and in the United States at the end. In 1944 I got a Guggenheim fellowship. My stay in the United States was a great experience, no less decisive than that in Spain. On one hand there was the amazing and terrible reality of North American civilization; on the other, my reading and discovery of a number of poets: Eliot, Pound, William Carlos Williams, Wallace Stevens, Cummings. Years later I met William Carlos Williams, who translated my poem "Himno entre ruinas" (Hymn among the Ruins), and also Cummings. I saw more of Cummings, and translated some of his poems. But let's go back to those years . . . When the war ended I was in Paris. There I met Peret. He took me to see Breton and that was how my friendship and collaboration with the surrealists began. I was very fond of André Breton and Peret. . . .

What do you remember about those years in the diplomatic service?

My career wasn't brilliant and my advancement was slow. That didn't worry me because what I wanted was to work more or less anonymously and have the opportunity to write. Above all to write poetry, which was and is my first love. I always wrote somewhat against the current—and against myself. *The Labyrinth of Solitude* cost me a lot of appallingly hard work. While I was writing it I felt a huge weight in my stomach. Pregnant women must feel like that. I was secretary to our embassy in Paris at the time and I could only devote my weekends to my book. On Friday nights I shut myself indoors and worked until Sunday. . . .

Did you have financial difficulties?

A lot. Before entering the diplomatic service I went through some very difficult times. I had no fixed profession, and I jumped from one job to another, all of them temporary. At one time I was employed counting old banknotes. The Central Bank of Mexico issues money and also destroys it. They paid us to count packets of unserviceable notes. Each packet contained three thousand notes. The already counted packets were put into sacks. And every month a large furnace on the roof terrace of the bank was lit and millions were burned. A hellish business. Money is an abstraction, a symbol, but that symbol became a dirty piece of paper and had to be burned. So as not to catch any diseases we wore rubber gloves. I was bad at counting, I always had too many or two few notes. At first this worried me, but afterwards I decided that the world wouldn't be any poorer or richer because of five or six notes too few or too many. In the end I decided to give up counting, and spent ten hours composing poems in my head. I used fixed meters and rhymes so as not to forget them. In this way I wrote a number of pretty mournful sonnets.

And in the United States?

I had some bad times in San Francisco. I was living in a little hotel but I came to the end of my money. I told the manager of the hotel what a fix I was in—he was an excellent person, a Mr. Mendelson—and he offered me a bargain: to live in the basement. An old ladies' club met there every afternoon. There was a small cloakroom, practically a closet, and this was my room for months. The only trouble was that I had to wait for the old ladies to go before I could enter my cellar. But those San Francisco days were marvelous—a sort of physical and intellectual intoxication, a great mouthful of fresh air. That was where I embarked on my path in poetry—if there are paths in poetry.

When did you first come in contact with the Orient?

In 1951 I was in New Delhi for some months and from there I went to Tokyo.

As ambassador?

No! No! No!

But you did finally become ambassador in India?

Yes, for six years, until 1968.

Were you interested in Indian religion?

No, I was interested in Indian traditional thought, especially the Buddhist current —Nagarjuna and his commentators.

What influence did those years in India have on you?

Mainly a personal one. In India I met my wife, Marie-Jo. After being born, that's the most important thing that has happened to me.

Were you married there?

Yes, under a big tree. A very leafy *nim*. That tree was full of squirrels, and eaglets would sometimes perch on the highest branches and a lot of ravens as well. Close to our house there were some Moslem mausoleums. Every morning we used to see flocks of parakeets coming from the farther end of the city to the tombs; and at dusk we saw the same flocks of birds flying above our house. More than once, while we were having breakfast in the garden, suddenly we saw descending over us, in a straight line, a dark shadow that clashed against the table and disappeared. It was a sparrow hawk, a thief of food. At dusk, the garden's sky was covered by birds flying in lazy circles. Then I discovered that they weren't birds but bats. No, they aren't disgusting creatures. . . . On winter afternoons, that garden was flooded by a smooth light beyond time—I would say, an impartial, reflective light. I remember saying to Marie-Jo: "It will be difficult to forget the metaphysical lessons of this garden." Today I would put it differently. Why metaphysical? "It will be difficult to forget the lessons of this garden."

What lessons were they?

I don't know—friendship, a feeling of brotherhood for plants and animals. We are all part of the same unity. For Westerners, nature is a part of reality to be dominated and used. That belief is the basis, the foundation of our science and our technology. For the Indians nature is still a mother who may be benevolent or terrible. And there are no definite frontiers between the animal and the human world. You know that India not only suffers from an excess of human but also bovine population. Well, I read a very serious editorial in a Delhi newspaper suggesting—this was before the days of the pill and the loop—that a factory should be set up to produce millions of uterine diaphragms of two types, one for women and the other for cows. . . .

Rules for writing are a very individual matter. For instance, is solitude necessary to you?

One has to write in front of something—noise, the city, trees. . . . Literature is transgression, of language first of all. And the subversion of language is also revealed in the writer's attitude to reality. A writer always writes in front of something, and often against something. When I say *against* I don't mean with hatred. *Against* could be love. In any case poetry is a breaking up the language.

Does this make actual writing painful?

Sometimes, not always. Sometimes it brings great happiness.

Have you favorite hours for writing?

No, my timetable is irregular. I work in the mornings or in the afternoons. I work a little every day, and I read too. That's one of the things I enjoy most, reading. Reading and talking. The thing I like least is writing.

Before you answer some of my questions—a great many of them, in fact—you make a a few brief notes. Why is that?

Lack of confidence in the spoken word. I still belong to the generation of the book, not of the tape recorder. Writing and talking are different and in a way opposite activities. That's a curious thing. In France, today, writers often use the word *écriture*. Like Derrida, they think that writing came before speech. I don't believe that. But without going into this problem, it's curious that the concept of *écriture* should predominate in France, while in the United States and in England the notion of "speech" predominates. They are two different ideas of literature. In France writing comes first, and therefore reading: eyes and silence. In the English-speaking countries poetry is the spoken word: the voice and hearing. . . .

When you write a poem, do your associations flow freely, or are they the result of elaboration?

I don't usually have a clear idea of what I'm going to do. Many times I feel empty, without ideas—and then suddenly the first sentence appears. Valéry used to say that the first line is a gift. It's true: we write the first line to dictation. Who presents us with that line? I don't know. In the past people believed it was the gods, the muse, God—some power outside ourselves. In the nineteenth century it was thought to be a gift from the poet's genius. But what does *genius* mean? Later on it was the unconscious, just another word. The fact is that line appears and that line controls the whole poem. The poem is a development of that line: sometimes it is written against it; at others in support of it; sometimes, when the poem is finished that first line disappears. In fact, I write that line and it is also written by someone other than myself.

And the elaboration?

Then a dialogue develops between the person who wrote the first line and the other, who goes on with the writing. There's a splitting-up, a plurality of poets. Of course that doesn't happen only to writers: we are all several people at the same time. And we all have a tendency to destroy that plurality in favor of some supposed unity. In the case of literature, when one of the voices suppresses the others, we say that the writer has found what is called a style of his own. We can also say that the writer has met death as a writer, petrifaction. A writer should live by dialogue, not only with others—his public, his style, fame, eternity, or what have you—but also with himself. Great writers—yes, the word "great" is repulsive—living writers, even if they have written no more than five lines, those are the ones who preserve their plurality, the dialogue between their egos. Suppression is self-mutilation. The suppressed ego, the corporal ego, the indecent ego, the cynical ego should all speak through the writer's voice. The page comes alive when the suppressed voices appear on it. I've always thought of literature as a language, but by language I mean the plurality of visions of the world. That is: I am talking about the suppressed voices. There's nothing I love more than verbal perfection, but only if that language suddenly opens, and as it does so we see and hear another reality in the abysmal—literally abysmal—breach. A reality that we didn't know and a voice we had hoped never to hear: the voice of death, the voice of the flesh. Great poetry, great literature, doesn't reveal man as an affirmation, as a unity, as something solid, but as a cleft, a fissure. Man fighting with himself. This seems to me the true modern vision of man.

Does this plurality also emerge when you write essays?

There's always someone collaborating with me. And he generally collaborates by contradicting me. The danger is that the voice refuting what we say may be so strong as to silence us. But it's worthwhile running the risk: it's better for the contradictor to silence us than for us to silence the contradictor. When we silence him our writing becomes pedagogic, moral, and boring. It turns into a declaration, a lesson. If I opposed "*engagé*" art, "social art," and all the rest of what was being written for many years in Latin America, it was because it seemed to me immoral that a writer should assume that reason, justice and history were on his side. It's horrible for a writer to claim to be right, not only in front of the world, but in front of his other self. . . .

Do you make a lot of corrections to your writing?

Yes, because the other keeps on talking. The other is a pretty perverse and unbearable being who says *no* to everything I say. The result is this continual stammering, this continual indecision, this continual change in all I say.

Doesn't this contradiction destroy spontaneity?

Well, spontaneity is nourished by the dialogue. If there's no "other," there's no spontaneity. The monologue is the enemy of spontaneity.

Do you compose your poems on a typewriter?

No. And that's a pity: the machine provides greater plastic possibilities than writing does. Cummings used to write his poems directly onto the typewriter. Handwriting is too subjective, it's infected with too much that is personal, sentimental.

Do you like to discuss what you're writing at the moment?

I used to formerly, but not now. I used to think what I was writing was important. . . .

What were the first books you read?

My grandfather had collected a fine library and I had completely free access to it from childhood. The first pornographic works I read were some of the classics. I remember being extraordinarily disturbed by *The Golden Ass*. There was also a lot of French literature and the poets and novelists of the end of the last century in our language. The Latin American "modernists" had a prominent place in the bookshelves. Those years of my childhood and adolescence saw a great explosion of avant-garde poetry and painting. It was also the time when our great baroque poets were discovered, especially Góngora. I read a lot of Góngora, and I go on reading him all the time. Also Quevedo. At school they made us hate our own classics, but afterwards I went back to medieval or traditional poetry. I also read and keep reading the Archpriest of Hita. But that was much later.

Did you also read the modern poets?

I discovered Hispano-American and Spanish poetry at about that time. I oscillated successively and passionately between Jiménez and Lorca, Guillén and Alberti, Neruda and Borges, Pellicer and Villaurrutia. The magazine *Contemporáneos* gave me an unforgettable jolt: I read in it and in the same issue the first Spanish translations of *The Waste Land* and St. John Perse's *Anabasis*. A little later, another jolt: André Breton's *L'amour fou*. Thanks to Villaurrutia I read Blake. Those were the years too when I first read Hölderlin and the German romantics.

Only poetry?

No, I read a lot of the publications of the *Revista de Occidente*, edited by Ortega y Gasset, and it was through it that my generation became familiar with modern German philosophy, the phenomenology of Husserl and his followers. We were deeply impressed by Heidegger's *What Is Philosophy?* in a Spanish translation by Zubirí published in Jose Bergamín's review, *Cruz y raya*.

Did you feel very cut off in Mexico?

As you know, unlike Argentina which is an open country, Mexico is concentrated and closed to outer influences. But the years before the Second World War were cosmopolitan, even in Mexico. We were fairly well informed as to what was happening, because there were some excellent magazines in Spanish at that time: the *Revista de Occidente* and *Cruz y raya* in Madrid, *Sur* in Buenos Aires, and *Contemporáneos* in Mexico. There's nothing of the sort today. And we were interested in politics and read a lot of revolutionary books, particularly those tending toward Marxism. Strange as it may appear I read Nietzsche with equal enthusiasm. For months and months I drank—that's the only word for it—maxims of *The Gay Science*. A unique form of spiritual intoxication. But we were none of us acquainted with modern English and North American philosophy. Russell we only knew through a collection of his essays, *Marriage and Morals*. Nothing of Wittgenstein . . . I was a great reader of novels. Whereas now I prefer books about anthropology, history, or travel.

In one of our conversations "without the tape recorder" you mentioned that one of your favorite books was the dictionary.

I read it every day. It's my adviser, my elder brother. It's magic, a fountain of surprises: you look for a word and always find another. The truth about the world ought to be found in the dictionary, since its pages contain all the nouns in the world. But it's not: the dictionary presents us with a list of words, and it's for men, not only writers, to link them together so that one of those precarious associations formulates the truth about the world, a relative truth that dissolves as it is read. My favorite book is *Diccionario etimológico de la lengua española* (Etymological Dictionary of the Spanish Language). It is the work of a Catalan. A salutory lesson for Castilians, a further lesson given by great Catalonia to proud Castile. Because in the old dispute between Castile and the other provinces of Spain, I'm not on the side of the centralists but of the rest, the Basques, Galicians, and Catalans. In the introduction to his dictionary Corominas says that no other Western language contains so many phantom words as Castilian. I tremble to think that there are words that have become disembodied, floating words, whose meaning we no longer know.

What other books besides the dictionary do you read?

I'm always reading poetry. Like Christians saying their prayers every night, I try always, every day, to read a poem or poetical text. During my last years in India I read Mallarmé passionately and patiently. That led me to translate one of his sonnets (the "Sonnet in ix"), and write a commentary on it. Last year, when I was in Pittsburgh, I read Dante. It was a great experience. I discovered that Dante was the great poet of the West. I hadn't known that . . . I also read Spanish and Latin American poetry. In the last few months I've been rereading the medieval poets. They are a mine of rhythms, a continuous spring of verbal forms. Originally, Spanish poetry was rhythmical, accentual: the scansion of syllables was not as importnt as tonic accents. Afterwards, at first through Italian influence and later, in the eighteenth century, through that of France, syllabic versification and metrical regularity prevailed. Thus, modern free verse is a return to irregular, rhythmic versification: to the origins of the language. . . .

Do you like reading your earliest poems?

Whenever I reread my work I feel embarrassed. And not only embarrassed, sometimes I feel nausea. But now and again I say to myself, well, that wasn't too bad.

Which of them "weren't too bad"?

The most recent. It's natural, isn't it? For instance *Conjunctions and Disjunctions*, my essay on the relation between the *body* and the *non-body*. In poetry, of course, *Ladera este*. It seems to me my best book. . . . And the one I wrote this summer, *Le singe grammairien*. Everything I'd ever done before in prose and poetry converges in this little book. It all converges . . . and then vanishes. There's also that same convergence between thought and poetry in another book of mine: *Eagle or Sun?* This was an exploration of the mythical subsoil, so to speak, of Mexico, and at the same time a self-exploration. An attempt to create a world of images in which modern and ancient sensibility were fused, the images of the buried Mexico and those of the modern world. A North American friend pointed out that there was an analogy between my book and one by William Carlos Williams, published years earlier: *Kora in Hell*. The similarity isn't textual but as to aims. In fact, both books are poems in prose, inspired by French poetry. However, *Kora in Hell* is a deeply American book and could only have been written by a North American. In the same way I think *Eagle or Sun?* could only have been written in Mexico. . . . Another similarity: William Carlos Williams also wrote a very beautiful book called *In the American Grain*, a collection of essays on American themes. Well, *The Labyrinth of Solitude* fulfills a corresponding purpose. I wrote *The Labyrinth* first as a confession or to relieve my feelings, and immediately afterwards I wrote *Eagle or Sun?* . . .

Do you think we are witnessing the end of an epoch?

You have asked me for my ideas on various subjects which appear now and then in my writings, especially in *Corriente alterna* and *Conjunctions and Disjunctions*: the rebellion of youth, the revolt of the countries of the Third World, the rebellion of women, the possibility of founding a new erotism, the reinvention of love, as Rimbaud called it. . . . All these themes are connected to a central theme: the end of lineal time. Yes, I think we are at the end of an epoch. It's an idea I share with a great many others. It has been one of the commonplaces of contemporary thought for some forty to fifty years. . . . I'll explain myself. I begin with this: all civilizations and cultures possess an idea of time and express a vision of time. In general, from primitive man to the Greeks, Chinese, and Aztecs, men believed in cyclical, circular time. Societies that postulate this cyclical concept of time nearly always go to the the past for their archetype and model. The past is the repository of values. Other civilizations have thought that perfection and essential values lay outside of time. Time is an illusion, but there is a time outside time in which temporal contradictions disappear. Indian civilization looks upon time as an illusion, and therefore ignores history; nevertheless, there is a point outside of time where the illusion disappears and true reality appears: Brahman, Nirvana. Christianity postulated two separate times: historical time with a beginning and an end, and a time outside time, the eternity of heaven and hell. . . .

Octavio Paz, one last question: what are your plans for the future?

To abolish it.

Selected by Tom J. Lewis
Translated from the Spanish By Frances Partridge

Poetry and the Reader

By RUTH NEEDLEMAN

As a poet Octavio Paz has always maintained a belief in the power of words to reveal in one form or another the path that would lead to our liberation. Faith in language, poetic language, lies at the base of his whole life's work. His understanding, however, of the nature of language and human communication, of the nature and function of art, has changed considerably over the past thirty years. New philosophical schools of thought as well as the realities of contemporary Western society have influenced Paz's world view significantly. By analyzing one aspect of Octavio Paz's poetry and poetics, we can observe more closely the development and modifications which characterize his writings.

In his earliest essays as in his most recent writings, Paz has been concerned with the relation of the reader to the work of art. The question of the reader's participation in the creative process became a central one during the *entre-guerre* period. The surrealists, in particular, popularized the Comte de Lautréamont's declaration that one day poetry would be written by all. In an essay dated 1938, Octavio Paz refers to "el lector de poesía, que, cada día más es un verdadero reconstructor de ella" ("Pablo Neruda en el corazón," *Ruta*, 4, 15 Sept. 1938, p. 25). Years later in 1954 in an essay on surrealism, Paz writes: "Si mi voz ya no es mía, sino la de todos, ¿por qué no lanzarse a una nueva experiencia: la poesía colectiva? En verdad, la poesía siempre ha sido hecho por todos. Los mitos poéticos, las grandes imágenes de la poesía en todas las lenguas, son un objeto de comunión colectiva" (*Las peras del olmo*, Mexico, UNAM, 1957, p. 174). Here and on other occasions, Paz does not distinguish clearly between "la poesía colectiva" and "communión colectiva." The surrealists wrote poems together, experimented directly with the possibilities they inferred from Lautréamont's proclamation. This kind of poetry, however, written collectively and based on participation in the creative act itself, places only minimal importance on the actual art work. For Paz, in contrast, it is always the poem itself which is of primary importance. Although he cites or alludes metaphorically to the ritual participation or "re-creation" achieved by the reader, Paz bases his central theoretical ideas on the poem, on the nature of poetic language. It is, above all, through his changing conception of language that the role of the reader is defined and modified.

In his earlier writings published during the decades of the thirties and forties, Octavio Paz stressed the importance of the artist's ability to draw the reader into a creative relation with the poem. Communication with a broad public and the creation of a poetic community were conceived as priorities. In more recent works, on the other hand, in *Corriente alterna* or *Marcel Duchamp o el castillo de la pureza*, Paz emphasizes the necessity of transforming the reader into a "poet" by confronting her/him with difficult and very demanding literature, "a poem by Mallarmé or a novel by Joyce" (*Marcel Duchamp or The Castle of Purity*, Donald Gardener, tr., London, Cape Goliard, 1970, n. pag., leaf 40). According to this view of reader participation, the interpretive act becomes synonymous with the creative process itself.

To account for the changes in his poetics we must look to the years that separate the first edition of *El arco y la lira* (1956) from the second and revised version published in 1967. During this period Paz reevaluates many of his ideas in light of structuralism and Buddhist philosophy. The influence of these two epistemologies can be observed in a comparison of the two editions. In the first edition of *El arco y la lira*, in the chapter on "El lenguaje," Paz writes:

> Todo aprendizaje principia como enseñanza de los verdaderos nombres de las cosas y termina con la revelación de la palabra—llave que nos abrirá las puertas del saber. O con la confesión de ignorancia: el silencio. Y aun el silencio dice algo, pues está preñado de signos. No podemos escapar del lenguaje. Cierto, los especialistas pueden aislar el idioma y convertirlo en objeto. Mas se trata de un ser artificial arrancado a su mundo original ya que . . . las palabras no viven fuera de nosotros. . . . Las redes de pescar palabras están hechas de palabras. Para salir de este laberinto es menester resignarse a desechar la idea del lenguaje como un "objeto" independiente o separable del hombre que lo estudia. (*El arco y la lira*, México, FCE, 1956, p. 31)

The final sentence of this quotation was deleted in the second edition and replaced by a footnote in which Paz explains that the new perspectives introduced by linguistic analysis and structural linguistics no longer support his previous hypotheses. In the earlier version Paz had denied the possibility of separating language from its human context, of analyzing language as an object in isolation from usage. Such an undertaking seemed impossible since "los redes de pescar palabras," according to Paz, were "hechas de palabras." After reading Saussure, Jakobson and Chomsky, however, Paz began to absorb and adapt for his own purposes the principles of structural analysis. At first, his contact with these new theories of language and communication, which now include cybernetics, resulted in a confused or sometimes contradictory attitude, a distrust as well as an anxiety over the semantic nature of language. If language could be severed from any individual mind or particular society, then where would meaning originate? How could the poet, for example, control the semantic dimensions of her/his poem?

Many of the disturbing questions which arose in response to new or unfamiliar philosophical approaches led Paz to examine his own poetics and poetry within the historical perspective of the modern period. During the interval between editions of

El arco y la lira, Octavio Paz wrote *Los signos en rotación* (1965). By means of this inquiry into the past, Paz attempted to resolve the crisis in meaning; that is, he sought to redefine the nature and function of his own poetry to accompany his revised understanding of both contemporary art and society. *Los signos en rotación* describes the condition of poetry in the modern world in terms of the effects of philosophical rationalism and critical thought. Paz searches back to uncover the origins of the modern period in Cartesian logic and enlightenment ideology. As reason displaced faith, the foundations of the old world view were undermined and finally superseded. What replaced them, however, was a form of skepticism disguised as rationality and an opportunism clothed in the garb of technological progress. In some ways, Paz regards the past few centuries less as an Age of Enlightenment than an Age of Alienation. According to Paz, Christianity provided a coherent and significant world image, but, once those structures ceased to determine our understanding, a formerly unified image was shattered into fragments. Unfortunately, the dissolution of the old image did not in this instance herald the creation of a new one. Religion had yielded to its successor, technology. For Paz technology signifies the very absence of a coherent image, since it works on and molds the world but does not reflect it.

With its utilitarian objectives, technology appears to Paz as the inevitable consequence of empirical or rational knowledge. Based largely on his interpretation of Martin Heidegger, the mystery of *Dasein* and the nature of truth, Paz has conceived of "knowledge" in terms of a manipulatory relationship, as knowledge over something rather than as an understanding of essence. Paz's analysis resembles Heidegger's in *An Introduction to Metaphysics,* in which he attempts to show that the sundering of mythos and logos by the logical copula leads to a necessarily manipulative relationship between subject and object. To know or understand something empirically is to be able to control it. Technological progress, then, is the practical culmination of enlightenment thought as Paz views it. Power and progress in contemporary society have replaced wisdom and meaningful direction; technology by itself lacks precisely what art and human life require.

Coherence, as a result, has ceded its place to fragmentation, so that the meaning, no longer immanent, resides in the very search for meaning. As should be expected, the absence of a shared representation of the world has yielded a language whose meaning is sometimes private, usually uncertain, and rarely the same for both reader and poet, or for two different readers. Once participation implied a collective sharing of language and experience, whereas now it tends to be more individualized and fragmented like the world we inhabit. As a consequence, Paz considers the role of the reader in a different light than he had previously, because the certainty and common social experience are no longer there.

The degree to which Paz's ideas are altered by his revised understanding of poetic language can be substantiated if we examine one other modification introduced into the 1967 edition of *El arco y la lira.* In the same chapter on "El lenguaje," Paz discusses the importance of certain modern French, Spanish and English poets. His observations on Valéry in the original version stand in direct contrast to those included in the second edition. In 1956 Paz criticizes Valéry's withdrawal into solitary philosophical speculation, which he (Paz) relates in turn to a certain disregard for the reader:

> Ahora bien, si la poesía es creación y communicación, es algo más que grito o automatismo puro, sin referencia al oyente que implica todo lenguaje. Pero sospecho que Valéry nunca dió demasiada importancia a ese oyente que entraña el "desarrollo" o recreación de la exclamación original. No es accidental esta ausencia: es el resultado de la voluntaria soledad del especulativo. Para Valéry, temperamento predominantemente intelectual, el lenguaje consistía en un sistema de signos. Su actitud nunca fue diversa de la del filósofo y la del matemático. Con frecuencia el intelectual olvida que las palabras nos sirven para communicarnos con nuestros semejantes. Cuando se dice que un hombre está "abstraído," perdido en sus pensamientos, se afirma implícitamente que las palabras que contienen esos pensamientos han perdido sus valores comunicativos. Son signos que sólo valen para él que los piensa. Así, tanto el que vive dominado por la ciega afectividad como el que se encuentra bajo el imperio de la lúcida razón ignoran a ese "otro" a quien está dirigida toda palabra. Lenguaje afectivo y lenguaje intelectual coinciden en esta ausencia de oyente.
>
> (*El arco y la lira*, 1956, pp. 46–47)

Using Valéry as a stepping stone, Paz develops his ideas on the function of poetic language and its orientation toward the reader. Implicit is a criticism of poets and poems that seal themselves off hermetically because of a very private and self-exploratory use of language. In other words, either too much emotion or too much intellect leads poetry in the wrong direction. Paz criticizes a poem that, rather than opening outward to the reader, maintains an almost exclusive relationship with its creator and with itself. In the second edition of *El arco y la lira* no more than a few phrases from the original remain. Not only does Paz delete the criticism and the discussion on the importance of the reader and communication, but he reverses his position on Valéry's poetry. Due to the growing intellectualization of Paz's own poetry, he now considers Valéry more in terms of a model. Emphasis shifts from the need of a poem to take cognizance of the reader to a stress on the closed or "self-sufficient" nature of a poem. Paz opens the revised passage with the same definition, borrowed from Valéry: "el poema es el desarrollo de una exclamación."

> El *desarrollo* es un lenguaje que se crea sí mismo frente a esa realidad bruta y propiamente indecible a que alude la exclamación. Poema: oreja que escucha a una boca que dice lo que no dijo la exclamación. . . . El *desarrollo* no es una pregunta ni una respuesta: es una convocación. El poema—boca que habla y oreja que oye—será la revelación de aquello que la exclamación seña sin nombrar.
>
> (*El arco y la lira*, Mexico City, FCE, 1967, pp. 46–47)

With the changes in Paz's ideas, the poem as he conceives it gradually disarticulates itself from both its creator and its reader, recoils into itself to become a reality replete and self-sufficient. The poem, as "boca que habla y oreja que oye," incorporates in its own language the connotative plenitude formerly associated with the reader's recreation or interpretation. What Paz referred to as the necessary involvement of the reader in the creation of meaning no longer seems so essential. Now it is primarily the semantic qualities inherent in poetic language that infuse words with new connotative dimensions.

According to Paz, in *Los signos en rotación* for example, the truly critical poem, the poem of the modern period, has been developed under the aegis of Mallarmé and modeled after *Un coup de dés*. The poem incorporates a possible reading within its own contextual development. "La palabra dicha," a poem collected in *Salamandra*, reflects this period of experimentation in Paz's poetry. During the late fifties and early sixties, he concentrates on the possibilities inherent in linguistic forms and structures in order to convey his new awareness of the complexities of meaning. In "La palabra dicha" images harbor concealed paradoxes, and the significance of a word multiplies as the word itself divides into the constituent elements of sound and sense. Morphemes and phonemes rearrange themselves in turn to suggest other words and other meanings. The normal process of communication tends, according to Paz, to limit a word's associative field. In its everyday usage language broadens the disjunction between phonology and morphology, by assigning meaning to sounds on an arbitrary or "utilitarian" basis. It is the poet's task to reunite sound and sense, to end, so to speak, the alienation of language. What becomes apparent here is the degree to which the responsibility falls on the poet to create a language that denies the utilitarian basis of communication and that, as a consequence, defines the possible experiences of the reader. In other words, the reader recreates the poet's poem. The meanings are inherent in the poem, and the reader realizes them by rendering them conscious. For example, the phrase from "La palabra dicha," "Simiente no miente," taken as a series of phonemes, has multiple possible interpretations (Paz, *Salamandra*, Mexico City, Joaquín Mortiz, 1962, p. 32). The reader does not create them; the reader can only discover them or overlook them. The poem requires such an awareness of structural and linguistic elements that only a few readers will be able to experience it, to be transformed into that ideal reader-poet envisioned by Paz. What of those readers who fail to comprehend the poem's hidden semantic dimensions? Is participation, real participation as Paz sees it, confined only to the initiate of poetry? On the basis of his own poetic evolution, it would be fair to assume that Paz's audience has become increasingly a public composed of other artists, poets and scholars. Octavio Paz has become the poet's poet as was Mallarmé. It is the most difficult art which allows for the quality of participation that Paz seeks. Participation means the ability to interpret poets whose language and meanings are not easily deciphered. Poetry, as Paz defines it in *Corriente alterna*, is the "*conocimiento* experimental del sujeto mismo que conoce." "En el caso de la poesía moderna, el sujeto de la experiencia es el poeta mismo: él es el observador y el fenómeno observado" (*Corriente alterna*, Mexico City, Siglo Veintiuno, 1967, p. 80). By this theory, art, instead of turning outward to the reader, turns inward to the poet. The function of poetry becomes the exploration of the poet's own mind and her/his own methods of cognition.

In *Corriente alterna*, Paz reconsiders and reevaluates once more the relationship between reader and poem and, at the same time, modifies his earlier conception of language and poetry as expressed in *Los signos en rotación*. In addition, he explores the future possibilities and ideal form of the reader-poem relation. He suggests that poetry is moving closer to ritual, so that participation no longer will be a theoretical problem or a secondary aspect of a work of art. Once again he invokes Lautréamont, although once again he interchanges metaphor and reality. In his prose, Paz refers to the necessity of the reader's participation in the poem's creation, but, in his poetry, our participation still seems symbolic. Paz envisions art, nonetheless, in the process of bridging the distance between itself and ritual, the transformation of a metaphor into reality. The role of the reader should resemble that of the Indian musician to her/his piece, that of the *juglar* to her/his poetry—an active and necessary moment in the creative process.

> Ahora el lector y el oyente participan en la creación del poema y, en el caso de la música, el ejecutante también participa del albedrío del compositor. Las antiguas fronteras se borran y reaparecen otras; asistimos al fin de la idea del arte como contemplación estética y volvemos a algo que había olvidado Occidente: el renacimiento del arte como acción y representación colectivas y el de su complemento contradictorio, la meditación solitaria. Si la palabra no hubiese perdido su significado recto, diría: un arte espiritual. Un arte mental y que exigirá al lector y al oyente la sensibilidad y la imaginación de un ejecutante que, como los músicos de la India, sea, asimismo, un creador. Las obras del tiempo que nace no estarán regidas por la idea de la sucesión lineal sino por la de combinación: conjunción, dispersión, y reunión de lenguajes, espacios, y tiempos. La fiesta y la contemplación. *Arte de la conjugación.*
>
> *(Corriente alterna*, p. 24)

This sense of "arte espiritual" sheds light on the notion of participation that Paz implies at this stage in his thinking. It embraces certain contradictions which are exceedingly difficult to reconcile but which Paz does, in fact, attempt to overcome in *Blanco*. *Blanco* represents the culmination and synthesis of this understanding of poetry. In a more personal sense, the poem stands for poetry as "un arte espiritual," because it traces out the form of Paz's own mandala. As Giuseppe Tucci explains in his book *The Theory and Practice of the Mandala*, the mandala is a "psycho-cosmo-grammata" that reveals "the secret play of the forces which operate in the universe and in us, on the way to the reintegration of consciousness" (Tucci, *The Theory and Practice of the Mandala*, Alan Houghton Brodrick, tr., 1961, rpt. London, Rider and Co., 1969, p. vii). The reader's participation, however, necessitates considerable intellectual research into Paz's sources. Without an understanding of the Tantric books, the language, symbols and layout of *Blanco* do not disclose their significance. In addition, Paz refers to this poem as an attempt to open the poetic form in order to allow the reader freedom in choosing how to read the poem. Yet this freedom is elusive. In the guidelines, Paz provides us with various ways of reading the poem. It is highly structured and unfolds according to a very conscious and carefully worked-out plan for spiritual liberation. As presented in *The Hevajra Tantra*, the book cited at the very beginning of *Blanco* along with Mallarmé's "Sonnet en ix." If we choose our own way of reading the poem we may not discover the shape of the Tantric mandala. Besides the Tantric book, however, there are other structural influences in the work which we would not uncover without a careful study of Paz's sources. Mallarmé is one; structuralism is another. Together with Tantrism, these three converge to form the world view that Paz incorporates in *Blanco*.

In order to understand what Paz means by "arte espiritual," we must sketch out briefly the parallels between *Blanco* and *The Hevajra Tantra*. *Blanco* is a poem of language, the symbolic matrix where "todo se corresponde porque todo es lenguaje." If, as Paz now maintains, language shapes the world we know, then *Blanco* represents the poet's efforts to capture symbolically the relationship of the word to reality, "un momento del discurso del universo" ("La nueva analogía," *ECO, Revista de la Cultura de Occidente*, 16, No. 2, December 1967, p. 121). Spatial and temporal experience are merged as in consciousness on the unfolding leaves of *Blanco*. There are three distinct typographical faces or layouts. At the beginning and end of the poem, words are dispersed over three columns. On the second leaf, printed in bold face, the central poem opens; its movement represents the flow of language as it shapes its river bed out of the white space of the page, the unformed dimensions of reality. This flow is interrupted by the four poetic moments which open out on the page like the two wings of a bird. These interludes divide and then merge in a dual extension of a single instant. Printed in italics, the left and right side are held separate the first two times they appear but then become continuous as well as simultaneous. The left-hand poem is in black, an erotic poem in four stages, reflecting the four traditional elements of the cosmos. It is juxtaposed and/or continuous with a cognitive poem, printed in red, which carries us through sensation, perception, and imagination to understanding. The two aspects of each poetic interval correspond to body and mind, matter and spirit, female and male. Each represents one pole of a dialectical rhythm whose resolution is an affirmation of both. If we compare *Blanco* in form and content with the mandala presented in *The Hevajra Tantra*, we can see clearly to what extent the poem is meant to serve the reader as a mandala, a method and means of achieving spiritual liberation. Part One of the Tantra joins body, mind and speech as in the beginning of *Blanco*. The four-fold sequence in the poem, including the erotic and cognitive poems, corresponds to the Four Moments in the Tantric book: Variety, Development, Consummation, and Blank (D. L. Snellgrove, *The Hevajra Tantra*, II, iii, "The Basis of All Tantras," London, Oxford University Press, 1959, p. 94). The final moment is attained through the union of Means and Wisdom, which is symbolized in the poem typographically as well as in the unity of the dual poetic aspects. As Giuseppe Tucci describes it in his book:

> a mandala delineates a consecrated superficies and protects it from invasion by disintegrating forces symbolized in demoniacal cycles . . . . It is, above all, a map of the cosmos. It is the whole universe in its essential plan, in its process of emanation and reabsorption . . . which develops from an essential Principle and rotates round a central axis.
>
> (Tucci, p. 23)

The usual representation according to Tucci is the lotus: "its four or eight petals disposed symmetrically about the corolla symbolize the spatial emanation of the One to the Many" (Tucci, p. 27). In *Conjunciones y disyunciones*, Paz comments extensively on Tantrism, revealing a thorough familiarity with its symbolism. Prejñāparamitā or "Sabiduría en la vacuidad" is "un loto rojo de ocho pétalos . . . hecho de vocales y consonantes" (*Conjunciones y disyunciones*, Mexico City, Joaquín Mortiz, 1969, p. 86).

> en cada fonema y cada sílaba late una semilla (bīja) que, al actualizarse en sonido, emite una vibración sagrada y un sentido oculto. *Rasanā* representa a los consonantes *y lalanā* a las vocales. Las dos venas o canales del cuerpo son ahora el lado masculino y feminino del habla. . . . El lenguaje ocupa un lugar central en el tantrismo, sistema de metáforas encarnadas.
>
> (*Conjunciones*, p. 83)

In addition to the eight poems, which emerge in *Blanco* from the central column as a symbolization of the lotus petals or design of the mandala, Paz refers here to the central place of language with the two channels, masculine and feminine. Tantrism incarnates literally the form of the mandala in the human body. There are two veins, left and right, feminine and masculine, Wisdom and Means, and a central canal that passes through six *cakras*, "nudos de energía sexual, nerviosa y psíquica." Examining *Blanco* according to Paz's guidelines, we find that in addition to the eight poems— feminine on the left and masculine on the right—the central poem breaks down into six parts equal to the number of *cakras*.

In reference to the highly formalistic qualities of *Blanco*, Paz comments in an interview that he does not fear running into "un manierismo formal": "porque el sistema no es gratuita, sino una necesidad derivada del poema mismo para conseguir una pluralidad dinámica en su significado" (Laus, "Octavio Paz: La crítica de la significación," Interview, *Diorama de la Cultura*, 16 abril 1967, p. 1). The "necesidad" mentioned seems to derive more from the Tantric formulas, however, than from the poem itself. The plurality of meanings that Paz sees as completely integral to and integrated in the poem can only be considered as internally necessary if the reader has already studied the external texts. Although Paz has managed to minimize the effect of such conscious structuring, there are still problems. At this point, though, we shall not go into other parallels between the two texts because they are too extensive. We should, nonetheless, question the importance of the Tantric tradition to this poem as, for example, Paz himself has questioned the importance of the Christian tradition in the meaning and structure of the *Divine Comedy*. We can certainly "understand" the poem quite well without the external guides supplied by the Tantric Books, but it is likely that we would be unaware of the poem's mandala structure and, therefore, of the spiritual uses or purposes of the poem. As readers we would remain very much on the periphery of the poem's significance.

On the basis of *Blanco*, we can see how Paz conceives ideally of the function of the work of art and specifically how it relates to the reader. It is not a question of participation in the way that the surrealists envisioned it, based on the ideal conceived by Lautréamont. Paz cites Lautréamont, but his own poetry and poetics do not coincide with those of many of the avant-garde artists who did, in fact, stress the reader's primarily artistic role in the creative process. Through a poem like *Blanco*, we can judge the intellectual demands which Paz places upon his reader. Consequently, the poem rather than the act of creation itself acquires the most importance. It provides the structure for a meditation that should direct the reader on a path toward spiritual liberation. The problem still remains, however, with all those readers who cannot or do not undertake to interpret and decipher the poem's secrets. As Paz's poetic language becomes more defined in terms of its spiritual function, the reading public grows more limited. The poet-reader gives way to the poet-initiate.

Wallace Stevens once commented that a way through the world was much harder to find than a way around it. This still seems to hold true. In *Los signos en rotación*, Paz refers to certain reservations expressed by Benjamin Péret in regard to the possibility that someday poetry might be made by all. Péret did not accept Lautréamont's prediction without his own qualifications. Paz attributes to Péret the following words: "la práctica de la poesía sólo es concebible en un mundo liberado de toda opresión, en el que el pensamiento poético vuelve a ser para el hombre tan natural como el sueño" (*Los signos en rotación*, Buenos Aires, Sur, 1965, p. 56). We have not, needless to say, reached such a juncture in history nor is language as yet a sufficient instrument by which to achieve our liberation. We should not, however, underestimate the power of words, nor of Paz's attempts to restore to language its original coherence, its ability to communicate.

University of California, Santa Cruz

43

Borges and Paz:
Toward a Dialogue of Critical Texts

By EMIR RODRÍGUEZ MONEGAL

> . . . *ese mundo de ideas que, al desplegarse, crea un* espacio intelectual: *el ámbito de una obra, la resonancia que la prolonga o la contradice. Ese espacio es el lugar de encuentro con las otras obras, la posibilidad del diálogo entre ellas.*
>
> Octavio Paz, *Corriente alterna* (1967)

There are few more tantalizing names in contemporary culture than Jorge Luis Borges and Octavio Paz. Both men have for a number of years transcended the somewhat parochial limits of their respective regions and have directed their work toward America (Latin or non-Latin) and Europe. To mention Paz or Borges in an international context today is to speak of writers who can demonstrate the intuition with which *El laberinto de la soledad* ends: today we Latin Americans are "for the first time in our history the contemporaries of all men."[1] The frequency with which the works of Paz or Borges are quoted or alluded to in French or American, English or German criticism is sufficient proof of that contemporaneity, achieved with such difficulty by a culture which until very recently had been considered marginal, peripheral and merely colonial. What Borges has to say about Henry James or Kafka (and not merely what he has to say about Lugones or Carriego) is now carefully discussed in the West; what Paz has to say about Lévi-Strauss or Tantrism finds an intelligent response among the specialists. The names of Paz and Borges have become symbols for a mode of being and of reading in contemporary culture. Interpreting them is the task of every educated person regardless of origin. Borges and Paz have achieved in our day what was impossible for Bello and Sarmiento, for Darío and Rodó, Reyes and Mariátegui: They have attracted the attention of a truly international audience which gives their texts the same care it gives those of its European or North American contemporaries, and interprets them unhurriedly and without condescension.

In the context of present-day Spanish-American culture the names of Borges and Paz have even greater importance. In more than one sense they embody certain traits that should be taken into account before passing on to a more detailed analysis of them and their work. They share a certain intellectual attitude toward the esthetic phenomenon: an attitude which of course does not offer identical solutions to the same problems. Neither Paz nor Borges are disdainful of the day-to-day exercise of intelligence and erudition. They are highly educated poets, even in their impulsive or anguished moments. Lucid intelligence and intellectual enlightenment pervade their works and those works can sustain critical, profoundly personal meditation. Neither Paz nor Borges have renounced intellectuality: they realize that a poet cannot main-

45

tain an attitude of ignorance before the problems of language, esthetic phenomena and rhetorical speculation. As critics, they have both analyzed foreign works as well as their own; they have submitted the (ultimately unexplainable) phenomenon of poetic creation to tireless scrutiny.

To say this is not to assert, as some pretend to believe, that Paz and Borges are unaware of or hold in disdain the other faculties without which poetic creation or criticism is impossible. Paz's lyrical work begins with lucidity in order to reach the blinding glare of ecstasy; that of Borges makes use of the intellect in order to undermine and definitively destroy its own arrogance. Overwhelming intuition, the electric spark that leaps between two distant poles, the ability to seize by oblique methods the elusive core of reality are also characteristic of Paz's and Borges's works. But if their intelligence does not function in a vacuum, it is certainly the conducting medium of that poetic or critical charge both of their works contain.

They also share a deliberate, conscious and programmatic acceptance of a cultural tradition that comes to us from the West and transforms our literary task into the renewed construction and destruction of a dialogue begun many centuries ago on the shores of the Mediterranean. In both writers Americanism does not exclude but embodies that Mediterranean tradition. Too brilliant to ignore the fact that they are using a European verbal instrument, both look at reality from their respective Americas with the discipline they have acquired in vast multilingual libraries. Their Americanism is open. Open to the multiple linguistic reality of that Mediterranean tradition which is also embodied in the Anglo-Saxon world, and more recently, in the Slavic. But also open to the shifting and circumstantial realities of Argentina and Mexico. For this reason both Paz and Borges have been able to give us a vivid image of Latin American machismo in "Hombre de la esquina rosada" or *El laberinto de la soledad,* and they have been able to explore in their more poetic works (*Fervor de Buenos Aires, Piedra de sol*) the primary and most occult symbols of their respective realities. Their Americanism is also open to other non-Mediterranean traditions. For both Paz and Borges the East is part of that inclusive cultural tradition that is centered in the Mediterranean. It should not be overlooked that both interpret oriental culture with the aid of European books. Borges discovered the East in a sinological library which, once in Geneva, is now in Montevideo. Paz began to *read* the East in books obtained in France. Of course he later visited the East and even came to live in India for six years as his country's ambassador. Likewise, Borges's East is (even today) that of the *Thousand and One Nights* read in his father's library, the East of Kipling and Captain Burton, of apocryphal Chinese encyclopedias, of the no less apocryphal histories of widows dedicated to piracy in the vast Yellow Sea. But that Paz has established roots in Indian soil and can write with authority about his direct experience there does not alter the fundamental fact that his interpretation of the East is also rooted in the Mediterranean tradition. And it could not be otherwise. For him the East has been above all an inner experience: the trial by fire, the rebirth of a poet more authentic than ever from the ashes of other avatars. But this is another story.

One does not have to overemphasize the similarities in Paz and Borges. Many things separate them, and in a profound way.

A gap of fifteen years (Borges was born in 1899, Paz in 1914), with what that implies about generational distance, separates them considerably. One example: the Russian revolution of 1917 finds Borges with his 18-year-old fervor intact; he dedicates an expressionist poem to the red dawn of Moscow; but his enthusiasm soon gives way to disenchantment and an anticommunism with a Manichean bias, which is almost inconceivable in a man so subtle in other ways. For Paz the Russian revolution is a historical fact (he was three years old when it happened) and it is the later struggle between Stalin and Trotsky that awakens his political conscience and from then on marks his commitment to the world. Just as disillusionment with Soviet totalitarianism drove Borges to anticommunism, Trotskyite criticism serves Paz as a stimulus for an exploration of the nature of the political universe.

Nor is the historical distance of Mexican and Argentine cultures negligible. Whereas Mexico has its deeper roots in the pre-Columbian past, Argentina founded its culture on a barely native soil, almost unpopulated, but generously fertilized by waves of Mediterranean immigrants. Borges can only be a European American; Paz is also an American Indian. On the other hand, geopolitics, which has emphasized Mexico's proximity to the United States, has contributed to the development of a powerful nationalism in that nation, a nationalism which Paz has criticized so masterfully in *El laberinto de la soledad* and *Posdata*. For Borges, however, nationalism is only an anachronistic romantic concept, or a private inheritance from ancestors who helped make the country. In his friendly attitude toward the United States, Borges reflects the geographical distance between Argentina and the powerful and remote nation to the north; but he also reflects an inability to understand a continental destiny that reaches beyond the battles of Junín or Ayacucho to the present-day struggle for freedom.

Nevertheless, these differences are not purely individual. To a greater or lesser degree they are differences other Argentines and Mexicans from the same generation would also reflect. The most important differences and distances, I think, are those created by the individual destinies of the two writers. In Borges one finds the image (pluperfect, as he wrote of Valéry's Monsieur Teste) of a writer whose life is nurtured only with books. He himself has said it a thousand times. Once in the epilogue to *El hacedor* (1960) he remarked:

> Few things have happened to me, but I have read about many. Rather, few things have happened to me that are more worthy of remembering than Schopenhauer's thought or England's verbal music.[2]

Paz, however, is a writer in whom intellectual activity is always situated within a wider and more varied social context. Like Borges, no passion is foreign to him, but whereas the Argentine writer lives out his passions within his breast and rarely expresses them in naked reality (as he would say), Paz is a man who lives what he dreams; or, rather, he lives twice: in the dream of reality and in the dream of writing.

47

Because of this, Paz has never shied away from political and human commitment (nor does he today). From his participation in the Spanish civil war to his recent intervention in the Mexican political debate (a debate which the daring pages of his *Posdata* have given a deeper meaning), Octavio Paz has known how to "suit the action to the word, the word to the action," as Hamlet said in another context. In Borges, protest or political participation (which isn't lacking, though at times it is regrettable) is always verbal. His eyesight was very weak from adolescence on and in the course of his life he underwent no fewer than six operations, until, on the threshold of old age he is practically blind. Borges lives a reality in which everything is shadows or reflections of shadows on the walls of a cavern of words.

If we leave the biographies in order to examine the specific cultural circumstances of their destinies, the distance between Borges and Paz grows even greater. The influence of an English grandmother who taught him to read in the language of Dickens before that of Galdós; the tutorial model of a father who was a professor of psychology in an English high school in Buenos Aires marks Borges (or Georgie, as he was called at home) with the stamp of Anglo-Saxon culture, which repeats at a distance the patterns of imperial culture. The Argentina of the upper classes is oriented more toward England than toward France. Borges was educated in Europe and obtained his M. A. (*bachillerato*) in Geneva, not Paris, and there he learned not only French, but German, thus deepening and diversifying his contacts with the roots of that Anglo-Saxon culture that is his blood heritage. Much later, as a professor of English and American literature in the Faculty of Philosophy and Letters at the University of Buenos Aires, Borges became immersed in the magic territories of early Anglo-Saxon poetry to emerge later (it was inevitable) in the even more remote and splendid monuments of Scandinavian culture. Today Iceland attracts him with the fascination of a remote, secret and inaccessible land. All that is Spanish, and thus obvious, in the River Plate culture; everything Italian that has so enriched the letters and music of his native country is foreign to Borges, or is hostile to him. He read the *Quijote* for the first time in English, and although he has dedicated many subtle pages to Cervantes, his authors continue to be De Quincey or Stevenson, Browning or Chesterton, Swinburne or Kipling, Poe or James, Emerson or Whitman, Mark Twain or Faulkner, Schopenhauer or Kafka. He, who has written so much and so well on *The Divine Comedy*, Ariosto and Croce, assures us that he does not understand a word of the Italian films and deplores the influence of Italian immigrants as reflected in the sentimentalism of Argentine letters.

Octavio Paz, on the contrary, begins by consciously assuming hispanic roots, which in Mexico is a sign of independence. Not only did he hurry to Spain in its hour of agony in 1937, but all his early poetry and critical work derive from a very personal reading of the great voices of contemporary Spain. The works of Unamuno and Machado guided the young Paz and the traces of both are very apparent in all his early writings, at least up to *El arco y la lira*. Another Spaniard, José Bergamín, also influenced Paz as a young man: Bergamín's presence in Mexico during those years just after the Spanish civil war served as a catalytic agent. He stimulated Paz to a more imaginative reading of Spanish literature, of the German romantics, of Lautréamont and the surrealists and Heidegger. The other great European source for his work is French literature, to which his critical thought returns incessantly as a point of reference. In this is one of the great differences between him and Borges. For although the Argentine writer was nourished in his youth on Mallarmé and Valéry, Flaubert and Apollinaire, Maupassant and Henri Barbusse, Marcel Schwob and Léon Bloy, his interpretation of French culture is too heterodox, too personal and arbitrary to be compared with the ordered, systematic and avid reading which Paz practiced from at least as early as the forties. It is not only a matter of keeping up to date and reading Sartre and Camus in 1945, and Robbe-Grillet and Lévi-Strauss in 1965. Nor is it a matter of the live and vivid experience of André Breton deeply marking Paz's critical thinking since those years when he visited the master of surrealism in Mexico, or at his own abode in Paris. (Only the heterodox, lazy Socrates, Macedonio Fernández has had a similar influence on Borges; but Macedonio was the opposite of Breton; he was a master without disciples or a cult, without a visible work, without any kind of literary strategy.)

Thus, when one thinks of Borges one thinks of a writer who is partly unexplainable unless the Anglo-Saxon cultural context within which his work is written is taken into account. With Paz it is the context of French culture, or France, that is essential. For even that which is not French comes to Paz by way of France: it was through Albert Béguin that Paz discovered the German romantics, as it was by way of French structuralism that he came to know the work of the Russo-North American linguist, Roman Jakobson. The fact that Paz and Borges appear to be the bearers of two of the richest currents of present day culture stresses even more their individual differences. For the rivalry between the French and Anglo-Saxon worlds (a rivalry that can only be understood in the parochial context of Europe at the end of the Middle Ages, but which lacks any meaning today) has prevented the incredible contributions of both cultures from becoming harmoniously integrated within Europe itself. This is one of the roots of mutual misunderstanding, which a dialogue between Borges and Paz texts can reveal.

Before I go any further, let it be known that while I assert that Borges and Paz are bearers of those parallel cultural currents, I do not intend to diminish in any way their originality, nor (which would even be less tolerable) their relationship with the national cultures to which their works belong. Only someone little versed in literary or cultural matters would lead us to believe that foreign influences are unfortunate, or that they should be eradicated. Those who support this theory today (and unfortunately they are numerous in Latin America) seem not to know that it had already been formulated in imperial Rome and that it was in opposition to this theory that Horace wrote his "Epistle to the Pisans." But the xenophobia of some of our compatriots on the continent prevents them from recognizing the foreign origin of the very nationalist doctrines which they profess with so much ardor and ignorance.

49

Borges and Paz have both been attacked for taking up foreign matters in their books, or for trying to reformulate foreign theories. Generally, the level on which these attacks are carried out is almost ridiculous. In 1954, an Argentine professor who today enjoys a considerable reputation in his country, wrote a pamphlet that denounced Borges's Byzantinism, supporting his argument with a very literal reading of some concepts of literary sociology popularized by Lucien Goldmann (a Romanian) and Jean-Paul Sartre.[3] In a recent review of *Configurations*, the most recent book by Paz translated into English, a Northamerican poet, whose name I prefer not to recall, discusses the poet's credentials for writing about the East because he considers Paz "a tourist"—this in spite of the fact that he has lived in India for six years.[4] Would it have occurred to the distinguished reviewer to ask Ezra Pound how many years he lived in China, or in the Provence of the troubadors? We should now turn to the text of a conference in which Borges responded to some of these so-called nationalists. It was written in 1951 and is included in the volume entitled *Discusión*, the sixth in his complete works.

> ... I don't know if it is necessary to say that the idea that a literature ought to be defined by the distinguishing traits of the country that produces it is a relatively new idea; just as new and arbitrary is the idea that writers should use themes from their own countries. Without going further, I believe Racine would not even have understood a person who would have denied his right to the title of French poet merely for having used Greek and Latin themes. I believe Shakespeare would have been surprised if someone had tried to limit him to English themes and had told him that as an Englishman he had no right to write *Hamlet*, a Scandinavian theme, or *Macbeth*, a Scottish theme. The Argentine cult of local color is a recent European cult that nationalists ought to reject as foreign.
>
> *   *   *
>
> I want to point out another contradiction: the nationalists pretend to venerate the abilities of the Argentine mind, but they would limit the poetic exercise of that mind to a number of impoverished local themes, as if Argentines could speak only of riverbanks and ranches and not of the universe.
>
> *   *   *
>
> Thus I repeat that we shouldn't be afraid and we ought to think that our patrimony is the universe; we ought to test all themes, since we cannot concentrate on what is Argentine in order to be Argentine: because either to be Argentine is a matter of chance, in which case we are Argentine no matter what, or to be Argentine is merely an affectation, a mask.
>
> I believe that if we give ourselves to that voluntary dream called artistic creation, we will be Argentines and we will also be good or tolerable writers.[5]

It would be easy to find similar points of view in Paz's works. In both Paz and Borges that tradition, originally Mediterranean, but now Atlantic and American, is still polemically alive.

In a certain sense, Borges and Paz renew in our day the dialogue (in mere reality, or in the imaginary confrontation of their texts) which Bello and Sarmiento, Darío and Rodó, Alfonso Reyes and Mariátegui kept up in other periods of our culture. It is a dialogue made up of apparent coincidences and profound discrepancies, of voices

Octavio Paz in 1971. Photograph by Nadine Markova

Josefina Lazano de Paz, Octavio's mother, at age 18.

Young Paz in 1924 with his aunt, a cousin, and his grandfather.

Octavio Paz at age 10.

Paz in 1930.

Early issues of *Taller*, the journal Paz helped to found in 1938.

Paz in Afghanistan, 1965.

In New Delhi, India, 1965.

Paz with Indira Gandhi, 1966.

Paz in India, 1966.

Paz and John Cage, 1966.

Visiting Ceylon in 1967.

Yves Bonnefoy with Paz at the Taj Mahal, Agra, India, 1968.

Paz and Julio Cortázar, 1968.

Charles Tomlinson, Paz, and Eduardo Sanguineti in Paris, 1969.

With Robert Creeley, 1969.

With Charles Tomlinson in Cambridge, 1970.

Claude Esteban, Paz, and Jorge Guillén at Cape Cod, 1969.

Octavio and Marie José Paz. Photograph by Nadine Markova

Paz at Teotihuacan, 1971.

With Elisabeth Bishop, 1972.

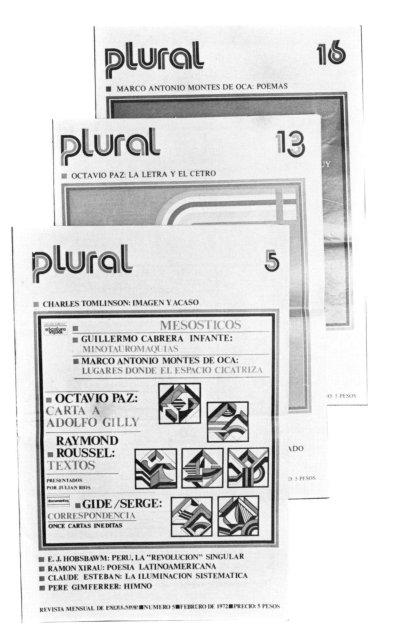

The review *Plural*, edited by Paz.

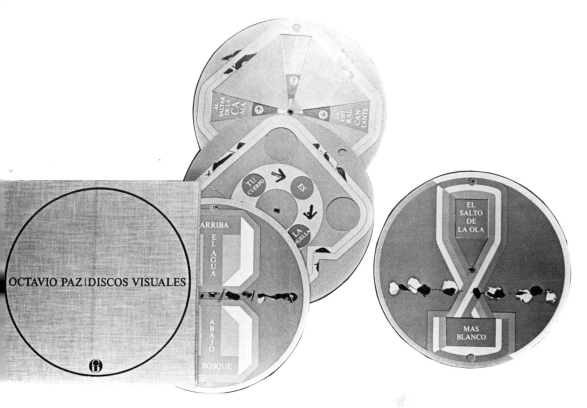

Paz's *Discos Visuales* (1968).

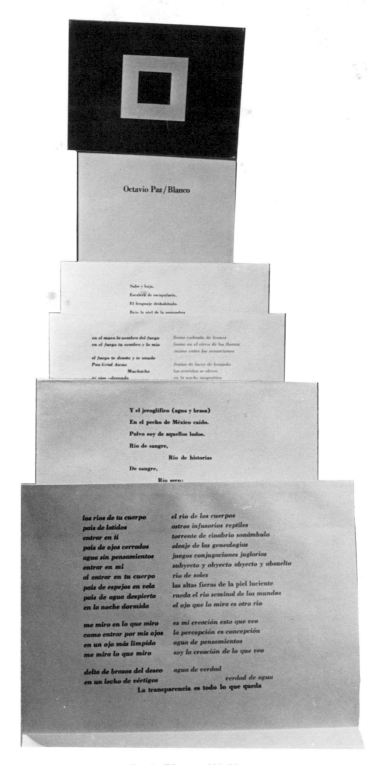

Paz's *Blanco* (1967).

that cross continents and seas in order to say the same things in a very different way, or to say things diametrically opposed in a similar way. It is, at times, a lively dialogue in which a kind of harmonious synthesis occurs at the end. But it is also a dialogue of deaf men; or a battle of careful duelers in a fog of words. To listen to their voices united and discrepant, to recognize echoes and resonances, to interpret a profound, inevitable opposition, is to submit to the most tantalizing process there is in reading: the palimpsest created by the reader's imagination, the photographic super-impression on a retina that still retains the image of a previous text, the memory tape on which one records directly over a previous recording.

I have been a most devoted reader of Borges almost since I can remember. I discovered him by chance, a matter of destiny perhaps, when I was 15 years old, leafing through a woman's magazine, *El hogar*, from Buenos Aires, to which my aunt was a subscriber. In it every two weeks Borges wrote a most erudite page entitled "Foreign Books and Authors." Since that time, reading Borges has been my profession. To read Paz after having read Borges has been a frustrating and challenging experience, one of discipline and confusion, a rare Tantalic torture. Paz came into existence for me in the pages of *El hijo pródigo*, one of the basic literary reviews of new hispanic literature. Reading *El laberinto de la soledad* at the beginning of the 1950s confirmed what I had found in the texts of that review. Then came *Libertad bajo palabra* and *El arco y la lira*. And what was to follow? All of Paz was implicit in the first texts.

But I insist that to read Paz after having interpreted Borges, or to return to Borges after having examined Paz is a singularly tantalizing experience. How many times have I lamented, for example, the fact that Paz had not developed a little further in *El arco y la lira* his ideas on the modern novel in the light of those hypotheses Borges had written fifteen years earlier in the prologue to *La invención de Morel*? But at that time Paz did not seem to have paid attention to Borges's prologue or to the extra-ordinary novel of Bioy Casares, the one which years later Robbe-Grillet would celebrate in a review and in the film-script of *Last Year at Marienbad*. And likewise, how many times I have lamented the fact that Paz spent too much time with French books and did not make a first-hand exploration of the unusual bibliography in English which Borges handled with so much familiarity and erudite peevishness? But also how many times, returning to Borges after an exhausting excursion through the pages of Paz, have I lamented the fact that the disconnected and capricious erudition of the Argentine master had so many times prevented him from rounding his argument with the Mexican's precision? How often, after following Paz in his readings of Heidegger or Lévi-Strauss, have I felt that Borges had remained (as if magically petrified) in the books of his youth, or in those of the maturity of his father, that Don Jorge Borges who has extended such a long intellectual shadow over the work of his child, his alter ego, his creation, his Golem?

To read Borges and then Paz; to read Paz and return to Borges, has been for me an exercise of quiet desperation but also an exercise of infinite learning. Some day I will have to attempt (with the space that is lacking here) a parallel examination of the critical works of both: an examination that will include, naturally, their poetic works, since in both writers poetry and criticism are not mutual opposites, but are integrated into a superior unity. Then I will attempt to emphasize some central aspects of that dialogue between critical texts: a dialogue that has never taken place in naked reality but which, nevertheless, continues to go on in my imagination.[6]

Yale University
Translated from the Spanish
By
Tom J. Lewis

[1] Octavio Paz, *El laberinto de la soledad*, Mexico City, Cuadernos americanos, 1950, p. 192.

[2] Jorge Luis Borges, *El hacedor*, Buenos Aires, Emecé, 1960, p. 109.

[3] Adolfo Prieto, *Borges y la nueva generación*, Buenos Aires, Letras Universitarias, 1954.

[4] Robert Bly, "Configurations," in *The New York Times Book Review*, 18 April, 1971, pp. 6, 20, & 22.

[5] Jorge Luis Borges, *Discusión*, Buenos Aires, Emecé, 1957, pp. 155–56, 158 & 162 respectively.

[6] This is the first part of a more extensive study on Borges and Paz which was read at the Third Oklahoma Conference on Writers of the Hispanic World: Octavio Paz, held on 15 October 1971.

Octavio Paz:
Critic of Modern Mexican Poetry

By ALLEN W. PHILLIPS

In view of the proverbially comprehensive nature of Octavio Paz's literary criticism, it is perhaps amazing to recall that he has devoted so much time to his own literature. It is equally true that for this very reason he is genuinely universal in his outlook, at the same time rejecting forcefully any spurious nationalism. Paz clearly does not believe in Mexican literature in the abstract, but rather in certain Mexican authors and in certain poems written by Mexicans who are progressively taking a major role in the literary dialogue of our times. However, from the decade of the thirties when he began to practice what he modestly called literary and artistic journalism, up to the panoramic prologue to "Poetry in Movement" (1966), he has not failed to be deeply concerned with Mexican literature, its past and its present.[1]

To begin with, let us venture a rapid description of Octavio Paz's literary criticism in its general lines, taking as a special base his works on Mexican literature, but without at the same time excluding others on different themes. As an essential note I should like to emphasize that his is a creative criticism, inseparable from poetic activity, always highly personal and the product of wide and careful reading. It is an *open* criticism, made in lively response to the works studied, which establishes the multiple resonances they wake in his spirit. To read his pages is to embark on a voyage through all cultures and all literatures, although it is not difficult to perceive certain preferences or families of writers that especially attract him. Without speaking of oriental sources, there are among the French: Baudelaire, Mallarmé, Lautréamont, Rimbaud, Apollinaire and the surrealists; Novalis and the German romantics; Blake Donne, Whitman, Eliot and other figures in poetry of the English language; the Spanish baroque writers (reading Góngora and Quevedo was decisive for him) and certain contemporary writing in Spanish from Darío and Lugones to Cernuda and Guillén.[2] Among the Mexicans to whom he is devoted alongside Pellicer, Villaurrutia and Cuesta, three national authors seem to be particularly distinguished by his preference: Alfonso Reyes, José Juan Tablada and Ramón López Velarde.

Paz's criticism is also in a certain sense fragmentary, which is not to say that he has not written organic books like *El arco y la lira*, revised in later edition, or *El laberinto de la soledad*, with its *Posdata* of 1970. Usually he chooses the form of brief notes and approaches authors who awaken his enthusiasm or admiration: fluctuation between direct commentary on some specific poem, the concentrated essay embracing the work of a single author; or more general topics like surrealism or pointed definitions of the modern literary adventure. Such, for example, are the pages collected in *Las peras del olmo* (1957), a selection of early works that have lost none of their freshness and mastery of direction in spite of having been written, for the most part, some twenty or twenty-five years ago. The book is composed of essays of various kinds, in which certain clichés of criticism undergo fresh examination, their partial truth failing to correspond with reality ("Emula de la llama . . ."); studies in revaluation ("La estela de José Juan Tablada"); or texts which perfect and complete earlier studies of other critics ("El lenguaje de Ramón López Velarde"). And it is appropriate to recall Octavio Paz's interest, still persistent, in the plastic arts, evident on many pages of this same book.

These brief essays were followed by a companion volume *Puertas al campo* (1966) intimately related to the earlier title and then at a later date by *Corriente alterna* (1967). In my judgment the prologues to the last two books are particularly significant. In the one to *Puertas al campo*, Paz explains that the volume is an extension of the earlier essay except that time separates them. He further states that this volume of 1966 coincides with a moment of great richness in Mexican letters, as opposed to one of indecision in the preceding volume of 1957, and in this flowering he takes great faith and joy.[3]

In the brief introduction to *Corriente alterna* he defends the fragmentary nature of his criticism, only superficially disperse, and in the same pages he insists on two key ideas: the moving reality of which we are part and books as a system of relations and interrelations. The critical fragments of Octavio Paz have an internal unity and a consistent train of thought holds them together. It is important to note how certain critical themes and concerns appearing in early pages are later more fully developed, a question of a clear process of growth and maturing; a constant return and an enrichment; a prolongation and refining of what was in him already from the first stage of his literary criticism.

Paz has never proposed arranging Mexican poetry in a systematic or systemized history. In this connection I am not forgetting his introduction to the *Anthology of Mexican Poetry* (Indiana University Press, 1958) which covers the Colonial Period up to and including Ramón López Velarde. Here he reveals his enthusiasm for some Mexican baroque poets as well as his lack of sympathy for the very limited success of Mexican romantics. With a few exceptions (among them the fascinating personality of Sor Juana), it is only natural that he is more interested in the poetry after modernism and especially contemporary expression. If he frequently condemns the novel of the *Revolución*, he is attracted to its more modern counterpart (Yáñez, Rulfo, Fuentes and some of the younger novelists).[4] Paz also gives importance to the essays of certain Mexicans, above all to those of Reyes and Cuesta. Nonetheless, the critical texts of Paz, indeed partial, tend to form a rather complete panorama of modern Mexican literature, above all from modernism to today.

Another element inseparable from his literary criticism and in effect of all his prose work, is the synthesis, sure and brilliant, often expressed in a terse phrase, almost aphoristic, which sums up or lights up clearly the meaning of his critical thought. I believe, in fact, that to characterize this criticism, based on a precise play of queries and answers (he questions himself and the works) there are two words of equal significance: illumination and revelation. I dare even propose two others: self-examination and self-portrait. Paz's literary criticism is the recreation of the poem by a poet-critic exceptionally gifted and committed to the practice of literature, who knows how to identify himself in feeling (which does not at all exclude lucidity) with the experience of another, make it his own and communicate to the reader a personal response to it.

The foregoing description of Octavio Paz's criticism corresponds to my personal way of reading it and being enlightened by it. Now, more objectively, I find myself forced to refer to a few texts in which the writer himself speaks of the function of that criticism. It is not surprising that a spirit so clear and passionate at the same time should have always had full consciousness of its mission and should now and again have complained of a certain poverty of good critical writing in Spanish.[5] He rejects, naturally and immediately, the journalistic criticism full of facile enthusiasms and useless conformism, and sees great danger lest criticism be prostituted by commercialism and politics (*Puertas*, 1966).[6] Nor is he a defender of a traditional science of literature and classifications imposed by traditional rhetoric ("to classify is not to understand"), although he may write: ". . . rhetoric, stylistics, sociology, psychology and all the other literary disciplines are indispensible if we wish to study a work, but they can tell us nothing about its intimate nature" (*Arco*, p. 15). There are, however, texts to which one must refer here: in one Paz explains the inner process of his criticism; in the other he defines the role of criticism, offering at the same time recommendations for Spanish language critics.

In his pages written in 1960 about the painter Rufino Tamayo, Octavio Paz reflects on the esthetic experience which is essentially pleasure, and since in the critical act of judging (and he judges, he confesses, to add pleasure to pleasure, which is or should be the starting point of all criticism) there enter reflections and the senses, thought and feeling, activities of diverse origins, but complementary in the adjustment of a truly critical vision. The senses cannot be eliminated; they must be guided and made more lucid. And then, as Paz says, judgment, sometimes an ally, at others an adversary, but always an incorruptible witness, "teaches how to distinguish living works from the mechanical. It reveals to me the secrets of clever fabrications and traces the frontier between art and artistic industry. In short, in enjoying works, I judge them; in judging, I enjoy. I live through a total experience, in which my whole being participates" (*Puertas*, pp. 216–17). Lastly in the same essay Paz speaks of how he takes possession of the work with careful scrutiny and how he conceives criticism again, always as an active and creative experience. In the critical act, he says, the work of art becomes a part of him. In judging it he also judges himself. No longer passive, he tries to go back to the origin of the artistic expression and rebuild the road which the creator has traced. Criticism, then, for Paz is always creative in nature and in the ultimate analysis is the description of a personal esthetic experience (Ibid. p. 217).[7]

A second fragment, highly significant and collected in *Corriente alterna*, is entitled "About Criticism." His point of departure is partly negative: he laments that there is not in Spanish what he calls "intellectual space," which would permit a meeting of works, one with another, in true dialogue involving its extension or negation: ". . . Criticism is that which constitutes what we call a literature and is not so much the sum of the works as the system of their relationships: a field of affinities and contrasts" (*Corriente*, p. 40). Once again Paz insists on the close relation between criticism and creation, criticism as nourishment for modern artists and as literary invention.

The mission of the literary critic, then, is to relate works of art and discover their place in the totality of literary expression. The function of criticism is to invent a perspective and an order. This points precisely to the failure of criticism in Spanish America; Spanish American critics must describe the frontiers, the forms, the structure, the dynamic movement of their literature and place its work in communication with one another, reading them in a universal context (Ibid. p. 41). Although Latin America still lacks a literary center ("Argentinian Europeanism and Mexican nationalism are distinct forms with a common infirmity: deafness"; Ibid. p. 43), Paz seems to glimpse the possibility of establishing authentic communication at some future time. Inasmuch as good literary criticism, operating by negation and associations, affinities and oppositions, brings order and stresses relationships, he even goes so far as to say that in our epoch criticism is the foundation of literature.

In an article about Paz as a critic of modern Mexican literature one cannot evade another idea conceived as fundamental and reiterated with marked frequency in his criticism of recent years. It is possible that Paz believed vaguely at an initial stage in the possibility of defining and differentiating the specifically Mexican in its literature.[8] It seems to me now that he has doubts about the conception of what is truly Mexican. At one moment he asks himself: what is it that unites poets so different as López Velarde, Lugones and Laforgue? It is not, it cannot be, the so-called national genius but the *spirit of the time* and he goes on to say:

> The existence of a French, a German or an English poetry is debatable; the reality of baroque, romantic or symbolist poetry is not. I do not deny national traditions nor the temperament of peoples; I affirm that style is universal, or better, international. What we call national traditions are almost always versions and adaptions of styles that were universal. In the last analysis a work is something more than a tradition and a style: a unique creation, an individual vision. To the extent to which the work is most perfect, tradition and style are less visible. Art aspires to transparence.
>
> (*Poesía*, pp. 3–4).

Literary styles are not national but international, and the individual accent of each artist is more significant than elusive national character (*Puertas*, p. 219).

Paz does not tire of repeating that styles travel; they are temporal in nature and "do not belong to the land but to the centuries" (Ibid. p. 220); they are, in a word, more ample than any geographical frontiers. And even more: in his opinion, modern literature is a single literature (*Corriente*, p. 42), and, now that time and space have become intermingled "a synchronic vision of art is superimposed over the diachronic" (Ibid., p. 23–24).

There definitely exists a Spanish American literature, different from the Spanish above all because of its destructive and polemic attitude with reference to language and tradition,[9] but the plurality of nations, each with their own peculiarities, does not destroy a unified culture and language. But this unity does not imply uniformity. Literary tendencies do not correspond to geographical labels, to political or ethnic entities. If an artistic movement is important, it does not take long to go beyond national boundaries (*Puertas*, p. 12). And Mexican literature is, after all, a portion of that literary dialogue, and the Mexican writer of today feels himself to be not only a part of Spanish American literature but also immersed in the universal artistic expression of our modern world.[10]

In *Cuadrivio* (1965) are collected four long essays on Rubén Darío, Ramón López, Velarde, Pessoa and Cernuda, dissident poets whose "creation was also critical, breaking with the language, the esthetics or the morality of their time" (*Cuad*, Prólogo) and their work, according to Paz, establishes a tradition of scission, the characteristic note of modern poetry. In the essay on Darío, "El caracol y la sirena," definitive pages and in my opinion among the best written by Paz as critic, modernism is correctly presented as what it really was: the great beginning, the end of which is not yet, the importance of which is double: ". . . on the one hand it produced four or five poets who renewed the great hispanic tradition, broken and detained at the end of the 17th century; on the other hand, having opened all doors and windows, revived the language" (Ibid., p. 12). It is enough to say that Paz emphasizes the most lasting and vital of that splendid movement, seeing it as a linguistic renewal without neglecting its profound ideological content. In summary, then, with modernism is created a new poetic language and in Hispanic America a dialogue with other literatures is really begun.

In modernism Paz usually and with good reason isolates the importance of Lugones and above all of his great *Lunario sentimental*, a book of open revolt already in a position outside of modernism. I believe, however, that Paz would be little interested in Lugones's final poetry, more narrative and traditional, but one cannot insist too much on the significance of the *Lunario*, in which a new poetic vision and extraordinary language have held so transcendant a place in the evolution of Hispanic-American poetry, from López Velarde to the *ultraístas* of Argentina and beyond. It surprises me a little that Paz has not given more attention to Herrera y Reissig, who is mentioned occasionally in lists, for this is another unconventional poet, moving surely toward the vanguard by way of metaphor and a language that mingles with lyricism certain prose elements that give new tension to his poetic expression. Naturally, Octavio Paz has at various times concerned himself with Mexican modernism, and he does not consider its poets to be of the same stature as the great figures of the movement. He believes that the Mexicans were not aware of the profound meaning of modernism and that their work was usually limited to the exoticism and purely external aspects of this tendency (*Peras*, p. 17). An example, not mentioned by Paz, could be Efrén Rebolledo, perhaps the most faithful of all Mexican poets to the modernist esthetic, with all the defects and virtues implied in such a statement. The verdicts of Paz on Gutiérrez Nájera as a poet (he does not refer to his prose) and Amado Nervo are not on the whole favorable (at one point he even calls them "authors of some of the clumsiest and most prosaic of our poetry" [Ibid., p. 69]); his reticences are equally eloquent. Personally, I believe that his opinions are correct and will stand the test of time. More kindly are his brief words about Othón and Salvador Díaz Mirón, and we can see how he relates them to each other in the following admirable summary: "If Othón is an academic who discovers romanticism and thus escapes from the Parnassianism of his school, Salvador Díaz Mirón undertakes a voyage in an opposite direction: he is a romantic aspiring to classicism . . ." (Ibid., p. 15). Paz all the same notes how Icaza and Urbina, less applauded in their time ". . . approach more nearly the electric zone of poetry" (Ibid., p. 18). There is, naturally, one modernist Mexican poet saved from this almost total condemnation: Enrique González Martínez who closes the period before the break that comes with the work of Tablada, López Velarde and Pellicer. Paz's opinions about the serious and austere González Martínez are definitive: he does not break with modernism, he strips it bare; he veils its light; makes from it a consciousness; and with the work of this writer from Jalisco "poetry ceases to be description and plaint to become again spiritual adventure" (Ibid., p. 19). His strength and example is to have returned to poetry what Paz calls the *gravity* of the word. This is the positive side of González Martínez, but the critic is not slow in referring to his moralistic symbolism and notes how his verse sometimes lapses into sermonizing (Ibid., p. 59). Furthermore: his poetic work lacks the unexpected and lacks movement, being essentially hostile to innovations. The treatment given González Martínez is courteous but distant and hardly enthusiastic.

Among the special predilections of Octavio Paz are three Mexican writers, very different one from the other, but each in the best of his work existing outside the modernist stream: Alfonso Reyes, José Juan Tablada and Ramón López Velarde.

In many pages, from some of the earliest to others of more recent date, Paz never stints his praise of Reyes as a writer and an example. "It is enough to say," he once wrote, "that without him our literature would be half a literature" (Ibid., p. 71). In his vast and varied writing, Paz praises the humanist and the universal writer, the erudite scholar refined by humor and the poet in love with words. In his literary output he fuses criticism and creation (another devotee of Mallarmé); prose and poetry mingle (for example, *Visión de Anáhuac*); and even in a few poems the direct language is infused with a secret poetic tension (*Poesía*, p. 13). The key and summit of Reyes, *Ifigenia cruel*, a dramatic poem commented on extensively in the beautiful essay "El jinete del aire" was written directly after Reyes's death.

And in summation of these statements about Alfonso Reyes, which sometimes take the form of enthusiastic portraits,[11] it is important to remember what Paz says about his books dealing with poetic theory. In the final section of the introduction to the first edition of *El arco y la lira* Paz writes this great tribute:

> Stimulus from him has been double: on the one hand his friendship and his example gave me courage; on the other, the books dedicated to subjects closely related to these pages . . . and so many unforgettable essays, scattered in other works— made clear to me what had seemed obscure, the opaque transparent, the wild and tangled easy and orderly. In a word: they enlightened me (*Arco*, p. 8).

In another way Tablada awakened in Octavio Paz enthusiasm and fascination, an attitude not shared by many commentators on modern Mexican poetry. And more: certain poems of Tablada have been, without doubt, on more than one occasion a model for Paz's own poetry. It is not hard to explain what he found in a part of Tablada's work: movement and severance, surprise and humor, adventure and travel, cosmopolitanism and curiosity. It is important to add to these substantives, already become commonplaces with reference to Tablada that he is always in the vanguard, friend of painters and devoted to prehistoric culture. With the exception of El Abate de Mendoza and, to a lesser degree, Villaurrutia, no Mexican or foreign critic has done more than Paz to revaluate the almost forgotten work of Tablada so that it can be said that he has *created* a poet whose work, nonetheless, is still awaiting complete evaluation. Octavio Paz has not only done this but has also separated the worthiest part of his poetry from the more lifeless part, in accord with what Villaurrutia asked for in an earlier time.[12] Dissenting with González Martínez, unmoved in his classicism, Tablada and at his side his young friend López Velarde, who was one of the very few who understood Tablada's attempts in spite of his grave doubts about certain poetical experiments of the older poet, broke with the language of modernism and initiated a new lyric adventure. And it is not irrelevant to recall that in 1914 Tablada was one of the first to recognize the originality and worth of López Velarde. Nor is Paz unaware that between these two poets and the next generation of *Contemporáneos* there exists an obvious continuity (*Peras*, p. 70). Paz's most complete essay on Tablada dates from 1945, but it is enough to mention here what Paz wrote about possibly "our youngest poet" (*Poesía*, p. 10) in 1966 and his opinion has not changed:

> In Mexico the tradition of the open work, not in the strict sense but in the broadest and most general, begins with Tablada. One part of his work fascinates me: that written at the end of his poetic life. There are not many poems but nearly all are amazing. Haiku and ideographic poetry, humor and lyricism, the natural world and the city, women and travel, animals and plants, Buddha and insects. His poetry has lost none of its freshness, none of its novelty . . . (Ibid., p. 13).

The longest essay that Paz devotes to a Mexican poet is "El camino de la pasión"

(1963) on Ramón López Velarde. It is difficult for me to summarize my judgments on this brilliant work. They shift from frank and unqualified enthusiasm to certain minor disagreements (perhaps the most pertinent is in reference to the slight value Paz seems to give the poems collected posthumously in *El son del corazón*, excepting "La suave patria"). What I have already said in print, is that after this memorable study by Paz there is practically nothing new to say of the Zacatecan poet, even in this year 1971, the fiftieth anniversary of his death, which has produced critical writing to the saturation point. Yet in my own inescapable share in the homages presented in the month of June, I had the uncomfortble feeling that I was repeating in another form many things said already, and better, by Paz.

His was an early interest in López Velarde. Exemplary is his note about this writer's innovations in language, and this work of 1950 completes and continues an earlier essay of Villaurrutia. Here for the first time something fundamental is studied: Lugones and Laforgue as fruitful stimuli to López Velarde's own original instrument of expression. I believe that Paz's statements made twenty years ago have not lost their freshness and they have passed, with hardly a correction, into his more extensive work of 1963. In parenthesis, if Paz has not changed his word on Laforgue, the pages on Baudelaire and López Velarde have undergone some fundamental modifications.

"El camino de la pasión," always precise and illuminating, places López Velarde on the threshold of worldwide modern poetry (and in the Spanish language, according to Paz, this saw the light in Hispanic America earlier than in the peninsula). The essay is important also for what it tells us of the modern poem, its form and structure; of the esthetic of López Velarde and the metaphor which reveals and strips bare; of his eroticism and his love; of his beliefs and his literary tradition. Especially meaningful also are the textural commentaries on one of López Velarde's most intense poems, "El sueño de los guantes negros," where the central verse is a question ("is not your flesh preserved in each bone?") and one with no answer.

This essay seems to be the happy climax of long years spent with the brief and concentrated work of López Velarde; it succeeds in illuminating many obscure corners that characterize the poet's mature work in prose and verse. Having commented thus upon some of the friendly judgments Paz gives on Reyes, Tablada and López Velarde, three writers related, though differently, to later poetry, we are in a position to move on to two ultimate nuclei in our long voyage through Paz's criticism of modern Mexican poetry: the generation of the *Contemporáneos* and that of the young who follow them.

In this final part of our subject it would be little short of impossible to make a complete collection of the critical judgments given by Paz on the poetry of the twenties to the present. They are, with a few notable exceptions, more fragmentary, but not for this reason less authentic or penetrating. This is the literary period that critic and poet lived through intimately. Above all I should like to avoid a sort of catalogue, and therefore will be content with pointing out certain enthusiasms and reservations that influence his personal way of evaluating or placing in focus the evolution of the national lyric in some fifty years of intensified production.

To the decade of the twenties belong the beginnings of the generation of *Los contemporáneos*, a group of distinguished writers, accused of being neglectful of Mexico but united by their absorption with universal questions and their high esthetic ideals, by their critical position and their tireless activities in behalf of culture (reviews, experimental theater, love for the plastic arts). Among these writers Paz seems to be enthusiastic about four in particular: the three great poets (Pellicer, Villaurrutia, Gorostiza) and the essayist Jorge Cuesta. He is less interested in two figures slightly more to the right: Torres Bodet and Ortiz de Montellano, although as regards the latter he does mention his sympathy for the prehispanic. All the same he points out the importance of Gilberto Owen, because his work is a milestone in the development of the prose poem in Mexico. As for Salvador Novo, only his first stage seemingly merits Paz's praise (*Poesía*, pp. 14–18).

In *Las peras del olmo* two critical essays are collected, from 1951 and 1955, devoted respectively to Gorostiza and Pellicer. There is no specific article on Villaurrutia, whom he greatly admired, none that we know of, except that he excuses himself for not having written one (*Peras*, VI). Certainly he comments warmly on his poetry on many occasions, and I believe, besides, that Villaurrutia's literary criticism on Mexican and foreign authors was always stimulating to Paz. He perfects and prolongs in more than one sense Villaurrutia's critical appraisals. And in 1966 Paz offers a splendid summary of his poetry (*Poesía*, pp. 16–17).[18]

In the case of Cuesta, who claimed Paz's intellectual sympathy because of the originality of his thought and his capacity for analysis, he valued him above all as an essayist preoccupied with research in the meaning of the Mexican tradition. Paz writes of him in a page of *El laberinto de la soledad* (*Lab*, pp. 143–45), alongside other thinkers (Vasconcelos, Ramos, Reyes and others), and besides a few other brief phrases alluding personally to Cuesta (for example, *Peras*, VI), Paz explains his exclusion from *Poesía en movimiento* as follows: ". . . The influence of his thinking upon the poets of his generation was very deep, and on my own also, but his poetry was not in his poems but in the work of those lucky enough to have heard him" (*Poesía*, p. 9).

In an early note (1942) entitled "Emula de la llama . . ." that received a prize in the Editorial Seneca contest, the earlier title being "Pura, encendida rosa," Octavio Paz undertakes a critical examination of Pedro Henríquez Ureña's often abused statement about Mexican sensibility and its twilight tones. Here are delineated the hour of Pellicer (the brilliant light of morning), of Gorostiza (early morning) and of Villaurrutia (night), (*Peras*, pp. 57–59). In a later essay on Pellicer he goes deeply into the work of this poet of sun and sea; sees in him the first really modern poet of Mexico, already far from the manner of González Martínez (*Peras*, 95); and completes his judgment by stating: ". . . he is the richest and most vast of the poets of his generation. There are more perfect poets; or more dense and dramatic; keener or deeper; but none has his deep breadth, his dazzled and dazzling sensuality . . . ." (Ibid., p. 103). I cannot resist the temptation to copy an opinion of 1966 about Pellicer in which Paz reiterates with increased certainty some earlier points of view:

> We also grow enthusiastic about this poetry which puts the world in flight and turns rocks to cloud, the woods to rain, a puddle to a constellation. Word-kite, word-helix, word-stone to fling at the sky. We shall never tire of this winged reality. Each time I read Pellicer, I truly *see.* To read him clears the eyes, sharpens the senses, gives body to reality. Speed of a glance into diaphanous air; to arrest that moment in which energy flows invisibly, matures and bursts into tree, house, dog, machine, person. Like the rivers of his land, Pellicer's work is broad and, like them, true to itself: his latest book could be the first. In another poet this might be a defect. In him it is a virtue, the greatest of his gifts. He preserves intact the original force: enthusiasm and creative imagination (*Poesía*, pp. 14–15).

The reflectiveness of Villaurrutia is contrasted with the magic of Pellicer, but in a revealing earlier page, Paz believes that there are wings in the poet of Tabasco ". . . but not a 'somersault,' nor change from one state to another" (*Peras*, p. 102). And on various occasions he repeats that those three poets, the best of their generation and each with his own remarkable, distinguished personality, were condemned to staying within the frontiers of their poetic universe (Ibid., pp. 101–102). Gorostiza, sparing and complex, is according to Paz, the author of "one of the most important works of modern poetry in the Spanish language," a poem ". . . summoned to last as long as the loftiest creations of the language" (Ibid., p. 71). In his introduction to *Poesía en movimiento,* he gives us, as in the case of Pellicer and Villaurrutia, another admirable measure for establishing what "Muerte sin fin" represents in the modern tradition (*Poesía,* p. 20).

After the generation of the *Contemporáneos* comes that of Octavio Paz himself, which in its time, the thirties, was grouped around various ephemeral reviews before the founding of *Taller* in 1938, its principal and most permanent organ. In 1954 Paz wrote his polemical reply to *La poesía mexicana moderna,* the anthology published by Castro Leal. He did it because it seemed clear to him that in the second part the compiler failed to understand and therefore did not represent the latest generation of Mexican poets very well. In this text, as opposed to the desires and predilections of the earlier group—many of them certainly admired and sympathized with by Paz—he defines clearly the ideals of his own generation of *Taller.* I confine myself to a short summary at best risky: poetry as an action and experience lived through, in which the writer realizes and transcends himself; repudiation of the earlier intellectualism; new influences (the young Spanish poets, the surrealists, Neruda, et cetera); and, as Paz says, "love, poetry and revolution were three burning synonyms" (*Peras,* pp. 72–75). A new conscience vis-à-vis the world, society and the word.

In two brief essays written in 1959 and later collected in *Puertas al campo,* Paz first hails the "verbal explosion" (*Puertas,* p. 125) of the first book of Marco Antonio Montes de Oca and next the appearance of *La paloma azul* of Manuel Durán. This is a cordial and sympathetic critique, enthusiastic but demanding, implying certain slight disagreements with the authors. In the same volume there appears a long essay

"El precio y la significación" (1963) which includes in its last part (Ibid., pp. 271–75) an extensive list of young writers (Rulfo, Arreola, Sabines, Xirau, Segovia, García Terrés, García Ponce, Fuentes and others) who contributed toward 1950 to the birth of a new epoch in Mexican literature, after the relative pause in the decade before. From the fifties must be mentioned also the experimental group of *Pocsía en voz alta* and the publication of the *Revista mexicana de literatura*, both undertakings animated by the presence of Octavio Paz in Mexico.

There was a delay of a few years, indeed until 1966, when Paz wrote his most organic pages about Mexican poetry of the last fifty years. This constitutes the introduction, already quoted, to *Poesía en movimiento*, an experimental anthology compiled in collaboration with Alí Chumacero, Pacheco and Aridjis. The anthology incorporates a total of forty-two poets, among whom about thirty belong to recent generations.

Certain basic ideas govern the selection of poets and poems. The aim is to show poetry in all its mobility and mutation; indicate the spirit of adventure and search which characterizes it from the point of view of the break initiated years before by Darío and Huidobro, the break which for Paz is the mark of modern poetry. Their criterion then, is change, not the stalemate implied by the collecting of the best poems of an author and not necessarily those showing an intention to do something distinctive. The method used to reflect this dynamic quality is not completely exclusive, and therefore, to the benefit of the whole panorama, some poets are included who have sought novelty in only a few instances (I am thinking at the moment of Torres Bodet, Rosario Castellanos). Besides in constructing this book, there is a departure from traditional order, since the authors do not regard the past as a beginning, but the reverse: "to see in the present a beginning, in the past an end" (*Poesía*, p. 7). Hence the order of the poets. The work begins with Homero Aridjis and Pacheco (the youngest), and ends with López Velarde and Tablada (the oldest). Lastly it seems to me highly proper to include poems in prose of Julio Torri, Owen, Paz, Aridjis and Pacheco, and I wonder, in parenthesis, why not some of López Velarde?

In his introduction, solid and complete, Paz moves freely, treating historical or chronological schemes and general historical groups (*Los contemporáneos, Taller, La espiga amotinada*), but, as he himself confesses, he lets himself be guided not by an objective criterion but by his own preferences and even his caprice. His judgments are always personal and imaginative and in them can often be seen the play of oppositions and affinities helping to determine the exact position of the authors. While individualizing them, he establishes contradictory and complementary relationships among them. Remember, for instance, the stratagem of using for the younger poets the system of coordinates derived from the *I Ching*. Paz insists that his opinions do not belong to literary criticism; clearly I do not agree; but let me repeat the closing words of the introduction:

> . . . the significance of poetry, if it has any, is not in the judgments of the critic or the opinions of the poet. The significance is changing and momentary: it flowers from the encounter between poet and reader (Ibid. p. 34).

One final word: Octavio Paz believes fervently in youthful Mexican poetry (he would probably say in some poets and their work); youthful Mexican poetry believes in him. He has oriented many of them, from Montes de Oca on; he is an inciting presence among them; they read and study him. It would be tiresome to recount here what during different periods of his wandering life Paz's sojourns in Mexico have meant to literary youth. They have acted as a catalytic agent. Even more: they are become a fundamental presence.

University of Texas, Austin

Translated from the Spanish
By
Esther Whitmarsh Phillips

[1] Having decided some months ago on the topic for these pages, I have since read the excellent article of Luis Leal entitled "Octavio Paz y la literatura nacional: afinidades y oposiciones," *Revista iberoamericana*, No. 74, January-March 1971. I shall try here to do something different and, despite certain inevitable resemblances, this earlier article excuses me from transcribing certain quotes and lists of authors.

[2] Especially illuminating in this regard, namely that of literary influences, is the interview with Paz published in *Insula*, Nos. 260–61, July-August 1968.

[3] Octavio Paz, *Puertas al campo*, Mexico City, 1966, p. 5.

We shall use in the present essay the following abbreviations in referring, both in the text and in the notes, to the works of Paz which we quote:

Peras: Las peras del olmo, Mexico City, 1957.
Lab: El laberinto de la soledad, 2nd. edition, Mexico City, 1959).
Arco: El arco y la lira, 2nd edition, Mexico City, 1967.
Cuad: Cuadrivio, Mexico City, 1966.
Puertas: Puertas al campo, Mexico City, 1966.
Corriente: Corriente alterna, Mexico City, 1967.
Poesía: Poesía en movimiento, Mexico 1915–1966, Mexico City, 1966.

[4] Certain articles by Paz about the novel appeared in *Taller* in about the years 1939 and 1940; they have not been collected in book form to date. At various times he has judged the novels of the revolution severely: e.g., in *Sur*, XII No. 105, July 1943, pp. 93–96. Elsewhere [Claude Couffon, *Hispanoamérica en su nueva literatura*, Santander, 1962, p. 75] he recognizes in them an historical importance and a documental value, and in the quoted interview published in *Insula* he seems to temper his views somewhat.

In 1961 Paz dedicates a splendid note to Yáñez's *Al filo del agua*, just published in French translation (*Puertas*, pp. 142–47). To this text, an admirable

summary of this great novel, he adds a very significant note in which he speaks in glowing terms of Rulfo, Fuentes, Arreola, Elena Garro and other young novelists (Ibid. pp. 143–44). For further reference to Fuentes, cf. "La máscara y la transparencia" (*Corriente*, pp. 44–50). The comments on Rulfo are frequent and always full of praise, cf. *Corriente*, p. 18, and Mercedes Valdivieso, "Entre el tlatoani y el caudillo," *Siempre*, no. 426, 8 April 1970, p. v.

[5] Cf. *El arco y la lira*, 1956, p. 84.

[6] With reference to the same subject, cf. "Sobre la crítica" (*Corriente*, pp. 41–42).

[7] Another very significant text in this regard and dealing with the painting of Juan Soriano is to be found in *Puertas*, pp. 233–34.

[8] The earliest text of importance is the "Encuesta sobre la poesía mexicana: Respuesta de Octavio Paz," *Letras de México*, V, Vol. III, No. 4, 15 April 1941, which should be quoted here if space so permitted. Luis Leal, in his above-mentioned article, devotes certain pages (pp. 246–48) to this matter of national literature.

[9] For an explicit statement in this regard, cf. quoted interview in *Insula* and also *Poesía*, p. 4.

[10] These ideas and others like them reach their maximum expression in a note appended to his book *Claude Lévi-Strauss o el nuevo festín de Esopo*, Mexico, 1969, pp. 131–32. In spite of its length I am copying it here: "Instead of being a succession of names, works and tendencies, the tradition would be converted into a system of significant relationships: a language. The poetry of Góngora would not be simply something that happened after Garcilaso and before Rubén Darío, but a text related dynamically with other texts; we would read Góngora not as an isolated text but in its context: those works that determined it and those that its own poetry determines. If we conceive of poetry in the Spanish language more as a system than a history, the significance of the works com-

posing it depends less on chronology and one point of view than on the relationship of texts themselves and the very movement of the system. The importance of Quevedo is not exhausted in his work or in the conceptualism of the 17th century; we find the sense of his words more fully in some poem of Vallejo even when, naturally, what the Peruvian poet says is not identical with what Quevedo said. The sense is transformed without disappearing: each transmutation in changing it prolongs it. The relationship between one work and another is not merely chronological, or, rather, this relationship is variable and constantly changes the chronology: to *hear* what the latter poems of Juan Ramón Jiménez say one must read a song from the 14th century (for example: "Aquel árbol que mueve la hoja" . . .

of Admiral Hurtado de Mendoza). Lévi-Strauss's idea invites us to see Spanish literature not as a combination of works but as one sole work. This work is a system, a language in motion and in relation to other systems: European works and their American descendants.

[11] Particularly well done are the following frag ments: *Puertas*, p. 58 and 65 and also *Lab*, pp. 145–48.

[12] Xavier Villaurrutia, Prólogo, *Poemas escogidos de Efrén Rebolledo*, Mexico City, 1939, pp. 13–14.

[13] For other texts about Villaurrutia: "Cultura de la muerte," *Sur*, VIII, No. 47, August 1938, pp. 81–85 in which Paz reviews *Nostalgia de la muerte* and also "El teatro de Xavier Villaurrutia," Ibid., XII, No. 105, July 1943, pp. 96–98.

Irony and Sympathy
in *Blanco* and *Ladera este*

By MANUEL DURÁN

To understand is to see patterns.

Isaiah Berlin's statement in *Historical Inevitability* might well stand as a motto for my critical approach. Possibly the relative security with which literary criticism has tended to deal with poetry derives not only from long experience—we have been at it since Aristotle—but equally from the structural emphasis of Aristotle's work. In a more contemporary context, the impact of Paz's poetry derives in no small part from its perception of patterns (which Frye prefers to call schematic rather than systematic) relating the parts of a poem or a book to each other and to the larger literary contexts which subsume them. Dr. Johnson would have been pleased.

Blanco appears in 1966, *Ladera este* in 1968. The first is a long, tight poem about a seemingly abstract subject, language. A philologist would turn to yards of gray prose. Paz explodes technicolor fireworks. *Ladera este* is a longer book, not more complex than *Blanco*, but rather less tightly composed, more varied. In both cases a yes and a no, enthusiasm and irony, provide a framework of polarities, and beat like the expansion and contraction of a heart. One does not pretend here, to make criticism (in this case criticism of Paz's poetry) what Harry Levin rightly observes it cannot be, an "exact science." What I rather propose to do is to explore structural units more systematically and fully than criticism has so far done. Insofar as literature is idea-form, a grasp of recurrent form is as essential and integral to a total literary comprehension as is a grasp of recurrent ideas or archetypes. My students have long since decided that to find patterns in a work is to please Professor Durán. I would make bold to suggest that in the intersecting of those patterns lies a unity: they are not a scaffolding but an inner frame holding the building erect.

To state that Paz is a living poet implies that he is subject to all the pressures, both positive and negative, that our time generates in abundance. Among them is an increase in the tempo, the rhythm, of change. The period of Paz's production that concerns us now is the decade of the sixties. During this time Paz discovers two facts that are bound to affect his writings. On the one hand, a fact which has its roots in a personal experience: his residence in India. He gains a direct access to the reality of the orient in a most specific form. On the other hand, another fact influences his conscious life, his life as an intellectual: this is the impact of a theory, the nucleus of ideas that we can describe under the general label of "structuralism." Without ceasing for a moment to be a surrealist and moreover without dismantling the superimposed existentialist canopy that had been placed upon the surrealist background, Paz becomes a structuralist.

We are therefore dealing with a complex multilayered reality. It is perhaps impossible to sort out the strands; the labyrinth of influences challenges our ingenuity when faced with any poem written by Paz in the decade of the sixties. Yet there are certain basic facts that will help us. Change is always superimposed upon an enduring continuity. If we compare the latest poem by Paz with one, with any one of his early poems, we shall immediately see the difference between the two poems, but we should also be capable of seeing the line that unites them, the stylistic and ideological factors that allow us to recognize both poems as being the result of the same personal vision, of the same poetic mind. Therefore I think it prudent not to overemphasize the originality of Paz's latest poetry: it is, of course, a new departure, a fresh look at the world, a new definition of reality, which is what we can and should expect from a new book from a great poet, and yet the man who has written this poetry is the same man, the same writer, who gave us *Libertad bajo palabra* and the early Paz essays. "Plus ça change, plus c'est la même chose."

On the other hand, there are periods where evolution steps up its pace, where *ça change* at a new rhythm. This is what happens for Paz, I think, during the decade of the sixties. We still do not have a biography, official or otherwise, of Paz as a man and as a writer. Usually one has to wait until the death of a man in order to have a complete image of his life. (Isn't this observation the same one made by a character created by Cervantes in *Don Quixote*, where Ginés de Pasamonte explains that he could not possibly write the story of his life, since he had not stopped being alive?) Some day, however, some day which I hope is still very far in the future, we shall have a biography of Octavio Paz. If it is a good one, it shall underline the importance of the decade of the sixties in his life. If I may be allowed for a brief moment to place my explanation within a Jungian framework, I shall remind my readers that according to Jung's interpretation of the evolution and maturing of the human psyche, a man cannot be considered as having successfully become an adult until he has killed a dragon and married a princess. These terms are of course symbolic and have to be translated into the language and the circumstances of the twentieth century. Yet it is clear to me, in my interpretation of what we know of Paz's activity during this period, of his long and courageous battle with what we can define as the ugly dragon of Mexican official institutions, and his having found in India a woman he loved and made his wife, that Paz has finally fulfilled the Jungian requisites: he has done victorious battle with a dragon and married a princess. No wonder his poetry has gained in depth: it is now the fully mature poetry of an adult poet.

The decade of the sixties is crucial for Paz in another field, the one that should concern his readers most. During these years he discovers simultaneously the vast reality of India—and the intellectual tool of structuralism, specifically in its French version as represented by Lévi-Strauss. Of his discovery of India we find abundant traces in Paz's poetry, and also in his prose essays on Hindu art. His structuralist avocation has found a lucid outlet in essays such as *El nuevo festín de Esopo* and *Conjunciones y disyunciones*. I think it is significant, and helpful to us as readers of Paz, that these two discoveries took place at the same time. They seem to balance each other, to "need" each other. India is the place—the culture—in which borderlines are erased, identities blend, sharp lines become as blurred as colors in a bleeding Madras cloth. A gigantic cauldron, the original melting pot, much more efficient and hotter than its American equivalent. Any Westerner who lives in India not as a tourist or as a mere diplomat, but rather as a man sensitive to his environment, is bound to have his sense of identity, himself, his ego, both expanded and eroded. Paz was fully prepared for such a change. I do not know whether Paz has read Martin Buber or not. What matters is that Paz was always interested in the "I–Thou" relationship, and therefore was already prepared to surrender some sharp edges of the self, to make his self more available to dialogue and projection toward others, toward the world in general.

"Everything the artist invents is true," Flaubert said—a more profound remark than it might appear. Yet the emphasis in Flaubert's sentence is placed upon man, as an artist, as a cultural hero. From Descartes on, it is man's rational self which occupies the center of the stage—at least in the Western tradition. This view is reflected in the early Paz as a critic: in the first edition of *El arco y la lira*, published in 1956, the emphasis is upon the self, the poet as a cultural hero: "There is no poem," Paz writes, "without a creating mind" (p. 37). "Poetry is an act of free creation" (p. 38). "Poetic creation is merely the exercise of human freedom. What we call inspiration is only the manifestation or unfolding of such a freedom" (p. 188). Emir Rodríguez Monegal has carried out a careful confrontation of this first edition of *El arco y la lira* and the second edition of 1967. The changes are numerous and important. Under the twofold impact of structuralism and the oriental experience, Paz reaches conclusions which in many respects differ from his previous statements (see E. R. Monegal's "Relectura de *El arco y la lira*," *Revista iberoamericana*, No. 74, Spring 1971). As Monegal states, "now the orient is for him something more that a dazzling vision or an intuition captured reading between the lines of texts by Western specialists. This does not mean that Paz has ever ceased being a Western man. On the contrary, he is more Western than ever. But the East has now become part of his vision as a Western man. . . . Through the mask, or disguise, of Oriental culture, Octavio Paz can now reach the true face of his Western world." Summing up: as a critic of literature, Paz has recently de-emphasized the magic or heroic role of the poet, underlining instead a new role of language which has been suggested by structuralism—and probably also by the emotional impact of his oriental experience. He writes in *Corriente alterna*: "The problem of meaning in poetry becomes clear as soon as we notice that the meaning is not to be found outside, but rather inside the poem; it is not to be found in what the words have to say, but rather in what the words *have to say to each other*" (". . . en aquello que *se dicen entre ellas*"). In his essay on André Breton, published in *Mundo Nuevo*

(December 1966), Paz states: "A man inspired, a man who really expresses himself, does not say anything that belongs only to him: through his mouth it is language that speaks to us." And in *Festín de Esopo* he states that for Lévi-Strauss "it is nature that speaks to herself through man, without man being aware of it." Flaubert's sentence should now become: "Everything language invents is true," and man would be a mere vehicle, a bystander. We are now in a properly humble frame of mind. Paz is ready to show us, in *Blanco*, a poem which seems to be self-creating, self-sustaining, a slow and painful—but also graceful—dialogue in which one word seems to give birth to another, until a whole army of words marches on. His approach is subtle, modern, humble: the act of creation is displaced from poet to the language itself. Mallarmé, Valéry, and structuralism, are an obvious background. I can think of another image that comes to my mind: a boastful young boy riding a bicycle: "Look, Ma, no hands!"

And yet a break with the past has not taken place, at least if by the past we understand the role of the poet as *vate*, as the one who expresses the yearnings and the visions of the tribe, the anonymous sayer of lines and creator of myths. For this vision, which the German romantic poets were to resuscitate, puts its emphasis not upon the self, the individual man, but upon the obscure forces of collective inspiration. By his retreat from the center of the stage, by his giving the dominant role to the forces of language, Paz in *Blanco* has succeeded in modernizing and updating one of the oldest and most basic interpretations of poetry. When the composition of *Blanco* begins we are surrounded by silence. When it ends we go back to silence. What happens between these two moments is not clearly willed and controlled by a conscious mind, at least not one that is visible to the reader. (We are reminded of a Japanese Noh play, in which the prop men, all dressed in black, may move furniture around without the public becoming aware of it.)

Blanco is possibly the most difficult poem written until now by Paz. The author himself seems to challenge us, to taunt, to tantalize us, by offering a series of elusive clues. The poet, the true poet, he says elsewhere (in his book on *Lévi-Strauss*) is a man in love with silence—but one who cannot keep himself from talking. He partakes of silence and language, is suspended half-way between an acute feeling of loneliness and the need to share his vision with others. While describing the world around him and inside himself he not only recreates this world but gives us the clues so that we can do the same thing while reading his poem. These clues are necessary if we want to approach a poem such as *Blanco* through analysis—and let us add here, through an analysis that has gained some insights from the structuralist approach. As Roland Barthes himself has stated,

> the goal of every structuralist activity, whether reflective or poetic, is to reconstitute an 'object,' in a manner that will make clear, through this reconstruction, the rules of functioning (the 'functions') of this object. The structure is, therefore, in fact, a *construct* [*simulacre*] of the object, and yet a construct which has a goal, a purpose, since the imitated object makes evident for us something that seemed to be invisible, or if we prefer unintelligible, in the natural object [which is being

translated by art]. Structuralist activity takes what is real, analyzes it and then synthesizes it. This seems to amount to very little—which sugests to some that structuralist activity is 'insignificant, uninteresting, useless.' Yet from a different viewpoint this little effort is decisive, for between the two objects, or the two 'strokes' of structuralist activity, something new is brought to light . . . the representation is the object plus the human intelligence added to it, and this addition has an anthropological value, inasmuch as it is man himself, his history, his situation, his freedom, and the very resistence which Nature opposes to his spirit, which is being defined.

(Essais critiques, p. 215)

After this "structuralist cameo," let us return to *Blanco*. The poem carries an epigraph of Hindu origin: "By passion the world is bound, by passion too it is released" (*The Hevajra Tantra*), and one from the West, "Avec ce seul objet dont le Néant s'honore" (Mallarmé). They give us two clues. First, that Paz's mind is now operating as a meeting ground of East and West. Second, that the poem is about a meeting between passion and silence. Since we soon discover that the poem deals with language, with the birth of words, this point is not without significance. The poem unfolds in several ways: we can read it as a whole, from beginning to end; we can choose the central column, which deals with the birth of language; we can find to its left another column, an erotic poem divided into four sections standing for the four elements in nature; to the right, another column also divided into four parts deals with sensation, perception, imagination and understanding. Briefly, this is a poem in which space, the interaction of these segments within the framework of the blank space of a book, is as important as time. Language cannot be born, Paz seems to tell us, if space, time, passion, and silence are not combined into one single unit. The Hindu *Mandala*, the squaring of the circle, the labyrinth which points toward infinity but also toward the here and now, is its emblem.

As Paz himself has written in *Corriente alterna*, "modern poetry is an attempt to abolish all meanings because poetry itself appears to be the ultimate meaning of life and of man himself." If the German philosopher Ernst Cassirer defined man as the animal who could create language and myths, we can also state that it is language, myths, poetry, that have created man, that have made modern man into a poetic, myth-making, speaking animal.

Blanco begins with an untranslatable pun:

> el comienzo
>   el cimiento
> la simiente

(Beginning, foundation, seed: all are the same thing, all are contained in words.) In the beginning was the Word, according to St. John. Not action, the will, the deed, as Goethe claimed, but the Word. The people who usually discuss words and language are philologists and linguists, and although language in itself is fascinating, language as analyzed and classified by linguists and philologists (without mentioning psycholinguists) becomes sometimes extremely boring. But Paz is a poet, and we sense the newness of his approach right away: where the philologists use black-and-white, most-ly gray, Paz plunges into technicolor and images. This is how he recreates for us the birth of the word "sunflower," and with it the birth of the flower that the word al-lows us to see:

> Superviviente
> Entre las confusiones taciturnas,
> > Asciende
> En un tallo de cobre
> > Resuelto
> En un follaje de claridad:
> > Amparo
> De caídas realidades.
> > O dormido
> O extinto,
> > Alto en su vara
> (Cabeza en una pica),
> > Un girasol
> Ya luz carbonizada
> > Sobre un vaso
> De sombra.
> > En la palma de una mano
> Ficticia,
> > Flor
> Ni vista ni pensada:
> > Oída,
> Aparece
> > Amarillo
> Cáliz de consonantes y vocales
> Incendiadas.

The word "sunflower" appears after a long preparation, after we have images, sounds, light and darkness. It is a painful birth, yet it creates in turn other images, sounds, in a loud explosion which we could compare to the second stage of a rocket: the poem unfolds into two columns, eroticism and sensations of sound and light open up right and left: Paz has organized a *son et lumière* spectacle around the magic blessed event, the birth of a word which is a symbol for the birth of language.

The yellow of a sunflower is replaced by the blue of a river. Once more we realize that color, movement, the anguished presence of a man surrounded by "something"—something we may have to name, we may call it "river"—are not merely steps that unfold slowly and logically but rather simultaneous, interacting realities. By translating so close-ly human experience, sounds, colors, images, into a frenzied sensual embrace, Paz seems to abolish time and history, or at least to tell us that the interaction of these spatial and temporal elements is so fast and furious that the neat Western projections of histori-cism, rationalism, positivism, are to the real world what gray ashes are to a living body. New visions, red deserts, frenzied screams of *yes* and *no*, seem to shake the entrails of this poem like a vast earthquake. More than once we feel we are drowning in a sea of intoxicating sensations. Yet Paz is too great a poet not to know that every work of art needs a center. He has provided one, and of course this center is in tune with the rest of the poem: it is an explosion of paradoxes out of which, if we look closely, if we are not blinded by the light of the explosion, a crown—or is it a halo, or a mushroom-shaped cloud—of meaning will momentarily appear:

> El espíritu
> Es una invención del cuerpo
> El cuerpo
> Es una invención del mundo
> El mundo
> Es una invención del espíritu

A blind alley? A vicious circle? Rather, a self-sustaining irony. It is not always easy to tell apart irony and enthusiasm in *Blanco*. When we come to *Ladera este* the operation is much simpler. The whole book is organized around two poles, the ironic look and the enthusiastic, ecstatic vision. The world around the poet contracts, then expands, pulsating evenly from beginning to end of the book. Most of the short poems, at least a good many of them, are wrapped around a core of irony. The long ones offer us a look into vast spaces, timeless vistas. Perhaps the basic irony, the original joke (the joke is on the reader) is that a book which deals with essential being and transcendental beauty reads also most often as a travelogue, as a tourist's notebook. Paz has also taken care to provide bridges in order to make his contrasts less painful. Thus for instance in "Madurai," a short ironic poem:

> En el bar del British Club
> —Sin ingleses, *soft drinks*
> *Nuestra ciudad es santa y cuenta*
> Me decía, apurando su naranjada,
> *Con el templo más grande de la India*
> (Mainakshi, diosa canela)
> *Y el garaje T.S.V.* (tus ojos son dos peces)
> Sri K. J. Chidambaram,
> *Yo soy familiar de ambas instituciones.*
> Director de The Great Lingam Inc.,
> Compañía de Autobuses de Turismo.

An inane monologue around soft drinks—and the reader knows that "lingam" means "phallic symbol of Shiva" or simply "male organ." Yet behind the tawdry boasting of a Hindu Babbitt there lurk the eyes of a beautiful goddess.

And yet the contrast between some of the short ironic poems and a long poem such as *Viento entero* is still powerful. Paz knows the world is made up of pettiness and infinity, of saints, madmen, clowns, mediocre people. His goal is not only to see infinity in a grain of sand, as William Blake proposed, but at the same time not to forget the size, texture and color of the grain of sand. *Viento entero* is a love poem *and* a metaphysical poem *and* a description of a journey through the Hindu subcontinent:

> El presente es perpetuo
> Los montes son de hueso y son de nieve
> Están aquí desde el principio
> El viento acaba de nacer
>   Sin edad

And yet we have concrete glimpses, snapshots of everyday reality, "los gritos de los niños / Príncipes en harapos / A la orilla del río atormentado / Rezan orinan meditan." Fragments of history, legend, literature, merge with the eternal present. Opposites become fused: "Eres la llama de agua / La gota diáfana de fuego." Images and sacred presences lift up the present to a higher level: "En el pico del mundo se acarician/ Shiva y Parvati / Cada caricia dura un siglo." Enthusiasm has won the day, irony recedes. Ambiguity becomes a shifting, shimmering change of focus in the human eye, as when the poet describes the subtle trembling of a poplar: "Entre el cielo y la tierra suspendidos / Unos cuantos álamos / Vibrar de luz más que vaivén de hojas / ¿Suben o bajan?" A chord is struck, the world vibrates, enthusiasm wins over the ironic eye. As in *Blanco*, so in *Ladera este*: words, mere words, tightly organized in endless dialogue, can create a world—which in turn will give birth to new languages: the present never ends.

Yale University

The Universalism of Octavio Paz

By RICARDO GULLÓN

Before examining the universalism of Octavio Paz we should first specify what we mean by universalism, for it is a somewhat ambiguous concept and should be employed as precisely as possible. The term's ambiguity arises from a confusion of universalism with cosmopolitanism, which, far from being an analogous phenomenon as it might seem at first glance, is rather the opposite. The cosmopolitan is comfortable everywhere but takes root nowhere. The universalist is well-rooted, especially in himself, but also takes an interest in what is foreign to him, thereby transcending his localism. The cosmopolitan is superficial, the universalist prefers the depths. In the recent past, Juan Ramón Jiménez, hostile toward all cosmopolitanism (whether it was Bonafoux's or Gómez Carrillo's), was justifiably called "the universal Andalusian," while Alfonso Reyes could, with as much accuracy, have been termed "the universal Mexican." Both are perfect examples of Andalusianism and Mexicanism, and yet both are universal writers who find nationalism and linguistic purism too restrictive.

Universalism can be defined as a conception of the world which, by a thorough assimilation and expression of what is essential, communicates with everyone, or anyone, regardless of cultural origins. The universalist is apt to be censured as an anti-patriot and an ingrate by the stubborn provincials who have come to enjoy the limitations of their *costumbrismo*. But the fact is that those provincials are rarely capable of understanding themselves as well as the universalist motivated by a desire to probe beneath the surface. Furthermore, the eager desire for universality impels the universalist to find in a particular characteristic—or if he prefers, in a national characteristic—a means by which he can communicate with common humanity.

There are no cultures, but rather there is culture—in the singular—and all its manifestations deserve our attention, as a matter of principle. Through some we come to understand others better, and Octavio Paz offers the clearest demonstration of this fact in *Conjunciones y disyunciones* (Conjunctions and Disjunctions, 1969). Beginning with the collection of short tales, dialogues and extravaganzas in the curious book *Nueva picardía mexicana*, he concludes by drawing a parallel between Christian and Oriental religions (particularly Buddhism and Hinduism).

Conjunciones y disyunciones allows us to see the roots of Paz's universalism, or at least one of its roots. Paz is an erotic poet, one of the competent erotic poets of the contemporary lyric, and *Nueva picardía* is a collection of stories and jokes about sex. Through the poet's analysis, the reader discovers problems, such as the duality of being, reflected in their opposites—fate is identity, *cara-culo*. Delving into José Guadalupe Posada, Quevedo, Góngora, Lévi-Strauss and Velázquez, among others, and making a crucial reference to Yeats and Juan Ramón Jiménez, who both associated excrement with love, Paz emerges with an unexpected statement: "the pleasure principle is subversive."

At times I have the impression that instead of carefully arguing from A to Z, Paz omits certain intermediary steps in order to save time and assumes that the reader will be able to follow him. This obliges us to make a violent effort to fill in gaps and grasp the thread of his argument. And at times Paz tends to get caught up in his obsessions, for his argument can lead to a conclusion which does not at all follow from the exposition leading up to it.

In *Conjunciones y disyunciones* those ruptures, disequilibria and the constant oscillation from one thing to another arrest one's attention with an unusual effect: "one thing" and "another" are abstractions. They are terms which allude to an opposition or contradiction but are not necessarily analogous to the two elements of the contradiction they refer to. Paz's thought moves like a shuttle that knots the thread neither at its beginning nor at its end but somewhere beyond those points or between them: for example, he does not go directly from the Protestant Reform to Hindu Tantrism, but instead attempts to make a link with Taoism or Confucian doctrine. As the title indicates, his book is a compendium of interesting and, above all, curious similarities and differences. We may or may not agree with the author, but the richness of his imagination is indisputable, as is the power of his vision, which discovers analogies and antitheses in areas so disparate that they are difficult to encompass in a single field of vision.

It is, above all, a question of culture. And beyond that, it is the capacity to penetrate and the will to understand. If the latter fails, culture will not suffice. In disjunctions Paz seeks a conjunction, a possibility of coincidence which derives from some remote common origin. The idea is mythic but no less valid for that. To demand historical rigor from works of this kind is absurd: in preliminary remarks to the book he describes the pages that follow as "wanderings and divagations," which characterizes them well. Since Montaigne, there has not been a better definition of the essay. With this characterization of his own work, it is easy to see why what we find in it is a gathering of opinions, very vaguely supported in theory. And they—not the theory— are what count. Certainly a theory is interesting; but the validity of an opinion depends upon the sincerity with which it is expressed: sincerity makes it legitimate.

There is no reason to require an essay to be systematic: it is enough that it be enlightening. But Paz not only enlightens, he frequently arouses passion and sometimes irritates. It is interesting to follow the meanderings of his thinking with an expectant eye to the surprises his associative genius and the uniqueness of his knowledge can give us. To whom but him would it occur to note the lack of "a general history of the relations between body and soul, life and death, sex and the face"? At times he seems disposed to write it himself, or at least to attempt it. But he is content to recall that these are "distinct realities that have distinct names in each civilization and, therefore, distinct meanings" (p. 42). And this is the root of so many difficulties, of so many problems of communication between author and reader. What do the words *love* and *democracy* mean, for example, in Paz's vocabulary?

Even more interesting is his attempt to establish a relationship between certain words and what that relationship represents: life-death or sex-spirit. It is here that his discoveries occur with the greatest frequency, above all, when a relationship, instead of being resolved in a more or less metaphorical, more or less symbolic, identification, emerges in what he calls *circuits*: for example, the "biopsychic that passes from life to sex to spirit to death to life." This circuit and the relationships between opposites interest Paz because they are universals. Societies, he believes, are what the combination of their central signs proclaim: the signs in the circuit I have just referred to. Moreover, that which makes men what they are—"complex, problematic and unpredictable"—is the association of signs (the pleasure principle, the death instinct) and men's domination over them (for example, over what Paz calls "body" and "non-body").

The relationships of signs are by nature difficult. If, making use of relationships among them, one tries to establish a system of parallels and antitheses between different cultures, the exercise is hazardous and the positive results provisional. Even so, it is worth the trouble to attempt it for it is the only way to show precisely the affinities between those different cultures and the common roots shared by very different men. In sum, it is a way of showing that signs reveal a common identity among human beings, be they Protestant Europeans of the 16th century or Buddhists of the 6th century B.C.

The contemplation of these correspondences, correspondences which strike many readers as unusual, is reserved for those capable of understanding history in its symmetry, in patterns whose similarities are intuited rather than proven, and are intuited above all in rites and ceremonies (which sometimes have a lucid symbolism) and in works of art. Comparatists and historians of religion without doubt have contributed a good deal to Paz's work, but the substance of his conjunctions and disjunctions would not have crystallized without his own tendency to see the world as a unity, to confront without prejudice the diversities of culture and to explain their antinomies as different responses to identical questions.

If we turn our attention to love and death, it is easy to get to the root of the matter. And Octavio Paz gets to the root of the matter without apparent effort in *Conjunciones y disyunciones*. It's a pity, in my opinion, that at the end of the book, in explaining the significance of revolutionary political changes, he bogs down in considerations that recall those repeated with suspicious frequency in the texts of the cold war: to equate the gallows of the Third Reich with the people's commisars seems to me an inaccurate simplification.

It is not often that Paz falls prey to such simplifications. On the contrary, his work is so complex and rich that it is a delight to follow its meanderings and zig-zags in that visionary wandering which allows him to see "in some rocks from the Valley of Cabul . . . the birth, the apogee and the end of the gothic style." The exotic tempts him, but he overcomes, or better, transcends it. The exotic is assimilated, integrated and united with the other elements of a culture in which nothing is alien; it makes no sense to say that his interest in Mallarmé's poetry is exotic, for he is himself a direct descendant of the author of "Un coup de dés."

Looking about elsewhere, we will discover in a modest little book an appreciation and explanation of what Lévi-Strauss represents in the contemporary world and the silences and sonorous ruptures of John Cage sung in a poem. Exotic inclinations? Much more than that, for from the great diversity that preoccupies and lures—or seduces—him, Octavio Paz extracts corpuscles of light, meaningful forms which, joining with many others, trace the outline of his concern: it is an outline in which antinomies are made whole in an equilibrium that resolves them without eliminating them. Anything hybrid repels him, just as any integrated thing attracts him.

I don't know if I dare to express what is hardly an opinion; it is, in fact, little more than a suspicion or presentiment: Paz believes in ghosts. Furthermore, his world is populated by presences as strange as those imagined by Lovecraft, but minus their fearsomeness and hostility. This presentiment, this obscure sensation I have, is understandable if we recall that Paz considers culture a phenomenon approachable, not diachronically, but synchronically. History remains permanently an irreversible fact, and even a grievous one, but Paz's vision does not have recourse to chronologies: he considers time as a continuity in which beginnings and ends coexist, latently or manifestly present like shapes displayed in a river that one can contemplate as a single unit from source to mouth. It is no accident that the word "metamorphosis" frequently occurs in Paz, for metamorphosis implies both change and continuity; as he would say, the butterfly is in some way still a worm and elements of the cocoon can be seen shining through its wings in its ephemeral flight.

Nor is it an accident that Paz thinks of the history of literature and the plastic arts as a repetition within the process of change. Some details can be argued (such as the date of the beginning of the contemporary North American avant-garde, or the fact that Ezra Pound served in it the "same ambiguous and exemplary function as Reverdy in surrealism"), but the discrepancies have no influence on the effect of what he sets forth as the "rhythmical law" (*Corriente alterna*, p. 37): "a movement of the pendulum between periods of reflection and periods of spontaneity."

I would like to examine more thoroughly these peculiarities in Paz's thought, making reference to the general lines of his esthetic, but that is not my purpose here. I will only emphasize the connection with the universalist tendency I am trying to explain. I would say in passing that I think I find in the pages of *Corriente alterna* or *Las peras del olmo* certain coincidental similarities with the ideas of Eugenio d'Ors, and even with the cultural formulas Ors is fond of repeating.

If anyone raises his eyebrows at this, if only for a moment, then the association of such apparently dissimilar names is not at all accidental. I am not speaking of influences, for it is possible that Paz has not spent much time with the pages of the *Glosario*. The common link between Paz and Ors is an openness, a receptivity to diversities and the will to unify them in a theory, a theory of culture that disregards boundaries; the difference between them is Ors's exclusive interest in Graeco-Latin culture as centered at one decisive point: Rome. Paz, a Mexican rather than a native of the Mediterranean area and far from believing that culture is a specific product of the *Mare Nostrum*, emphasizes the beliefs and creations of America and Asia. He postulates a theory of cultures, not of culture.

Thus we approach what makes Paz's universalism a truly unique phenomenon, brought about by a series of circumstances that were very apparent, beginning with modernism: an American culture and the recognition of the fact that to have roots is a necessarily complex fact: *roots* and not *root*. The remote Indian ancestry (ancestry by blood or adoption) does not exclude what has come down to present-day man from Spain, France or Germany, or from occidental culture as a whole. This was the example of Alfonso Reyes. As the world became smaller, Paz was literally within arms' reach of Hindu wisdom, as well as the art works of China and the rest of Asia. In Paz there are none of the Chinese imports we find in Gautier, but prolonged experiences, living *in situ* and an intimate knowledge of what is essentially Asian in art, philosophy and religion.

When he laments the paucity of criticism in Spanish-American culture, he justifiably feels the lack of what he himself tries to create for others: "a resonance" that prolongs or contradicts the work of others; "a meeting place of other works." Through this we can understand Paz's universalism as a reaction against provincialism and the tribal spirit of Spanish Americans (the Spanish legacy, for one thing), a spirit which does not enter into a live and vigorous tradition. And I would even dare to add something more: this reaction has led him to unfurl his banners in the camp of criticism, giving criticism a value equal to that of poetry, since his purpose is not to "invent works" but to invent a literature by means of the relationships he is able to establish among literary and art works. His attack against short-winded critics ends with an affirmation we can accept without thinking twice: "for me modern literatures are one literature" (*Corriente alterna*, p. 42).

I do not hesitate in adopting this affirmation as one of my own, but in addition, aside from its accuracy, I offer it as another proof of Paz's universalist vocation. I recall that, in Paz's judgment, "contemporary literature tends to be world literature" (*Corriente alterna*, p. 50). Even if this is not so, even if it is not true that the historical conflicts among nations and civilizations are in the process of disappearing, it is revealing that Paz feels they are. It should not be surprising, then, that he recommends to Spanish Americans that they read those of their writers who are "from the modern tradition and read them as part of that tradition." He urges them to begin a careful examination of conscience, to delve into what is essential in order to know thoroughly what the beginning point is. This is what the author of *El laberinto de la soledad* did in his day in a book which, as an examination of conscience, is rigorous and sincere.

The domination of provincialism is inexcusable if our critics do their duty and fulfill their purpose. As a Spaniard, I understand this demand well, since our literature and that of Spanish America has a decisive and indisputable tie: language. The two literatures comprise the one great Spanish literature that groups Lugones and Neruda with Unamuno and Lorca; Huidobro and Borges with Juan Ramón Jiménez and Jorge Guillén; and one could place Rafael Alberti beside Paz. They are not equivalents, I know, but for that very reason they broaden and deprovincialize a Spaniard's circle of experience, opening up to him means of communication with the cultures of other languages, both near and remote, similar and dissimilar.

Paz's language is the language of passion—not only when he speaks of André Breton, which is understandable, but when he comments on Lévi-Strauss, which is much more shocking. His intelligence is not satisfied with understanding; he also has a need to vigorously register his own reactions. Coldness is not in his style, nor stand-offishness. He is not satisfied to approach problems: he gets inside them, looks at their entrails, examines intestines, inspects the nervous system, while he senses in his own nervous system the blows and counter-blows of the arguments those problems have engendered. Serenity yes, but impassioned.

And Paz, like André Breton, understands that the language of passion and the passion of language are on good terms with one another, that they are the recto and verso page of the same attitude. Moreover, language is where song happens. There is no song without words, even though a song can be diminished to a susurration or concealed in a number. Like Saussure, Paz understands that the act of speech is significant only when it is a part of a general system of expression, and though I do not recall if he has said so explicitly, I believe that he does not by any means consider language something bestowed upon him ready-made, finished, concluded. The passion, the urgency to speak, drives him to forge his own language, created from the potentialities Language offers.

To follow the lines of criticism written by Paz, above all when he speaks of works that are really important to him, is to become involved in the secret of his person: it is to recognize him in the mask and behind the mask. Never has that not altogether paradoxical assertion that criticism is autobiography seemed more true than in him. As he describes, he defines: In whom could "verbal splendor and intellectual and passionate violence" (*Corriente alterna*, p. 56) be more truly allied? When he says that the aim of poetry is to "support the apparition of our double, to create that other person we are and who we never completely cease to be" (Ibid.), perhaps he is thinking of Breton. But if we apply these words to Paz himself, we cannot go wrong, for his poems produce not merely the sense of a revelatory creation, but the sense of a revelation that is a creation, the creation of "another" creation, the creation of a being about whom Merleau-Ponty remarked, feeling its closeness: "Every 'other' is another self. . . . 'I' and 'other' are two almost concentric circles . . . ." And the problem remains where the French philosopher left it: "I make the 'other' in my image, but how can there be for me an image of me?" (*La prosa del mundo*, p. 125)

I have just used the word *revelation* and should stop with it, because it alludes, within Paz's ideological system, to a belief anchored more solidly in the poetic realm than the religious. He has looked around and has collided with that term everywhere, and with others that for him are associated with it, such as *rite, ceremony, initiation* . . . . Particulars change but not structures, which are identical even in the most distant latitudes. The small quantity of esoteric dross which I cannot help pointing out in Paz's lexicon arises from the reality of his universalism. If I once said of Unamuno that he was the heteroclite of heterodoxy, then it could be said of Paz that he is the orthodox of heterodoxy, although, let it be understood, in Paz's thinking ideas of orthodoxy and heresy achieve only a metaphorical value. Each initiation interests him, every rite has meaning in his eyes, every revelation he sees as a means of participating in the unknown, in whatever is different, in whatever must bring him to a more complete knowledge of man in the abstract and of a specific man named Octavio Paz.

I haven't the space here to attempt in even the most sketchy fashion a study of Paz's critical vocabulary; I will be content to point out that the terms I have just indicated, and others, like *magnetism, incarnation, predestination, myth, prophecy* et cetera, reveal his curiosity about the timeless phenomena that are recorded in all cultures and all epochs, from the caves of Altamira to Red Square in Moscow ("The happening is also . . . a rite," *Corriente alterna*, p. 70). It is a vocabulary with a religious origin. To explain this religious connection it will suffice to recall that Paz is one of the very few writers in Spanish in whom it is possible to discover evidence of a genuine surrealist. Paz's surrealism is another of those problems we should explore thoroughly (and I hope that my friend and colleague, Professor José Gabriel Sánchez, will soon reveal the results of his investigations of the problem). It is a surrealism much closer to Bretonian orthodoxy than any other phenomenon among those in Spanish letters often placed under this rubric. And surrealism, which is so Parisian, tried to become a universal movement and a nearly universal religion.

One would have to ask what the ultimate reasons were for Paz's decision to write a long essay, almost a book, dedicated to Marcel Duchamp, the smiling destroyer of art, both traditional and modern—and he destroyed perhaps more modern art than traditional—who played the most stupendous pranks of his time, an era which produced some very funny ones in different guises. Duchamp's intention goes beyond a desire to shock the bourgeoisie; he disconcerts the pretentious, and the placing of a toilet stool, nothing more, in an exhibition of art objects reveals indirectly an intention of unmasking the pseudo-artist, the commercializer of new things. Thus, Duchamp is the anti-Dalí, or more precisely, the antidote against the industrial exploitation of modern things, which has enriched and popularized the deceitful magus from Cadaqués.

Duchamp was a great, tireless demythifier and is himself on the verge of mythical enthronement. Did Paz want to initiate, in a subtle way, his canonization? in a certain sense his book is an apology for Duchamp and an explanation of why and how the Duchamp phenomenon came about. Explaining Duchamp implies a certain degree of assimilation of and identification with Duchamp's intentions. Closing the circle, mythification, demythification and return to the beginning.

Facing one of the most disputed and controversial issues of our time—drugs— Octavio Paz could not remain indifferent, even if only because, as he puts it, "Drugs provoke a vision of universal correspondence, give life to analogy, put objects in motion, make of the world a vast poem of rhythms and rhymes" (*Corriente alterna*, p. 82). Drugs' distortion of reality leads, as he himself observes, to "short-circuiting the universe," which is a serious matter. Beginning with a break with exterior reality, they take us, by hallucination, to "another" reality, to "the interior of another reality," our very own. What a drug makes visible cannot be outside the brain which it affects though it may be certain, as Paz indicates, following Baudelaire's lead, that "the temptation of drugs is a manifestation of our love of the infinite" (Ibid. p. 82).

If we are returned to the "center of the universe," if boundaries and antagonisms are erased, it is because the region in which drugs operate is precisely that stratum common to all men, the deep zone of contact where fears and hopes are resolved in deep perspective and in certain almost identical figures, as if they originated in the most remote past and were ultimately an unleashing of dark powers which in the obscurity of their own shadows take on the spectral consistency which hallucination has made of them. For many there is something perverse in submitting to drugs; it is to evoke that which under no circumstances should be brought to light, that which is more preferably kept quiet and dormant among the shadows of its normal habitat: chaos.

But delirium can approach what lucidity hardly succeeds in suggesting as the cause of differences: the recognition of limits, the discovery of a lack of openings. Entrance into chaos by hallucinations or delirium can imply, as Paz suggests, "a re-generation by immersion in the original fountain, a true return to the *previous life*" (*Corriente alterna*, p. 89). Primitive and esoteric religions attract him. A Tantric influence? Who knows? Let us simply recall that when for the first time he visited India in 1952, the universe seemed to him "an immense, multiple fornication." Thanks to this confession we understand that Paz's violent eroticism allowed him to accept the Hindu chaos as "a kind of ritual bath." Where we occidentals see disorder and experience fear, the oriental experiences a return to primal origins, which Paz shares with them.

Without forgetting that he is not a mystical oriental, nor anything remotely similar, but a poet from the other camp, it seems certain that the vision of chaos, which for us is traditionally negative (and the vogue of a science fiction novelist such as Lovecraft, who is so harried by this vision that he convinces us that it is negative for the majority of that indefinite entity called "the public"), in Paz is associated with resplendent lights, and it seems that if, after all, chaos drives away immediate realities —the present and history—that is no reason to consider it maleficent: that (abominable) face, or faces, which we are afraid of meeting in the darkness is only the immense whiteness of total calm and quietude. Lovecraft is afraid that a terrible and demoniacal inhumanity is holding us until immersion is complete; Paz insinuates that "perhaps our condition is not human" (*Corriente alterna*, p. 90), but his insinuation implies hope; it opens not onto terror, but onto the infinite.

The constant concern of Octavio Paz—I would almost say his obsession—is poetic creation. I speak not merely of poetry but of the secret roads and the technical resources by means of which this confluence of forces crystallizes in what we call a poem, an experience that does not derive from other experiences but from the art of combining words based on understanding, whether intuitively or not, the function of language. *El arco y la lira* (The Arc and the Lyre) is an attempt to clarify the problem posed by this function, and among the impressions a reading of Paz leaves, few are so clear as the one that modern poetry is closing all roads, even to the extent that the ideal poem is no longer content with the page being white, which was postulated by Mallarmé a century ago, but prefers the poem that liquidates poetry, the poem which is both "its negation and its culmination" (*Signos*, p. 13). And in the final chapter of what is definitely a poetics, it is not surprising, whoever is dealt with, to find observations, not at all extemporaneous, on poetry as an instrument of salvation.

Do I exaggerate, perhaps? I will try to adhere to Paz's thought as much as my synthesis will allow: "The modern phenomenon of noncommunication does not depend so much on the plurality of subjects as on the disappearance of 'thou' as a constituent element of each conscience" (*Signos*, p. 23). (We observe in passing that this is another universal phenomenon). The impossibility of communicating with others is, of course, based on the impossibility of making ourselves clear to ourselves, of knowing who speaks to whom when man speaks alone and by himself. If we are not sure how many selves live within us and how they live, we will hardly find out with language that reaches for the unknown, with imagery in which we see only ourselves. Poetic language can perhaps be reactivated and made useful if "I" and "thou" again take on a precise meaning. Poetry, as Antonio Machado reminds us, can only be a search for the essential "thou," the "thou" that accompanies us in silence and lives at our side without its face being as familiar to us as it should be. Or in Paz's phrase: "Poetry: the search for others, the discovery of otherness" (*Signos*, p. 24).

The function of poetry becomes a fundamental restoration of a community as a communion, a restoration of the participation in a relationship that originates in recognition. Once this supposition is accepted, it will be understood without difficulty that poetry is essentially social, that it always is and cannot but be social, and that those who invented "social poetry," were wrong to such a degree that they confused essence with accident and function with utilization. For this reason they have been so easily relegated to the warehouse of old-age while the people they killed, Juan Ramón Jiménez, for example, are still enjoying good health.

In this light certain youthful lines by Paz speak of the demands he makes on poetry:

> Insist, vanquisher,
> because I exist so alone because you exist
> and my mouth and my tongue took shape
> to speak so alone your existence
> and your secret syllables, untouchable
> and despotic word,
> substance of my soul.
>
> ("La poesía," *Libertad*, p. 13)

This poem is the first in *A la orilla del mundo* (On the Shore of the World; I have copied it from the first edition of *Libertad bajo palabra* [Liberty on Parole, 1949], a book that has accompanied me for more than twenty years and is still at my side). *A la orilla del mundo*, a 1942 title, is highly significant to my theme. It is about a world that for Paz is total reality, the universe in its diverseness and complexity, with the underground currents which nurture that reality. And every day that universe is more difficult to conceive as a unity; its image is fragmentation and disconnection, followed immediately by dispersion.

Paz understands that the poet is justified by the language that makes him what he is. When he recovers it, when he feels it beat and vibrate he begins to console himself as the being he is, precarious, inconclusive, vacillating, because in that language, or thanks to it, he will discover the reality of the other, of what the other is; but it is not irreducibly different, nor is it hostile. In *Signos en rotación* (Signs in Rotation) which is perhaps the most lucid part of his poetics, man is not denied as something incomplete, nor is the idea of living in a state of indecision, which is a vacillation, in a vacillation which is a rhythm, rejected.

I was reading, not long ago, the conversations Jean Paulhan had with Robert Mallet in 1952 on Radio France. One of the ideas Paulhan expressed made me think of what Octavio Paz has been saying for years. According to Paulhan, "if an author thinks a little too much about the work he is writing—his essay or his poem—he is deprived of sharpness and surprise" (Jean Paulhan, *Les incertitudes du langage*, p. 105). And the reason is that "our self-conscious reflection simplifies things and makes them false" (Ibid., p. 85). If I am not mistaken, Paz's essays—and we will say nothing of his poetry—are the product of an imagination that lets itself be carried away, that is not obsessed, does not concentrate obsessively on reducing problems to graphs and tables; thus his insistence on the inconclusive, on what is always open.

Whoever circulates so broadly through such diverse beliefs and ideologies, whoever has investigated so many differences and contradictions, cannot but contemplate man *sub speciae universalitatis* and leave his work open to the doubt that what breathes behind the concept of otherness—much more ambiguous than is often believed—perhaps is revealed, as he suggests, in the whirl of the breeze or in "the secret life of plants." (*Signos*, p. 40)

"Is not the poem," asks Paz (*Signos*, p. 41), "that vibrant space over which extends a fistful of signs like an ideogram that is a fountain of meanings?" (*Signos*, p. 61) And reading him I tell myself: this question or this definition is resolved in a metaphor which only he who is tinged with universalism could imagine. When, in the Spanish language, has the ideogram been sought as an illuminating term for what the metaphor is or can be? A step further and we find these surprising lines that leave no doubt as to the hand that writes them: "While imagining the poem as a configuration of signs or an animated space I do not think of the page of the book: I think of the Azore Islands seen as an archipelago of flames one night in 1938, of the black tents of the nomads in the valleys of Afghanistan, of the mushrooms of parachutes suspended over a sleeping city, of a tiny crater of red ants in an urban patio, of the moon that multiplies and is canceled and disappears and reappears over the gushing breast of India after the monsoon. . . ." (*Signos*, p. 42)

When he recently wrote a prologue to a book by Bashō—*Sendas de Oku*—he praised "that feeling of universal sympathy with all that exists" as "the best Buddhism has given us" (p. 14), and confirms the inclination I have commented upon. In the same prologue, a little later, in defense of the Japanism of José Juan Tablada, he rises up against those who in the name of classical culture and Christian humanism condemned the popularizer of haiku in the Spanish language, reminding them that Culture is *cultures*. And then he recalls the decision to compose a Western *renga*, a succession of sonnets, written in four languages by four different poets. This experiment, carried out in Paris in April 1969, is a rare example of universality; Italian, English, French and Mexican poets agreed that "a Japanese method of composing texts" could unite them in their effort to arrive at a collective poetry, a poetry by all, for all. Without discussing the experiment here, it is undeniable that individual and national characteristics, if not destroyed, were suppressed for a moment by this new collective and universal effort in favor of what has guided the creative impulse of Octavio Paz from the beginning.

University of Texas, Austin

Translated from the Spanish
By
Tom J. Lewis

Octavio Paz: Invention and Tradition, or The Metaphor of the Void

By GRACIELA PALAU DE NEMES

Octavio Paz occupies a key place among the writers of this century. His poetry expresses essential attributes of the Hispanic people and, at the same time, it breaks with the Spanish tradition to create a work which captures the spirit of our age and gives a distinctive character to the literature of Spanish America. Paz has invented a mysticism for our times reconciling contemporary man with his temporal condition and assigning to space a transcendental meaning which counteracts the nihilist preoccupation with the void.

In his poetic invention, Paz follows a long tradition. A consistent note in the poetry of the Spanish people has been the concern with the final destiny of man and the longing to transcend the limited space of their terrestrial existence. This preoccupation appears in the greatest creations of the language, in the "Ode on the Death of his Father," the fifteenth-century poem by Jorge Manrique; in the sixteenth-century poems of St. John of the Cross, "Dark Night of the Soul," "Spiritual Canticle," "Living Flame of Love"; in the great seventeenth-century soliloquy of Calderón de la Barca, "Life is a Dream"; in the nineteenth-century Romantic elegy "To Teresa" of Espronceda; in the anguished twentieth-century cry of Unamuno, *The Christ of Velázquez*. In the works of the fifteenth and sixteenth centuries death is accepted as the passage which allows man to fulfill his desire for more life, but this implies a renunciation of his dual nature. The mysticism of St. John of the Cross is the highest expression of the willingness of the Spaniard to renounce the flesh for the sake of the soul in order to transcend the limitations of this world. The ultimate goal, according to their religious beliefs, is union with God. In the seventeenth century, as man's horizons widened and beliefs were altered, the Hispanic poet began to struggle with his doubts about a life for the flesh and another for the soul. By the beginning of the twentieth century, the desire for transcendence became merely a yearning for more being, dissociating itself from the orthodox religious belief in a life hereafter.

The literary creation of the great Spanish writers of modern times, the well-known Generation of 1898, reveals this deviation from tradition, but their apparent preoccupation with the national crisis gives their works a definite Spanish character. Among the writers of that period only Juan Ramón Jiménez stubbornly expressed in his poetry his innermost conflict, which he resolved by inventing a poetic mysticism which embodied his modernistic belief in a harmonious universe where beauty reigns supreme. In *Animal de fondo* (1949), Jiménez attains union with his poetic deity and states his belief in Beauty which is "at the same time outside and inside of Being and unites Being with the Totality" ("Notas"). Poetry allows Jiménez to transcend consciousness and his vision comprises all the beauty of creation. Inflamed with love, the flesh becomes essence and the soul becomes perception ("En mi tercero mar"), and he experiences unity within himself and union with the All resolving the conflicting duality of Being without the traditional aggrandizement of the spirit at the expense of the flesh. He implies that he has reached, not the ultimate goal but a stage which satisfies his human quest. The metaphors of his poetry reveal his will to go no farther: "now I can stop my movement," "now I am paralyzed sea," ("El nombre conseguido de los nombres"). His experience is defined as the love of the body, "You are . . . the love in my body as a man, and in the body of the woman" ("En mi tercero mar"); the sexual act, per se, has no part in the experience. In this aspect, the mysticism of Jiménez differs from that of Paz and is closer to the Spanish tradition, although Jiménez is unwilling to renounce the flesh for the sake of the soul. Paz no longer thinks in terms of flesh and soul but in terms of body and non-body. Furthermore, not having felt the full impact of technology and the machine age, Jiménez lacks Paz's awareness of the fragmentation of being and the universe.

Beauty does not resolve the inner conflict expressed in the poetry of the Spanish American modernists, although unlike Jiménez, they sought it with greater persistence than their Spanish brothers. Equating poetry, beauty and woman, they aspired to transcendence through carnal love, but adherence to the traditional belief in the sinful nature of the flesh precluded the reconciliation of their dual nature. Darío, the great poet of the erotic, was unable to reconcile the parts with the whole. In his essay "El caracol y la sirena" (*Cuadrivio*, 1965) Paz attributes this failure to Darío's belief in dispersion as the manifestation of unity: he feels that "each form is a complete universe and at the same time, part of the totality."

Space plays an important role in the poetry of Darío. In the essay mentioned Paz explains: "Each time Darío searches for a symbol to define the oscillations of his being, the aerial space or the aquatic space appear. To the first belong heavens, light, the stars and by analogy . . . the incorruptible nameless realm of ideas, music and numbers. The second is the domain of blood, the heart, the sea, wine, woman, passions, and by magic contagiousness, the jungle with its animals and its monsters." Darío's beautiful poetry, like his passion, never left the plane of the terrestrial. This is not true in the case of the other Spanish American modernists, who persistently searched for the realm of the spirit. When historical changes altered their religious beliefs, agonized by their doubts, some of them became the poets of the void, acutely conscious of the passing of time, while others struggled to expand the limited boundaries of time and sought a transcendence in which their entire self could participate. They became as concerned with space as the first group was with time and they anticipated some of the essential characteristics of the poetry of Paz.

Paz's poem *Blanco* embodies his poetic mysticism. It is an outstanding work in form and content: the culmination of a quest, a poetics and a philosophy of life, an artistic spectacle which allows the reader full participation. It describes the act of poetic creation in its totality, fusing it with the description of the emotion which inspires it, erotic love. The concepts embodied in *Blanco* (in *Configurations*, 1971) appear in Paz's prose work *El arco y la lira* (2nd ed. rev., 1967), to which we shall refer.

According to Paz, love and poetry allow man to experience the unity and final identity of being. Both require him to give of himself completely, to come out of himself to be another and to become lost in that *otherness (El arco y la lira)*. In *Blanco*, while the body consummates the act of love, the non-body consummates the act of poetic creation. "Woman exalts us, makes us come out of ourselves and at the same time, allows us to return," states Paz in his prose work. "The word is a bridge by which man tries to overcome the distance which separates him from exterior reality." "Language is poetry in its natural state," and the task of the poet is to purify it and return it to that state, so that the word may acquire its original plurality of meaning. In *Blanco*, we witness the purification of language: the word, born from silence, advances through a *via mistica*, purging itself before illumination and final union with the poetic thought. When man purges his language, he purges himself: "The word is man himself. We are made of words. They are our only reality, or at least, the only testimony of our reality," Paz assures the reader in *El arco y la lira*. But language alone does not bring forth the poem, the poet must break the temporal walls to be another, and he does this in *Blanco* by entering the body of the woman. It is then that he is immersed in "the original waters of existence," in the "pure time," *the poem*. Paz has fixed the moment in which man comes to the encounter of poetry. In the aforementioned prose work he declares: "Being is eroticism. Inspiration is the strange voice which brings man out of himself to be all he is, all he wishes, another body, another self. The voice of desire is being's own voice, because man is but his wish to be."

To express his poetic transcendence, *Blanco* becomes an expansion of itself. It is, alternately, a single column and a double column poem with verses which face each other, coming to each other's encounter, fusing, expanding, separating. Their flux is parallel to the content of the poem and allows it to overcome the limitations of the page, the space it occupies. Space is the essential attribute of *Blanco*: as man projects his being outside himself for the consummation of his love and his inspiration of being and later resumes his natural self, the void acquires a positive meaning, it becomes a transcendental spatial dimension. This is the invention of Octavio Paz: the assignation of a transcendental meaning to space, and the Spanish American modernists are his predecessors in this quest.

Poetry provided a form of transcendence in reverse for the great precursor of modernism, Zorrilla de San Martín. In the introduction to *Tabaré* he brings back the dead *Charrúa* race from the spatial limbo where it dwells. In a speech on Núñez de Arce, Zorrilla defines this place he has invented. It is "between the worlds," a repository and dwelling for greatness and beauty without history. He refers to it again in his book of travels, *Resonancias del camino* (1930), and defines it as a place where the perfection of lines exists, the new-born color, the virgin sound, the pristine mold which gave form to the first man and the first woman, the echo of their first word of love (pp. 198–99). It is the place of origin, poetry resides there and in *Tabaré* it is a dark place where lines, color and dispersed harmony flow looking for the poem (Introduction, IV). In *Blanco*, this void is illuminated with "reflections, thoughts / The precipitations of music, / number crystallized," it is "an archipelago of signs" (Charles Tomlinson and G. Aroul, trs., in *Configurations*, p. 187).

Zorrilla shares the same views as Paz about transcendence through poetry. In his essay "The Dignity of Letters" he states that poetic creation is an act of spiritual reproduction accompanied by an ectasy of love whose purpose is to allow man to see himself, to love his self outside himself as his word, which is not his person but his own indivisible substance. He declares that man realizes his intemporality through poetry, fusing the past, the present and the future, experiencing simultaneity. Zorrilla is not a poet of the erotic, but he searches for an undefined quality in love which signifies ineffable union or accord, "what the waves in the fountain search for / when they follow each other, kiss and fuse" ("El dolor").

In the poetic production of José Martí, the initiator of modernism, love is an important theme, but erotic love does not play a role in his philosophy. Martí and Paz coincide in their poetic will to reconcile the opposites. In *Símbolo y color en la obra de José Martí* (1960), Ivan A. Schulman demonstrates the dual spatial character of Martí's symbolic language and calls attention to the fact that polarity in symbolic language is the esthetic equivalent of the philosophical conviction that the world is made up of inherent dualisms which in their struggle to overcome each other are reconciled in favor of more noble elements (pp. 82–83). When Martí wishes to exalt a theme, he creates a spatial imagery of transcendence. In "A los espacios" (from *Versos libres*), he expresses his desire to give himself to space, symbol of the highest poetry. In "Musa traviesa," from *Ismaelillo*, the collection of poems which initiated Spanish American modernism in 1882, his muse rides the air, enters the pink clouds, descends the deep ocean and travels through the eternal womb. Poetry allows Martí to break the temporal wall to become another, "I am a harp, I am a psaltery / where the Universe vibrates: / I come from the sun and there I go: / I am love: I am the poem!" (*Versos sencillos*, XVII). This sentiment of transcendence is found again in "Cual de incensario roto" in *La edad de oro*, "from whence I came I go: to the Universe." Schulman notices that Martí accords the sun the traditional connotation when he uses it as a symbol. We think that by his many references to the sun he is negating the void. In this respect, he anticipates Paz's metaphysics. This can't be said of the other three great initiators of modernism, Silva, Casal and Gutiérrez Nájera, who look upon poetry as a consolation rather than a means of transcendence. In Silva's poem "Ars," it is a balm; in Casal's "El arte" it provides unknown joys; in Gutiérrez Nájera's "A Justo Sierra," it is immortal consolation. They believe that the final goal of art is beauty, which they identify with truth. In their poetry, love and woman are sources of beauty. Their quest ends in futility because they continue to assert the superiority of the spirit over the flesh. In *Gotas amargas* Silva condemns eroticism; Casal repudiates woman in "A la castidad" and prays to Chastity for guidance. Beauty becomes the chaste vision of an unknown sanctuary for which he searches in vain in the poem "A la belleza"; while purity becomes a theme in the poetry of Gutiérrez Nájera and is symbolized by the reiteration of whiteness, as in "De blanco" and "Tan blanca vas . . . ."

Some critics label these poets as "escapists" believing that they escaped into a fanciful imaginary world as a protest against the hard bitter realities of our days, but this protest can be found without subterfuge in their works. Their escapism is the symbol of their quest for transcendence and it is the substance of their poetic expression. Silva's "Nocturno," one of the greatest poems of the language, is the reverse side of Paz's poem *Blanco*. It describes a metaphysical experience without terrestrial transcendence: the poet's shadow joins that of the departed one on the nocturnal plain. The form of the poem embodies its content: as in the case of *Blanco*, the verses lengthen as the shadows fuse, but the repetitive emphasis on the words *night* and *shadow* contribute to the extension, symbolizing the nihilist vision of the void.

Existential anguish, terror of the void, a conception of woman as the repository of beauty, an association of love and death, an identification of art with the spiritual realm alone and the same lack of reconciliation between the flesh and the soul characterize the poetic production of Jaimes Freyre, Valencia, Nervo, Herrera y Reissig, González Martínez and Lugones, the modernists of the second generation. The unreconciled dualistic vision of life is symbolized in the poetry of Jaimes Freyre by the struggle between the pagan and the Christian world. The visions of deity in his poems occur within the limited natural landscape as in the case of his open-armed god in "Aeternum vale," (from *Castalia Bárbara*). In the poem "Cristo," (from *País de sueño*), prayer, "winged and pure symbol of the divine" comes to the fallen apostle who could have been shown reaching beyond his confines to ascend with it. In "Lustral" (from *País de sombra*), the visions also descend to earth. The past is Jaimes Freyre's symbol of beauty and harmony and the inspiration and theme for his greatest poems, "Medioevales" and "Los antepasados" among them. In his poetic world, the night is "more beautiful than the sun and the dawn" ("Otoñal," *País de sombra*), the void is always beckoning ("Sombra," Ibid.); space is a void to be crossed to reach the sea of death in "Subliminar" (*Las víctimas*), a long poem about his inner life.

In the poetry of Jaimes Freyre, woman is art's most beautiful spectacle, but he is most concerned with her goodness and renders her the homage of a chivalrous knight. The Venus of his verses ("Venus errante" in *País de sueño*), is an errant goddess whose face the sailor has never seen, and the vision of "Eros" in *Anadionema* is white and candid.

In accordance with the modernists of the first generation, Guillermo Valencia believes that poetry is consolation rather than knowledge and that man is only transitory. His two great works, "Los camellos" and "Cigüeñas blancas," symbolize the poet's futile passage through life. Valencia's camel is a noble brute which suffers tedium, fever, hunger, thirst, celibacy; his storks are also fatigued birds forced to travel in search of milder climates; "intoxicated with the sky" they become lost at the vanishing point. In the poem, they are "the soul of the Past," "love departed." Most representative of Valencia's poetic nihilism is "La parábola del foso." All great spaces in this poem are voids: the ocean is but a void, veiled by the fine gauze of the foams, the sky is a void of voids; thought is defined as "time" and flesh as "a fragment of space" and both find their tomb in the void: "What exists is the grave of what is yet to come, / each instant, at birth, perceives its own sepulcher, / the instant buries our thought, which is time / and with it goes a shred of our feeble flesh / a fragment of space / burned in life's lasting fire." In "Exégesis," a philosophical sonnet, love is described as a hidden flame in the universe which seeks to fuse in its crucible the many forms of life: " 'Which is your destiny?' I inquired of the poet, / 'Love which unites, for reason separates' "; love, nevertheless fails to reconcile the poet who must eliminate the body to bring forth the verse. "Patmos," from his book *Ritos*, describes the moment of inspiration as the mute hour in which the soul assassinates the body and in the oblivion of its bare mansion the poet struggles with the untamed verb.

In his incessant search for transcendence, Nervo, the religous writer of Mexico coincides with the non-religious Paz. Bound by tradition, he seeks union with the divine and considers the poet a bridge between man and God ("El puente," in *Elevación*), there is diaphaneity in his poetic voids, but his artistic intuition is suffocated by his analytic disposition. In his writings, as in the work of Paz, man is time: "I learned, at last, that time does not pass by, we pass by" ("El viejecito," *Obras completas* I, p. 259). In "El sexto sentido," another short story, he suggests the possibility of a glimpse at the final destiny of man: "there are crevices . . . the visionaries have looked through them . . . .Consciousness and unconsciousness are bound by a fragile bridge. . . . Some privileged beings dare cross it and glimpse with more or less certainty the vast architectures of the future" (*Obras completas* I, p. 361). The attraction of space is in his verses, the man of flesh and soul finds himself there in "Yo estaba en el espacio" (*En voz baja, Obras completas* II, p. 1569) or in "El viaje" (*Serenidad, Obras completas* II, p. 1634), but these poems lack the lyric intensity of his religious production, they are not the answer to his quest. There is greater conviction in his poem "Bienaventurados," from his book *La amada inmóvil*, a song to the dead, "Blessed are those who have destroyed / the illusory wall of space and numbers, / those who finally returned to the Whole / those who already measured all the voids" (*Obras completas* II, p. 1712).

In "La hondura interior" (from *Elevación*), written in his last years Nervo reconciled within himself and repudiated the vast expanses, "why search the extensions! . . . the great mystery is not there!" (*Obras completas* II, p. 1731). The illuminated void within himself, he sees, *without seeing*, what Paz sees, *without thinking*, in *Blanco*. In Nervo's vision there are "pure lights / excess of radiance, architectures / of such vast conception, / such mystery, such depths" (Ibid.) as to terrify reason. In Paz's many-splendored vision, he *sees not* what he sees, he *thinks not* what he thinks, he advances in "the radiance of the void" and fuses with it to reconcile the opposites: "The spirit / is an invention of the body / the body / an invention of the world, the world / an invention of the spirit / no yes" (*Configurations*, p. 193). "Poetry is neither a judgment, nor an interpretation of human existence," declares Paz in *El arco y la lira*, therefore, he neither affirms nor does he deny the soul, the flesh or the world. The experience of *otherness* is his poetic goal; Nervo sought the experience of God.

"We are all afflicted by an impetus of flight / an attraction of space / an obsession of sky," said González Martínez, the Mexican poet, in "Alas" (*Los senderos ocultos*). Silence is the answer to his quest, and it symbolizes alienation rather than reconciliation. Death is "one of life's many rhythms" in his poem "Anima trémula" (*La muerte del cisne*); love and death "life's conjunction" in "Aleluya de la muerte" (*Bajo el signo mortal*), thus coinciding with Paz who considers life and death a totality and seeks to reconcile them through love, but González Martínez cannot abandon the idea of a soul apart, which Paz does, nor can he resolve the conflict of reason versus faith. But the expression of duality in his works shows a distinct change from that of the first modernists, "my spirit and my flesh have always been inseparable friends," he says in his autobiography *El hombre del buho* (1944, p. 135). The poem "Parábola de la carne fiel" (*Parábolas y otros poemas*) is an exaltation of the sinful flesh. Erotic love is a theme in his first books, especially in *Preludios*, but it provides no transcendence and it looses emphasis in his later works. The plea to adore life with passion, which appears in this famous sonnet "Tuércele el cuello al cisne," can be found in many of his great poems and in his prose works. In *La apacible locura* (Mexico, 1951), also an autobiographical work, he speaks of his "inner thirst," of his desire to go to the very sources of life; to commune with the visible world and to go farther, "to thrust myself into daring excursions toward what is beyond human perception; to interpret the mysterious soul of the world" (p. 14). In his book, *Los senderos ocultos*, the verse expresses this wish: in "Deux pays" he dreams of "a divine consortium between human life and the life of the world," and in "Me abrazaré a la vida" life's infinite love will bring the ecstasy by which the poet will pulsate in unison with the rhythm of the universe. But the fusion does not occur, the idea of a soul apart is consistent in González Martínez's verses. In a late poem, "Preludio de evasión," the metaphoric corolla of his soul reaches for heaven while the stem sinks deeper into the earth. In his famous sonnet "Mi amigo el silencio" he travels the unknown region in the company of silence, "but life no longer comes to hear the verse we do not say." According to Paz, fusion of the word and the thing, the name and what is named, demands a previous reconciliation of man with himself and the world.

Life and death are the two poles in Herrera y Reissig's poetry and love is the great mediator which allows him "to enter Paradise before entering the grave." In *Opalos*, poems in prose, love is equated with being: "Loving is the same as being, the two verbs are one and the same," coinciding, in this respect, with Paz who defines love in *El arco y la libra* as the simultaneous revelation of being and the void, as being's creation of being: "We annihilate ourselves when we create ourselves, and vice-versa." Herrera y Reissig says in *Opalos*: "love is the antithesis, the beauty and the beast, pleasure and torture, transparency and shadow, life and death"; "I love, therefore, I am, I have been, I shall be." He identifies possession with death, the act of love is a ritual; but while Paz considers woman part of self, in Herrera y Reissig's poetry she is an offering, a victim sacrificed before an altar. Faithful to the traditional belief in the sinful nature of the flesh, he relates erotic love to sin. These concepts appear in his "Emblema afrodisíaco," in which the lover is a barbarian conqueror who buries in the woman his sadistic emblem of death, while the afternoon assumes the red tones of a mass "of horrid holocaust." In Herrera y Reissig's quest for more being, space plays an important role. In his metaphysical poem "La vida," an expression of his quest, a metaphoric mount, the poet's conscious self, meets an Amazon who represents human attributes in the realm of the spirit and "the blind instinct of life." She offers him knowledge of the void: "my inflamed love / will make you feel the intoxication / of the Immensity and the void." The poet asks to be guided "to the beautiful fountains / of the unheard of Blue / where Infinity quenches its thirst." Leading him to a grave like a bed, she offers herself to him and in her embrace turns into a dark knight who pierces the poet's heart with a stroke of the sword. This poem constitutes the highest expression of the quest in the poetry of Herrera y Reissig.

The quest for transcendence in the works of the great Spanish American modernist, Leopoldo Lugones, is not an obvious theme. In "The voice against the rock," the introductory poem to his great initial book *Las montañas del oro*, he chooses to believe in God, for he needs Him to fill infinity: "Freedom denies him, science suppresses him / . . . 'but how will you then fill infinity?' " Metaphorically, faith is, in this poem, a mountain full of abysmal crevices, its pure summit represents the visible effort of the abyss struggling in the darkness to come out of itself. The soul also has its summit: God. In Lugones's profession of faith, the traditional and new beliefs of the Old World are repudiated. He wants to be known as a poet of the New World who takes "the side of the stars."

The spatial dimension has preponderance over the temporal dimension in his poetry. Cosmic space is the theme of an early poem, "Los mundos" (1892). In it, the modernistic thirst for space is expressed in positive terms, "the spirit feels the yearning of the infinite, . . . it makes the high immensity incarnate in an imitation of its being"; the scientist is a diver of the darkness who pries away secrets from space; space is like an open page, where the daring eye spells out revelations of higher things; the instinct of the high pushes those who have wings, genius is a legitimate child of the sky with the voracious yearning of a condor openly facing the sun.

Unreconciled expressions of the duality of being are found only in the love poetry of Lugones. He is, like Paz, a poet of the erotic but unlike Paz he longs for purity in love. Possession, a theme in *Las montañas del oro*, is sinful or sad: in "Oda a la desnudez" it is a blasphemous religious sacrifice: "give me your breasts—chalices of the ritual of our mass—of love; give me your fingernails, daggers of gold—that I may suffer your accursed possession." In contrast to this expression, we read in a later poem: "My life is this delicious torture / the purer you are, the more you are mine" ("El dolor de amar" in *El libro fiel*). In Lugones's poetry, love is a form of transcendence nullified by the sinful nature of the flesh: "To love is the entire destiny, / . . . and the passion that vilifies your human self, / reveals in your soul what is divine, . . . Only he is worthy of love eternal / who knows how to condemn himself by loving" ("El tesoro"). This is, perhaps, the reason why Lugone's love poetry is associated with death and sadness, elements present in "La blanca soledad," his lyrical work about the white immensity of a moonlit night. Time is negated: "the infinite [is] / run by the wheels / of clocks, / like a car that never arrives." The poet feels the proximity of death, a city in the air beckons, the attraction gives a sense of purity. As the poem ends, the immensity turns into a white stone and all that remains is an awareness of the absence of the beloved.

The transcendental search for more being loses impetus after the period of the great modernist writers in the first half of the century. Octavio Paz continues it and brings it to its conclusion in *Blanco*. This poem is a summation of the Spanish American characteristics of that quest, and a liberation from the notions inherited from the great Spanish poetic tradition. By binding together in his poem the hunger for time and the thirst for space, Paz comes closer to expressing the essence of life.

University of Maryland

Stone and Water Imagery in Paz's Poetry

By ELSA DEHENNIN

It is to a *seguro azar* that I owe having discovered the work of Octavio Paz immediately after having studied the work of Jorge Guillén. As a result, I have seen in these two great poets of Hispanic literature, in these two friends, temperaments which, though opposed, coincide in an identical humanistic attitude, through their unshakable faith in the light of this world and in human love. An article by Octavio Paz, entitled "Horas situadas de Jorge Guillén,"[1] drew my attention to the possible divergencies and convergencies. Divine Octavio—as Guillén affectionately titles him—certainly speaks of his elder in "Horas situadas," but he cannot resist telling us something about himself as well. I gathered from it that if neither is a baroque poet, the luminous serenity of Guillén is opposed to the tormented chiaroscuro of Paz. Further, if neither is an intellectual poet, Guillén integrates consciousness into existing reality, fully and immediately, whereas Paz, more Mexican in this respect, is obsessed, just as is a José Gorostiza, by their dissociation and seeks to transcend the multiple confrontations which the latter solicits. "A plena luz la calidad de ser" (*Cántico*, p. 120)[2] is the motto of a happy Guillén who further clarified "Aquí, sobre la cima / Ya clara, / Estar es renacer." For Paz, light is not the calmly original datum. It is born aggressively, as a disruptive element, at the end of a sleepless night: "El alba lanza su primer cuchillo" ("Máscaras del alba," p. 216),[3] or, as we shall see, it bursts forth into the delirium of noon.

These facts, perhaps less fortuitous than they may seem at first glance, were those which led me to seek to know better the originality of Paz. A contrastive procedure which could emphasize sufficient differences and similarities seemed appropriate. In such a limited study as this, I have concentrated on works which are generally recognized as having the greatest poetic density: *Cántico* (first complete edition, 1950) and *La estación violenta* (1958). Out of concern for perfect objectivity, I looked first at the words. Paz has observed "una cierta fatalidad en las palabras . . . no creo que quiera decir que el azar preside la creación, sino que una fatal elección nos lleva a ciertas palabras."[4] Still more explicit, he notes in *El arco y la lira*: "La palabra del poeta se confunde con su ser mismo. Él es su palabra . . . . La creación consiste en (un) sacar a luz ciertas palabras inseparables de nuestro ser. Ésas y no otras. El poema está hecho de palabras necesarias e insustituíbles.[5]" By "word" I mean especially "substantive," which, as its lexeme clearly indicates, carries the signifying substance; to which, moreover, the other elements of speech are secondary.

For Guillén—I believe that I have so demonstrated (cf. *Cántico de Jorge Guillén, Une poésie de la clarté*, Bruxelles, PUB, 1969)—*luz* is the most frequent word: the primary key word. The celestial constellation *luz, sol, cielo, aire, viento, nube* dominates by far. After *luz* and *sol, amor* is the third key word, their human equivalent in sum. Even if *noche* is more frequent than *día, luz* is far more frequent than *sombra*, as *sol* is far more frequent than *luna*; it also dominates the other elements, *agua, río* and *tierra*, signaled most often by *mundo* or by *realidad*.

In Octavio Paz the "fatality" of numbers leads us into semantic fields which are just as fundamental but clearly different. The primary key word is *noche* (57) and, with *sombra* (12), it contrasts with *luz* (40), *sol* (34), *día* (33) in a proportion of 69 to 107.[6] The second key word is *agua* (57), and it is opposed to *piedra* (48).

It seems to me that if we consider as a whole the semantic fields which have formed around these two key words, we reach the central zones of this poetry: *agua, río* (27), *mar* (17), *fuente* (15), *ola* (10), *manantial* (5), *corriente* (4), *arroyos* (3), *chorro* (3), *gota* (3), *lluvia* (3), *onda* (2), *oleaje* (1), or 93 words in all, as opposed to *piedra* (48), *tierra* (10), *cristal* (10), *polvo* (10), *roca* (19), *llano* (7), *monte* (4), *oro* (5), *diamante* (4), *plata, bronce, cobre, jade, silex, mármol, obsidiana* all once, or 114 words in all. Even though *agua* is the most frequent word, the group *piedra* is the largest. The same may be said of *noche* in the group *luz*.

But there is more than the opposition of light and dark, of moving fluidity and lasting fixity; in varying combinations with *luz*, there is the constellation *cielo* (9), *viento* (9), *nube* (9), *aire* (5), as well as *astro* (11), *luna* (9), *estrella* (6), or 58 words which laterally reenforce *luz*, the prime element of the collection, which is in the center of a vast constellation and which is opposed, of course, to the contradictory term *noche*, but especially to the opposing elements *piedra* (*tierra*) / *agua*. *Mundo* (22) and *universo* (2), as global terms, are hardly opposed to the elements which they carry within them; they are the abode of all things and certainly of man. *Hombre* (35) is not opposed to any antithetical term, neither to *dios* (13) nor to *mujer* (8).

However wretched he may be, man is the king of this poetry. His body (*cuerpo*, 32) is astonishingly present throughout all his anatomy, from head to toe. *Alma* (9) is of little significance in contrast to *ojo* (40), *rostro* (36), *sangre* (22), *mano* (19), *frente* (17), *pecho* (13), *cara* (10), *boca* (10), *hueso* (10), *pie* (9), *labios* (5), *diente* (6), *entrañas* (4), *vientre* (4), *piel* (4), et cetera. The extent and variety of this field —to which I would like to add *pensamiento* (26) and *palabra* (26), of equal importance—are such that they make of it the governing whole of the collection.

But that is not all! Around the body of man in the world, whose sensory and mental faculties are so active, the gifts of nature and the constructions of man, which are both most simple, most intrahistorical, if you will, are distributed according to a curiously balanced frequency. *Árbol* (24), for example, is contrasted with *cuarto* (24), the pivots of two semantic fields at once varied and coherent. Around *árbol* (with species such as *sauce, chopo, álamo, olmo*), there is *fruto* (10) (*uva, naranja, manzana*), *flores* (10) (*rosa, clavel*), *raíz* (9), *racimo* (9), *semilla* (4), *yedra* (4), *jardín* (4), *rama* (4), *hoja* (3), *grano* (3), *ramo* (2), *parque* (2).

Jardín and *parque*, just as *surtidor* (9), could be added to the following semantic field; that of *cuarto* (20), *espejo* (18), *muro* (16), *puerta* (10), *plaza* (10), *torre* (10), *calle* (9), *pared* (6), *patio* (3), *casa* (3), *ventana* (3), *escalera* (1), *balcón* (1), *banco* (1), *muralla* (1). The spaces which thus concretely situate the microcosm of man are made of stone and greenery: contrast occasionally gives in to complementarity. I must, however, detach from the last group the word *espejo*, the only significant word of the series which is not a constituent element of construction.

Aside from the semantic fields already set out, *espejo* is part of a line which goes from *luz* via *ojo* to *imagen* (18) and *reflejo* (3), which are opposed to *presencia* (18); that presence which, according to a whole Mexican tradition, is threatened by its illusory reflections and which must assert itself against its dreams. *Sueño* (12) is not without importance: it is often expressed by the verb *soñar*; but it is rivaled neither by *fantasma* (2) nor by *recuerdo* (2). We have now entered imperceptibly into more abstract semantic zones. They are limited in variety and in extent.

I call attention to the frequency of *tiempo* (4), which is scarcely opposed to *espacio* (6) but which is so much more frequent than it. Of course, time is shared, as is well known, between *noche* and *día*, to which one must add different moments of the day such as *alba* (9), *mediodía* (9) *mañana* (6), *tarde* (6), and even *verano* (4), all of which definitely confirm the unquestionable superiority of light, even though *luz* is not, I repeat, the key word of Octavio Paz. From a chronological point of view, it is interesting to note that *tiempo* is completed by *instante* (31), the latter being much more frequent than *siglo* (16), *año* (15), *hora* (14), *minuto* (7), *eternidad* (2). The moment is not necessarily present. Paz is pleased to upset temporal succession whether from the future toward the past or vice-versa. *Hoy* dominates, nevertheless, *ayer* (5), and *futuro* (2) or *porvenir* (2).

I must evoke one last semantic contrast, distinct from all the others and very significant for the Paz question: that of *vida* (43), *muerte* (24), *vivos* (6), *muertos* (9).[7] A Mexican contrast par excellence, which Gorostiza sums up very candidly, after having shown that intelligence, hostile to the dull weight of flesh, is incapable of resolving it. He speaks of

> *el escarnio brutal de esa discordia*
> que nutren vida y muerte inconciliables,
> siguiéndose una a otra
> como el día y la noche,
> una y otra acampadas en la célula
> como en un tardo tiempo de crepúsculo.[8]

Octavio Paz confirms this point of view indirectly in desiring that death be given, in an "open" vision, its original meaning: "muerte y vida son contrarios que se complementan. Ambas son mitades de una esfera que nosotros, sujetos a tiempo y espacio no podemos sino entrever."[9] Octavio Paz is not then content with the immanent complementarity of life and death, so characteristic of Guillén.[10] He wishes to conceive of it as a superior and mythical —should I say utopic—unit. Already in the first poem of the collection, which, just like the last, is a key poem, thesis and antithesis alternate without attaining a true synthesis.

Directly, a fabulous Mediterranean world is offered us. An elementary world made of sun and sea—light and water are powerful allies!—of rocks also and of ruins —"ruinas vivas en un mundo de muertos en vida" ("Himno entre ruinas," p. 211). In spite of the conflicting oxymoron of *muertos en vida*, all is for the best:

> Los ojos ven, las manos tocan.
> . . . . .
> Ver, tocar formas hermosas, diarias.
> . . . . .
> Como el coral sus ramas en el agua
> extiendo mis sentidos en la hora viva:
> el instante se cumple en una concordancia amarilla,
> ¡oh mediodía, espiga henchida de minutos,
> copa de eternidad!   (pp. 212–13)

The euphoria is quite Guillénian! There is no solitude; the unity with creation is established; all is harmony, *redondeamiento* Guillén would say, who sums up his cosmic vision with *todo es cúpula* (*Cántico*, op. cit. p. 250). Paz prefers another kind of metaphor, wherein he put at once a bit of humor and of "conceptismo":

> ¡Día, redondo día,
> luminosa naranja de veinticuatro gajos,
> todos atravesados por una misma y amarilla dulzura!
> La inteligencia al fin encarna,
> se reconcilian las dos mitades enemigas
> y la conciencia-espejo se licúa,
> vuelve a ser fuente, manantial de fábulas:
> Hombre, árbol de imágenes,
> palabras que son flores que son frutos que son actos.
>   (p. 213)

The *escarnio* of which Gorostiza spoke no longer exists. I shall emphasize only two aspects of the reconciliation. First, the reconciliation of the moment is divorced from its successivity with eternity, which is not artificially reduced but enters into each minute. Paz explained this phenomenon: "Es el tiempo mismo engendrándose, manándose, abriéndose a un acabar que es un continuo empezar. *Chorro, fuente.*" (*El arco y la lira*, p. 102). Here again the image of the saving water, with its Mexican connotations, is profitably used in the poem. For there is also the reconciliation, almost constant in Guillén and rather rare in Paz, between intelligence and flesh, between consciousness and life, between reflection and matter. Consciousness—*páramo de espejos*, for Gorostiza—can capture only the reflections of things of ourselves, beings willingly narcissistic who admire ourselves in what Gorostiza again calls "la imagen atónita del agua." At the privileged moment of union, consciousness becomes substance and the reflection, water—the life-source of the world since Thales of Milet!

For man, it is in the totality of the day—of its twenty-four hours—that he finds the reign of myth and a marvelous correlation of gifts.

Is this truly a synthesis? It seems to me more idyllic than real. The thesis, all light, in a privileged place and moment, implies so plain a harmony that the antithesis, quite dark, "Cae la noche sobre Teotihuacán", may be admitted to coexist with the thesis, remains separated from it. The former develops parallel to the latter, according to a strict alternation. The antithetical vision is not only Mexican or contemporary; it is just as universal as the first: "Acodado en montes que ayer fueron ciudades, Polifemo bosteza" (p. 212). The cyclops may contemplate "Nueva York, Londres, Moscú." Forever and always, "Abajo, entre los hoyos, se arrastra un rebaño de hombres," about which the poet makes a cynical remark which one would seek in vain in Guillén. That is, on the theme of human misery, thought is provoked: it sets out upon a blind path: "Mis pensamientos se bifurcan, serpean, se enredan, recomienzan, / y al fin se inmovilizan. . . ." It is a closed and fixed cycle. The metaphorical transpositions, borrowed as if by chance from water, are expressive: "ríos que no desembocan, / delta de sangre bajo un sol sin crepúsculo. / ¿Y todo ha de parar en este chapoteo de aguas muertas?" The question remains open. One remarks that the key words are endowed with determiners which negate them. And one wonders at this terrible never-setting sun. Is union possible between these two antithetical worlds? Is man not condemned to go from the one to the other? His euphoria may be such that he accepts the one *and* the other, that he permits their being joined, but can he live their union? An implacable alternation seems to be our lot, especially for us Westerners who do not assimilate the principle of the identity of opposites. "El mundo occidental es él del 'esto o aquello'; el oriental él del 'esto y aquello' y aun él de 'esto es aquello,'" says Octavio Paz (*El arco y la lira*, p. 102–104). The Buddhist initiate could serve as an example for the poet. So man is not totally disarmed. But before evoking his principal weapon—love—which is for both Guillén and Paz a maker of the absolute and of union, I would like to emphasize the torments proper to Paz, who certainly conceives of the joining of opposites, who dreams of their identity, but who lives in the tension or the vibration of their antagonisms. "¡Arco (tendido sobre la nada) y lira!" Even in a poem like "Fuente," where he has almost Guillén-like verses, such as, "El mediodía alza en vilo al mundo. / . . . . Todo es presencia, todos los siglos son este Presente" (p. 216–17) the present, which is for Guillén "el tiempo menos patético" (*El argumento*, p. 19) or further, the time of the "greatest gift," becomes here the time of bursting forth: "la presencia, el presente, estalla / como un espejo roto al mediodía, como un mediodía roto contra el mar y la sal" (p. 217). One better understands what has happened when the poet adds, "Y el caído bajo el hacha de su propio delirio se levanta" (p. 218). Without being a key word, delirium is significant. One will note that it is surrounded by verbal forms of opposite dynamism: *el caído* (nominalized, of course) and *se levanta*. There is a dynamic proper to Paz which one could not possibly find in Guillén, for whom even "la pleamar es una cima de equilibrio" (*El argumento*, p. 37). Though I do not have available numbered data, I would dare to affirm that *caer* and its synonyms, like *despeñar*, are key verbs; they are clearly opposed to verbs expressing a rising movement. "Todo se pone en pie para caer mejor" says Paz with a maxim-like tone before adding, "Y el caído . . . se levanta."

The fall may also be prolonged and transformed, then, into a nightmarish withdrawal. Such is the case in a long poem, "Mutra," made wholly of disparate enumerations, evoking a very heavy summer day: "todo este largo día con su terrible cargamento de seres y de cosas," stranded in "time standing still," in a "static confusion."

> Todos vamos cayendo con el día, todos entramos en el túnel,
> atravesamos corredores interminables cuyas paredes de aire
> sólido se cierran,
> nos internamos en nosotros y a cada paso el animal humano
> jadea y se desploma,
> retrocedemos, vamos hacia atrás, el animal pierde futuro
> a cada paso,
> y lo erguido y duro y óseo en nosotros al fin cede y cae
> pesadamente en la boca madre.
> (p. 223)

Whatever one does, temporality slips in, and with it reappears the opposite semantic field, this time in the Heraclitus image: "También las piedras son el río" (p. 224). Remarkable verse, expressly paradoxical, where Paz establishes neither unity nor union but the identity of two opposites which condition the very existence of man. "¿Dónde está el hombre?" Precisely in that contradiction of stone and water and in the time-river which carries it away: "También el hombre fluye." Under these conditions, Paz refuses the "beatitud de lo repleto sobre sí mismo derramándose," of which the temples of Mutra offer voluptuous images, filled with key words, joining, impossibly, water and fire:[11] "no somos, no quiero ser / Dios, no quiero ser a tientas, no quiero regresar, soy hombre y el hombre es / el hombre, el que . . ." (p. 224–25). There follows a long and painful definition of which I retain here, other than "arco / tendido sobre la nada," already cited, "*partido en dos* desde el nacer, *peleando* / contra su sombra, . . . disparado, exhalado, sin jamás alcanzarse" (p. 225)—which clearly seems a condemnation. Falling is everywhere: aside from *despeñar, caer* occurs four times. The conjunction *pero* permits, nevertheless, the beginning of the inevitable recovery. For one could say also that everything falls the better to rise up again. Among the resources of rebuilding, man has available other than poetic magic—"el poema que asciende y cubre con sus dos alas el abrazo de la noche *y* el día" (p. 226)—a truth which is also a determination: "el hombre sólo es hombre entre los hombres" (p. 226). Guillén would subscribe to this verse; Guillén, who observed à propos of the poem "Cara a cara," "El hombre no se rinde sin más ni más a sus enemigos" (*El argumento*, p. 35). What can this man do? A man divided, inevitably projecting his division into a world of stones and water, falling and always getting up again.

In *La estación violenta*, where night is certainly the most frequent word and where the poet is often prey to insomnia (cf. "Repaso nocturno," "¿No hay salida?,"

"El río"), he is tempted to follow his thought far form the body and far from the world, until he feels "ni vivo ni muerto," or better, "vivo para la muerte, muerto para la vida" (p. 219-20). That is what rhetoricians call a *commutatio*: the second antithesis is the inversion of the first; in this way, the tension is stabilized but in a horrible de-tension (cf. also p. 221, lines 70-74). In another poem, "El cántaro roto," binary too, with multiple correlative oppositions, the poet asked himself the question: "¿Abrir los ojos o cerrarlos, todo es igual?" (p. 235). From these feverish experiments he has retained at least a possibility of salvation, presented here through verbal forms (*hay que*, infinitives and subjunctives) open to a time *in posse* and not *in esse*. "Hay que dormir con los ojos abiertos, hay que soñar con las manos" (p. 235). He tells us: combine the sensory perceptions from the exterior with the intimacy of the dream. *Soñemos* becomes a watchword, of course, unknown to Guillén, who imagines dreams only among (*entre*) things (p. 196). Further, "hay que soñar en voz alta, hay que cantar hasta que el canto eche raíces, tronco, ramas, pájaros, astros" (p. 235). Poetry, which is not always so euphoric an exercise (cf. "El río," p. 230), may be, if not a canticle a fabulous song of progressive resurrection! And that is not all: "hay que soñar hacia atrás, hacia la fuente, hay que remar siglos arriba" (p. 236) which does not signify that one must undertake the painful regression of Mutra. Everything must be begun again: "volver al punto de partida, / ni adentro ni afuera, ni arriba ni abajo, al cruce de caminos, adonde empiezan los caminos" (p. 236). In a space of light and water, it is the splendid zero point, the absolute point, which, however, never seems to be reached, since friendly prepositions indicate all the way, to the last verse, the path to be followed: "*hacia* allá, *al* centro vivo del origen, *más allá de* fin y comienzo" (p. 236). A *más allá* which Guillén has taught us to know "cerca a veces / muy cerca, familiar" (*Cántico*, p. 30) and which Paz situates in a world reconciled and united—"vida y muerte no son mundos contrarios, somos un solo tallo con dos flores gemelas" (p. 236)—to which Cartesians do not perhaps have access, but which is open to poets, who have been able to "unearth the lost word" (12), and to lovers—*los dos*—gifted with the power not only of glimpsing "the undissolvable unity of opposites" but also of living it—be it only for a moment.

I can only evoke here the great poem-movement *Piedra de sol*, which ends both *La estación violenta* and *Libertad bajo palabra*. A poem without end, since the latter repeats the end. A poem of cyclical becoming which joins, strangely, in its last two strophes *all* the principal key words; a synthesis-poem, in some ways, where creation and destruction, union and solitude alternate exactly, according to the rhythm of all human adventure, according to an "exemplary" process:

> un caminar de río que se curva,
> avanza, retrocede, da un rodeo
> y llega siempre.
> (p. 254, p. 237)

A poem of pronouns, thus of desprendimiento of *tú* and *yo*, where *tú* is in the image of the world and is identified with it:

> voy por tu cuerpo como por el mundo,
> tu vientre es una plaza soleada,
> tus pechos dos iglesias donde oficia
> la sangre sus misterios paralelos,
>
> (p. 238)

Tú adapts beautifully to the desires of *yo*, then, inexplicably, she disappears, abandoning *yo* to his vain, closed research, pursued within himself. Condemned to the torments of the poetic act,[13] to the total enclosure of the moment, he is prey to an infernal torture:

> ardo sin consumirme, busco el *agua*
> y en tus ojos no hay agua, son de *piedra,*
> y tus pechos, tu vientre, tus caderas
> son de piedra, tu boca sabe a *polvo,*
> tu boca sabe a pozo sin salida,
> pasadizo de *espejos* . . .
>
> (p. 243)

The same metaphors—or should one say symbols?—recur constantly; in the middle of the poem, *yo* is "una larga herida, / una *oquedad* que ya nadie recorre"; *tú* is the cry of Melusine.

A considerable shock is necessary in order that the poet get hold of himself. It will come from outside, from what is called the history of events: Madrid, 1937. In the middle of the bombardments, "los dos se desnudaron y se amaron" (p. 246). Paradise opens in the hell of war. There are, once more, two antithetical worlds which *both* make the best *and* the worst of our human universe. The power of love is such that, "todo se transfigura y es sagrado, / es el centro del mundo cada cuarto" (p. 247). Man condemned, in the words of Carlos Fuentes, to ex-centricity, finds here the center which Guillén lives everywhere. For the "magnificent convergence of Creation" (*El argumento*, p. 36) occurs everywhere. Even though all the horrors of our world are once more here enumerated at length and in their atrocious confusion, they disappear:

> se derrumban
> *por un instante inmenso* y *vislumbramos*
> nuestra unidad perdida, el desamparo
> que es ser hombres, la gloria que es ser hombres
> y compartir el pan, el sol, la muerte,
> el olvidado asombro de estar vivos
>
> (p. 248)

And one thinks again of Guillén, poet of wonder, poet of love for whom all of *Cántico* must rise toward love (*El argumento,* p. 20): "Merced a ese acuerdo alcanzamos plenitud de realidad." The Castilian poet is destined to live everywhere and forever that unity which is existential plenitude. One will seek in vain in Paz that so simple, that so direct avowal: "¡Qué oscura es nuestra voz! / La carne expresa más. / Somos nuestra expresión." (*Cántico*, p. 106). Even here the poem is not the prolongation of an experience of unity ("vislumbramos"). The poet has of course been able to observe that "el pensamiento encarna" (p. 248), but we are not privileged to live the incarnation with him. We see through the prism of his hopeful consciousness, through the metaphorical and symbolic irisation of a consciousness seizing the immanent oppositions and declaiming the possibility of a superior reconciliation, which is told and retold to us. It is the only but also all the unity to which *La estación violenta* can lay claim.

In this avowal-invocation of the next to last page,

> *vida y muerte*
> pactan en ti, señora de la *noche,*
> torre de *clairidad,* reina del alba,
> virgen lunar, madre del *agua* madre,
> CUERPO del *mundo,* CASA de la muerte,
> (p. 253)

the principal semantic fields are joined and the poet accepts the alliance of opposites, which is succession and not fusion, which is on the human scale of *y* (tacitly enumerative) and not on the mythical scale of *es.* Yet *es,* the verbal index of identification, is not far away. It appears—in the first person—in the constant prayer:

> llévame al otro lado de esta noche,
> andonde *yo soy tú* somos nosotros
> al reino de pronombres enlazados,
> puerta del ser. . . .
> (p. 253)

Imperative, apostrophe: the situation seems one of injunction, opened, in addition, on a total world which always appears as a possible terminal (note again the repetition of the preposition *a,* even at the beginning of the verse): a terminal inside the circuit imperturbably designed by "un caminar de río que se curva" which always arrives without discord.

Université Libre de Bruxelles
Translated from the French
By
Wendell McClendon

---

[1] *Puertas al campo,* Mexico City, 1967 (2nd ed.), p. 75.

[2] We refer to the edition *Aire nuestro,* Milan, 1968.

[3] We quote according to *Libertad bajo palabra,* Mexico City, 1968 (2d ed.).

[4] *Las peras del olmo,* Mexico City, 1957, p. 199.

[5] Mexico, 1967 (2d ed.), p. 45.

[6] I indicate in parentheses the frequency of the word. Since the figures were not obtained by computer, they are relative. I require of them an indication, not an explanation.

[7] In Guillén's work, over more than 500 pages, *vida* occurs 77 times, and *muerte* 21 times!

[8] *Poesía,* Mexico City, 1961, Cf. *Muerte sin fin,* p. 120. My emphasis.

[9] *El laberinto de la soledad,* Mexico City, 1955, p. 55.

[10] *El argumento de la obra,* Milan, 1961, p. 20.

[11] Cf. *La estación violenta,* p. 224, vers 55–56: "agua de ojos, agua de bocas, agua nupcial y ensimismada, agua incestuosa, / agua de dioses, cópula de dioses, agua de astros y reptiles, selvas de agua de cuerpos incenciados."

[12] Cf. *El arco y la lira,* p. 113. See also a poem like "Fábula" in *Semillas para un himno,* p. 121.

[13] Cf. p. 241–42, verses 153 to 161.

Woman in Sleep: Some Reflections on the Eye of the Beholder

By RACHEL PHILLIPS

> *Temporal*
> En la montaña negra
> El torrente delira en voz alta
> A esa misma hora
> Tú avanzas entre precipicios
> Por tu cuerpo dormido
> El viento lucha a oscuras con tu sueño
> Maraña verde y blanca
> Encina niña encina milenaria
> El viento te descuaja y te arrastra y te arrasa
> Abre tu pensamiento y lo dispersa
> Torbellino tus ojos
> Torbellino tu ombligo
> Torbellino y vacío
> El viento te exprime como un racimo
> Temporal en tu frente
> Temporal en tu nuca y en tu vientre
> Como una rama seca te avienta
> El viento
> A lomos del torrente de tu sueño
> Manos verdes y pies negros
> Por la garganta
> De piedra de la noche
> Anudada a tu cuerpo
> De montaña dormida
> El torrente delira
> Entre tus muslos
> Soliloquio de piedras y de agua
> Por los acantilados
> De tu frente
> Pasas como un río de pájaros
> El bosque dobla cabeza
> Como un toro herido
> El bosque se arrodilla
> Bajo el ala del viento
> Cada vez más alto
> El torrente delira
> Cada vez más hondo
> Por tu cuerpo dormido
> Cada vez más noche
> (Octavio Paz, *Salamandra*, 2nd ed. Mexico City, 1969, pp. 80–81)

107

Woman, nature: dual images defining a unity of concept throughout Paz's work from his early love poems to the complexities of *Blanco*. The one analogy which escapes the clutches of irony, though all else in his work is a prey to this agent of erosion. On the shifting sands of reality, in the confusion of subjectivity and objectivity overlapping and inseparable, the concept remains of woman as creative principle, of nature as female mystery. Because, of course, the poet adds another analogous element—he also creates, the poem ultimately *is*, and the corrosion of the ironic glance is finally eluded when the dynamic process has taken place and the poem exists before our eyes.

To Paz, what counts in women and in nature is, then, the dynamism, the becoming, be it of the erotic moment or of the moment of fertility. In "Solo a dos voces" (*Salamandra*, pp. 109–15) the creative struggle in the poet and the winter solstice both end in the promise of fertility. In *Blanco* the moment of sexual climax is the Tantric enlightenment (*bodhi*), and also the emergence of language recreating the world in the new object, the poem. "Temporal" (*Salamandra*, pp. 80–81) has seemed to me yet another fascinating variation on the theme of woman, desired and desiring, emerging as it does through images and metaphors which the poet draws from the objectivity of the natural world, yet blends into his own perceptions in a delicious and delicate tension. The dynamic process—the poem—is mirrored in the motifs of the storm and the sleeping woman, yet is balanced and checked by our visual recreation of her sleeping form, producing in the reader an intensity of reaction exceptional even when one takes into account the powerful sensuality of Paz's verse.

For in the eroticism of this poem there is no physical fulfilment, though the tensions of the intricate emotional and sexual interaction between man and woman is simulated in the tensions of metaphor and image. The occasion of the poem is rare in Paz: the woman is asleep, watched or evoked by the poet, and his voice speaks to her, gaining in intimacy and poignancy through our awareness of its solipsism. Yet though this voice is neither heard nor answered, it speaks with a freedom and a fervency which come from a consciousness in which subject and object have become merged. The desire felt and the object desired are one, and the image which will carry such a theme is equally full of confused potency—a mountain stream raging during a storm. The poem moves between the two scenes, the sleeping woman and the raging stream, juxtaposing and superimposing images to build up the feeling of dynamism. Thus the stream is at once an objective correlative for the primeval power inherent in the woman's body and so deeply felt by the poet, and also for the turmoil which this body, itself passive in sleep, creates in the mind of the beholder.

Darkness and the sound of water open the poem ("el torrente delira en voz alta"), both creating an atmosphere of instinctive yet hidden passion. Water traditionally connotes fertility, life and sexual fluids, reactions heightened here by the personification of the verb "delira." The reader at once intuits the cries of a human being in troubled sleep, and immediately this impression becomes linked with that of the sleeping woman. She moves forward "entre precipicios," and her somnolent body is troubled by the wind, symbol of the pneuma, the breath of life, here the life-force inherent in sex: "El viento lucha a oscuras con tu sueño." The double image continues with the foliage on the mountain, and the tossing body—"maraña verde y blanca"— and the color green links the vegetative world with that of eroticism and procreation. After this confusion of tangled undergrowth the long *i*'s of the next line and the unexpected assonance produce a beautiful *rallentando* which keeps alive the peacefulness of sleep alongside the frenetic energy of the mountain stream: "Encina niña encina milenaria." The wind then becomes the dominant motif, and the girl's mind is tossed and buffeted, dragged and thrown—"abre tu pensamiento y lo dispersa." Her relaxed body is caught up in her psychic whirlwind: "Torbellino tus ojos / Torbellino tu ombligo. . . ." The wind storms around and through her: "Temporal en tu frente / Temporal en tu nuca y en tu vientre. . . ." And it is the wind which finally brings together the woman-image and the stream-image, then fused into one for the rest of the poem: "Como una rama seca te avienta / El viento / A lomos del torrente de tu sueño. . . ." Now the interpenetration of imagery and symbolism is complete. Mountain stream and woman become identical ("Manos verdes y pies negros"); her body is "de montaña dormida"; the stream flows between her thighs with the same delirium of pebbles and water; her forehead is a cliff where a river of birds passes, birds so often associated by Paz with desire felt or fulfilled. The mountain woods are personified and somehow subjugated to the wind of life within her, and the raging of the stream rises higher, while her body sinks deeper into sleep in an ever darker night: "Cada vez más alto / El torrente delira / Cada vez más hondo / Por tu cuerpo dormido / Cada vez más noche." The tension is not resolved but heightened in this climax where the polarity between opposites is made extreme—noise and silence, sleep and life force—to end in all the energy of unsatisfied passion. The delving into the sleeping mind, here not the poet's but his woman's, brings us close to the surrealists' deliberate penetration of hidden regions of the psyche. Likewise Paz has gone behind outer reality to explore inner realms and has set one in opposition to the other, the antithesis never being brought to synthesis but allowed to end in tense expectancy. For the expression of these opposing tendencies he has turned to the natural world and picked, in contrast to the relaxed passivity of a sleeping body, the turbulence of a mountain stream and a stormy wind at night. The erotic power of these images in an oblivious body communicates the antagonism between male and female principles, and between the subconscious world of the unbridled imagination and the controlled world of the conscious mind. While the sexual urge is left in unsatisfied tension, the brilliant fusing of the two images does present an esthetic synthesis of opposing forces. The poem itself, typically in Paz's work, is the point of union of the two poles of the creative mind, one imaginative, the other rational, or in other words the one drawing upon primordial impulses and the other filtered through the process of personal experience.

Woman, nature and the poet. The expected triangle, yet in "Temporal," woman ("tú") and nature become one, and both together absorb the turbulent energies of the speaker's "yo." The involvement of subject and dual object in the dynamism of becoming, which is this poem, must seek openness of form and must call upon the incantatory qualities of language. Hence the repetitions, sometimes of vowels ("Encina niña encina milenaria"), sometimes of syllables ("te arrastra y te arrasa"), sometimes of substantives ("Torbellino tus ojos / Torbellino tu ombligo / Torbellino y vacío"), and finally of the phrase "Cada vez más . . ." which appears three times at the close of the poem. The word must be sense and sound at once, and sound may often carry more of the magical property of speech in its most primitive function. Length of line is also determined by speech—"breath lines," to use Charles Olson's definition, lines which fall as naturally as the body rises and falls in motions of breathing and speaking. No artifice, just the magic of words and the power of images which grow and change, the "dynamic organicism" as Morse Peckham has defined this quality which was injected into man's view of himself, his world and his creation by the romantics, and which has stayed with us from their day onward. The poem grows according to the laws of its inner dynamism, its form is the "extension of (its) content," as Olson has phrased it, that is, open, undetermined, freely produced, and the images—even, paradoxically, the sleeping woman—move, grow, develop with the burden of the metaphors they carry.

Insofar as a similar motif, very differently treated, may provide a convenient clue to the esthetic attitudes and poetic worlds of two poets, close in time and space, but otherwise far removed from each other, I have turned to Paul Valéry's sleeping woman for contrast and comparison. The juxtaposition of "La Dormeuse" and "Temporal" may seem an odd one, but it points out, intriguingly, I think, Paz's inherently romantic vision of art and life, as opposed to the detachment with which the more classical Valéry approaches the same subject. The French poem appeared in *Charmes* (1922) and is written in sonnet form:

> *La Dormeuse*
> *A Lucien Fabre*
>
> Quels secrets dans son coeur brûle ma jeune amie,
> Ame par le doux masque aspirant une fleur?
> De quels vains aliments sa naïve chaleur
> Fait ce rayonnement d'une femme endormie?
>
> Souffle, songes, silence, invincible accalmie,
> Tu triomphes, ô paix plus puissante qu'un pleur,
> Quand de ce plein sommeil l'onde grave et l'ampleur
> Conspirent sur le sein d'une telle ennemie.
>
> Dormeuse, amas doré d'ombres et d'abandons,
> Ton repos redoutable est chargé de tels dons,
> O biche avec langueur longue auprès d'une grappe,
>
> Que malgré l'âme absente, occupée aux enfers,
> Ta forme au ventre pur qu'un bras fluide drape,
> Veille; ta forme veille, et mes yeux sont ouverts.
>
> (Paul Valéry, *Charmes*, rev. ed. Paris, 1926, p. 57)

A sonnet, thus, an exercise in the shaping of verse, in "mastery" as Valéry himself says in his notes on classicism (*Selected Writings of Paul Valéry*, New York, 1964, p. 152). For method—expertise combined with craftsmanship—was essential to Valéry's conception of the poem and was, indeed, identical with the poem itself. Not the word saying itself but "the acquired habit of always thinking, or combining, with the technical means as *point of departure*, and of never thinking of a work except in terms of its *means*: of never beginning a work with a subject or an effect which has not been imagined in relation to the technical means." (Ibid.) Not that he is talking about himself in these notes. The remarks are general ones but are relevant to his treatment of the image of the sleeping woman, contrasted with the interpenetrating dynamism of Paz's use of the same theme. Paz's woman blends with the natural images of stream and mountain so that the outline of her form is finally indistinct in the reader's imagination, and the sensation which remains is the surging eroticism within the gazing poet and the object of desire. As "Temporal" ends barriers are dissolved—reader becomes viewer becomes nature-woman, or, to use other terms, animus and anima unite in the imagined moment of erotic passion. Valéry reverses this process of undifferentiation. The poet's attitude is one of tenderness ("ma jeune amie"), certainly of sensuality ("O biche avec langueur longue auprès d'une grappe . . ."), but not of erotic desire. In the sexual embrace subject and object would lose their separateness and the esthetic moment be lost. To this poet what "la dormeuse" gives is the beauty of pure form: when the poem is read and remembered, it is the perfection of the sonnet echoed in the still beauty of the sleeping woman's shape which remains in the mind. Her outline, like that of the poem, is precise, and it is the eye, not the body or the appetite of the speaker which is satisfied: "Ta forme au ventre pur qu'un bras fluide drape, / Veille . . ." Subconscious thoughts and desires are not to be brought to light ("Quels secrets dans son coeur . . . l'âme absente, occupée aux enfers"), for what impresses the watching poet is the feeling communicated by the sleeping body of a sculptured mass. Alliteration and assonance add weight and solidity to the images—"paix plus puissante qu'un pleur," "l'onde grave et l'ampleur / Conspirent sur le sein . . ." "amas doré d'ombres et d'abandons . . ."—every aural and visual effect helps to achieve the stasis which for Valéry is the essence of the esthetic experience, and which is caught in the last perfect line: "ta forme veille, et mes yeux sont ouverts."

So this poet moves not toward the desired woman but away from the image which has occasioned his poem back into a detachment which observes the source of beauty and preserves it immobile in a closed and perfect form. We are reminded of Stephen Dedalus in his moment of rebirth upon the beach when the promise of life and beauty appears to him in the vision of a girl, motionless and expectant, "like one whom magic had changed into the likeness of a strange and beautiful seabird." She is a living thing, fashioned by life, and answers to the "new wild life . . . singing in his veins." Yet he too accepts the joy of the esthetic moment with a serenity in which the reactions of flesh and blood play no part. His soul worships and he turns away from her, keeping in his heart only the timeless message of her beauty. Valéry's vision is less celestial;

his sleeping girl is no angel in her youth and beauty. Yet he also stands back from the physical presence to worship the essence he finds there—art itself, perfect form, or in his own words, ". . . the suspicions of a diamond in a mass of 'blue ground': a moment infinitely more precious than all the others and than the circumstances that gave it birth." (Ibid.)

Vassar College

Poetry and Poetics in Octavio Paz[*]

By TOMÁS SEGOVIA

Since the romantic period, there clearly appears in Western poetry a division between poetry and poetics. Before romanticism, as well as after it, the work of all poets was based on an idea of poetry which was as much a program as it was a kind of knowledge, as much a conscious desire as it was an obscure tendency. But during the period of romanticism the role of the individual poet changed in relation to the idea of poetry. Previously, he had practically nothing at all to say in the debate on poetics. If his word contributed in any way toward changing (or perhaps confirming or structuring) the dominant concepts of poetry, it was only in an indirect and nearly always involuntary way. The action of a poet on the accepted idea of poetry resulted from an accumulation of small inevitable mutations, which were almost imperceptible when viewed individually. Such changes came about in a way that allowed each poet to maintain strict allegiance to the inherited program while at the same time submitting it to minimal alterations which, when combined with numerous other small changes, would result in a total disfiguration of the original program. From romanticism on, the situation is entirely different. Poetics is scrutinized in every work, it is the essence of every poem, and the poet is forced to take a personal stand in the poem itself.

Summarized in this way, the formula might appear exaggerated. It is true that the radical, incessantly renewed questioning of the idea of poetry in each poet, and even in each poem and stage of the poet's evolution, has not been manifested in a clear way until recently. It is, perhaps, an excessively contemporary mentality which conceives according to this perspective the work of the first romantics. But our view and that of the first romantics are not two views, but two aspects of the same view.

It is easy to distinguish voluntary and explicit poetics from involuntary and implicit poetics. The programs, rationales and stated positions of a poet are one thing; quite another are the obscure and unconscious representations, the unconfessed tendencies, the unconfirmed assumptions which one discovers beneath the surface in a writer's successful poems.

It would be arbitrary to decide beforehand whether or not there exists or even

---

[*]Ed. Note: This is the authorized abridged version of the paper delivered at the Paz Conference.

113

whether it is possible that there be a discrepancy between the explicit and implicit esthetic intention in a given poem. Even given the existence of a symptomatic interpretation of the unconscious meaning of a poem, it seems clear to me that such an interpretation is psychological and not esthetic; that it is indeed symptomatic, that is, that one does not just read the poem, rather one reads in the poem another text, just as we might read in the voice tone of a foreign speaker the symptoms of the sex to which the speaker belongs, without having understood a single word of what he says in his language. We are not interested here in discussing whether such a reading would be correct, or whether we might read for example in the tones of a Marlene Dietrich a virile gravity, or in those of some diminutive tenor a gracious femininity. The type of reading we seek is different, and it is one in which we can never be sure but that the intention of the poet is not exactly identical to the poem itself. On the other hand, it may also be possible that the esthetic of the poem and that of the poet do not coincide. In other words, it is possible that a reading—which is neither psychological nor symptomatic—can lead us to an idea of poetry which the poet himself would contradict on another level. And this other level is that of the poem itself.

The objective then of this study is to examine briefly the poetry of Octavio Paz from the perspective of the possible tension between poetry and poetics in the poetic work itself, that is the tension between that which the poem pretends to be as the realization incarnate of a poetics, and that which the poetics says and is as the implicit assumption of the poem.

The work of Octavio Paz is perhaps particularly rich in theoretical orientations. Not only because his poetics has always been amply explicit—and I am not referring to his essays, rather to the poetics included or assumed in the poems themselves—but also because his poetics and style have both evolved visibly, and these two evolutions have always demonstrated an especially clear parallel pattern.

It is well known that the effective poetics of Octavio Paz—what I call incorporated poetics to distinguish it from the other voluntary and theoretical poetics, the poetics of the essay—has conserved throughout its evolution a single predominant element: the concern for the Word and for words. I do not mean that this concern, and others of his incorporated poetics, are not found as well, even in the same way, in his literary theories. No serious reader of Paz will need a detailed demonstration of the fact that Paz's poetics is incorporated into his poems. As an example, I cite "Las palabras":

> Dales la vuelta,
> cógelas del rabo (chillen, putas),
> azótalas,
> dales azúcar en la boca a las rejegas,
> ínflalas, globos, pínchalas,
> sórbeles sangre y tuétanos,
> sécalas,
> cápalas,
> písalas, gallo galante,
> tuérceles el gaznate, cocinero,
> desplúmalas,

destrípalas, toro,
buey, arrástralas,
hazlas, poeta,
haz que se traguen todas sus palabras.
(Libertad bajo palabra, pp. 59–60)

Quite apart from whether we can discover here ideas which might coincide with those expressed in the theoretical writings, there is no doubt but that the poem is also the poetic expression of a real, lived experience: the relation of the poet with words is not just a rational representation; it has been incorporated, even though it might have been originally such a representation, into the poetic experience itself by means of a lived experience.

But Paz's concern for words is not just a personal reflection on the craft of the poet; rather it is instead a reflection on the poet's craft which is extended to the point of transcending itself, which thrusts its branches upward until it is uprooted, transplanting itself into another medium. I shall focus on the distance between surrealistic poetics (for example that of *¿Águila o sol?*) and the poetics stemming from the aleatory music or from Jakobson and Barthes's theories of polysemy which we can infer from *Topoemas* or *Discos visuales*. But I shall highlight this distance only to suggest that we should be able to find between these two poles a virtual center which makes them precisely two poles within the same force field. Because between surrealism and polysemy, the common element is the search in the word for what we could call, paraphrasing Lévi-Strauss, an indeterminant plurality of meaning. With regard to Paz's esthetic intention, we could say the same thing we said a moment ago regarding this poet's concern for poetic craftsmanship. His incorporated poetics, through its own movement, is uprooted from its natural habitat and puts down roots in another. The act of achieving meaning—that is, in general all human acts which are conceived as human—is that act which, when manifest, displaces its own origin; it is a river which as it flows takes along its own source.

The concern for the word by Octavio Paz, indeed the concern by all poets for the word, seems to be a search for, or a vision of, the structure of meaning which is inherent in the very nature of meaning. As Paz himself has said many times, this has nothing to do with the words of the philologists, or the critics, or even of the linguists. In spite of his book on Lévi-Strauss, in spite of the labyrinthine esthetic of the *Discos visuales* and the esthetic at the same time polysemical and orientalist of *Blanco*, Octavio Paz is today further from structuralism than is commonly thought. These lines of "Retórica" from *Bajo tu clara sombra* have never been totally negated:

1

Cantan los pájaros, cantan
sin saber lo que cantan:
todo su entendimiento es su garganta.

2

La forma que se ajusta al movimiento
no es prisión, sino piel del movimiento.

3

La claridad del cristal transparente
no es claridad para mí sufficiente:
el agua clara es el agua corriente.

These lines imply a rhetoric which reveals the transparency of meaning. It is a rhetoric which questions the adequacy of a type of expression applied to a content which in one way or another is independent of all expression, which is sufficiently removed from the more or less Jakobsonian theories of poetic function which conceives of the poem as a message on the message and as pure form which says nothing more than what is contained in its own occult—and necessarily mute—structure. It is true that in the first stanza a poetics of the unconscious is also manifested. But it is the unconscious of the romantics and not of the structuralists. The birds, the poets, do not know what they are singing. Their throat knows for them. It is sufficient for me to think that my throat is more me than my reason in order for me to say that I know what I sing. The metaphor, I realize, is sufficiently ambiguous to allow for other interpretations: it might not even be a metaphor, but rather metonymy, in which case the throat would be the song: thus the song would understand itself and again we are in Lévi-Strauss and Wittgenstein and others. I feel, however, that given the work and given the tone of the poem, the throat is more a reference to the bird than to the song, and as a result the song is more a function of the singer than of itself. To say, "In my language I understand myself," is not the same as saying, "I, who do not understand myself, am understood by a language which I do not understand." To say "The Word invents itself and invents me each day," is not the same as saying "I invent the Word, freedom which invents itself and invents me each day" (*Libertad bajo palabra*, p. 10).

But the most important thing is not what the poem states regarding rhetoric; what is most important is what the poetry of Paz does with these statements. Although he has probably gone as far as any other poet in our language in his attempt to put into practice a poetics of nullification of the senses and the circularity of meaning—in this sense symbolic of a metaphysics of nullification of contradictions and of the vacuousness of meanings—Paz's viable poetry has never ceased to be an attempt to leap from solitude to a communication which he himself defined in his first theoretical writings, just as his life has not ceased to be an attempt to remove itself from asceticism, renunciation or nullification of the self in illumination. If the Buddhist influence has been great in the recent Paz, the Hindu has been equally important. The *Bhagavad-Gita* teaches that one should "not renounce acts, rather the fruits of acts"; it teaches not ecstasy, but knowledge; not nullification of the world, rather a return to the world following a passage through death which, in turn, is illumination and the demise of illusions. As with all initiations, this book teaches one not to enter into death, rather to return from death. The destruction of the illusory hegemony of the senses likewise teaches Paz not to enter into silence, as the illuminations taught Rimbaud or as death without end or exit taught José Gorostiza, but rather to turn to words, because the poem is possible only in this impossible realm of meanings, in the same way that life is possible only in this impossible realm of poetry.

Poetics and poetry then are, if not in opposition, at least in a state of tension in the work of Octavio Paz. But if we can refrain from seeing this tension as a thwarting, as a negative product of human limitations, perhaps we can see it as an integral part of the poem itself. The poem always runs the risk of being devoured by its own poetics. Contrary to what the vulgar poet—the poet affirmed in secure values—thinks, the poem is devoured with much greater security when the poetics, rendered invisible by the magical cloak of consensus and undisputed acceptance, digests the entire poem without the happy author even thinking about it. Opposed to this placid digestion, the radical poet suggests another means of confronting the risk. The tension carried to its extreme between poetics and poetry constantly places the poem on the brink of an abyss; a fall into this abyss would be another form of devouring. If there is no fall, we are confronted with a great poet. I do not dare say that all great poets are of this type, but I do know that there is at least one class of great poets who are great not in spite of, but rather *because* of the fact that their poetry is indefensible.

I have left a question unanswered and a reference incomplete. I would like to suggest in which direction that answer and that completion may be found. Mention is often made of Saussure, Lévi-Strauss, Jakobson, Chomsky. But most people forget that modern linguistics has, as we all do, two parents. I would prefer to call Saussure the mother of this new offspring, an offspring whose father appears to be unknown, not because it is unclear who it is, but because he is unknown to so many of his descendants. The father is the Danish iconoclast Louis Hjelmslev. He deduced that the digestion of one metalanguage by another is not an infinite series, that meaning is not circular, and that the series of plural meanings are not indeterminant. For the Danish iconoclast, metalanguages are strictly limited. After the third meta-level, it ceases to be possible to create a meta-meta-metalanguage because it would be confused on the one hand with the none too exciting traditional phonetics, as acoustical as it is articulatory, and on the other hand with the even less stimulating Logic. While metapoetry would be the poem itself. Hjelmslev does not state it exactly this way; his formulation is even more scandalous. Thus, he reasons with exemplary simplicity that the most elementary binary rules of semiology imply that poetry may deal with anything except poetry; that the content of poetic language can be anything but poetic language. The reversibility of an ordering of meanings is not infinite: meaning transcends itself and this transcendence is called sense. Here, of course, we enter another realm too perilous to approach at this moment. We shall confine ourselves to seeing how the limits of reversibility can also be appreciated in our small ternary system of theory-poetics-poetry. We have seen how poetics may be the decentering of the meaning of theory, and how it may be the meaning which itself is decentered by poetry. But it is clear that these relationships are not symmetrically reversible. Because if it is true that the intentionality of the poetics and the corporality of the poem strip from each other hegemony with respect to the meaning of the meanings, they nevertheless do not as a result cease to be radically different in their relationships: poetics ends with the poem, while the poem does not end with rhetoric. Let us consider for example *Blanco*: this is what explains why so many readers for whom the esthetics of the poem is entirely lost, as well as the philosophy on which the esthetics is based, can nevertheless participate in the poetic experience itself, they can participate in the corporality of its words which say more than does the totality of their meanings.

Like that of Hjelmslev, the idea of language with which Chomsky renews linguistics breaks in another way the circle of reversibility. Because he reminds us that language cannot be described if one forgets that men communicate *through* language, and not the other way around. It is not true—I mean that it is not the only truth—that *Blanco* speaks to us through Octavio Paz. Perhaps the poet has managed to break through the isolation of the "yo," which is another matter. In this case *he* would not speak through *Blanco*; rather it is man who would speak. Man speaks through his poetry just as poetry speaks through man. Only in this way can poetry be an experience which illuminates and transcends the "yo"; otherwise it would illuminate and transcend itself in a solitude which is uniquely its own and which could not be called a "yo" or even an immanence. *Blanco* is on the edge of an abyss and this abyss is that of the infinite and indeterminant reversibility of meanings. But due to the corporality of the words, *Blanco* is opened up to us and to the world, it is flowing through us in a "chorro de evidencias" which disperses its signifying intent at the same time that it embodies it. This "chorro" is the meaning, and the meaning, even though it cannot envision itself as being signification—simply because it can never embrace all at once the totality of meanings—nevertheless does not allow its own disparity to propagate itself in a chain reaction until it is completely empty of itself. Instead it gives itself direction which makes the poem an oriented movement. Thus, the experience of the void of meaning is transformed into this: it is an experience, that is a meaning-for-us, just as the experience of the vacuousness of life is an aspect of knowledge and not a dissolving. The words which reflect each other, of which Mallarmé spoke, were reflected above all in the same Mallarmé. In the same way, what the words say to themselves alone constitutes the poem because "las palabras se dicen" means above all "nos dicen que se dicen." The silence of the Word is thwarted in words; at the same time it gives itself to us in these words. But the words give of themselves to themselves, and without being thwarted they give us silence: they name it. Thus, the final answer again belongs to Hölderlin: poetry permits us to manipulate the fire of heaven, the burning light of the immortals who are the givers of meaning. In the light we drink the ray of light: the union of water and fire. This is another way of understanding that union of opposites, the "agua quemada" of the Aztecs of which Octavio Paz is so fond.

Colegio de México

Translated from the Spanish
By
Nick D. Mills

Octavio Paz: Image, Cycle, Meaning

By RAMÓN XIRAU

In the present study I shall analyze three constituent elements of the poetry of Octavio Paz: linguistic elements—metaphor, description, image; cyclical and circular elements; and the sense and meaning of the images. Such an investigation requires a few preliminary definitions.* In his poems, Octavio Paz employs primarily three types of language: metaphor, description, image.[1] I would like to clarify here the meaning which I give to each of these terms.

It is well known that the analyses of metaphor in contemporary criticism and philosophy—from Ogden and Richards to Carnap, from Max Black to J. Cohen, from Jakobson to Max Bense—would fill the bookshelves of a library of considerable proportions. I shall not deal here with the in-depth, detailed analyses which descriptions of metaphor often entail. Rather I shall limit myself to employing the word "metaphor" in the sense which recently—and quite adequately—has been proposed by the authors of *Rhétorique générale*[2] who define the metaphor as "the product of two synechdoches" (p. 108), a definition substantially different from Roman Jakobson's. The authors of the Liège group see the metaphor not as "a substitution of meanings, but as the modification of the semantic content of one term" (p. 106). This modification implies the existence of an intersection of two terms and, by extrapolation, it means that the metaphor is based "on a real identity manifested by the intersection of two terms, thereby affirming the identity of the totality of the terms. The metaphor extends the *meeting* of the two terms of a property which belongs only to their intersection" (p. 107).

Octavio Paz used the following words to define poetic image: "El poeta nombra las cosas: éstas son plumas, aquéllas son piedras. Y de pronto afirma: las piedras son plumas, esto es aquéllo . . . . La imagen resulta escandalosa porque desafía el principio

---

*The first part of this analysis will be concerned with problems of semantics and the formal elements of poetry. I shall refer in particular to three works: *Viento entero, Discos visuales* and *Topoemas*. The study of these works could be extended to the majority of Paz's poems. On the other hand I believe that this investigation—dealing as it does with linguistic form and poetic semantics—amounts to a confirmation of certain observations made in my *Octavio Paz: El sentido de la palabra*, Mexico City, Joaquín Mortiz, 1970.

de contradicción" (*El arco y la lira*). And in *Rhétorique générale* there is mention of "small semantic 'scandals' " (p. 106).

What Paz calls image is what we here define as metaphor. A scandal of logic? Without a doubt; because even without going into discussions on the contradictory character of the metaphor, it is plainly evident that metaphors imply some type of paradox. In effect, the feathers that are rocks are not rocks either in logic or in common language.

Our use of the word metaphor is simple: a metaphor shall be the total or partial association of diverse, opposite, contrary or contradictory terms. Thus, the metaphor, which is often descriptive, will be a linguistic form which opens the way for the image.

But what is "image"? In a tradition that probably comes from German romanticism and, more specifically from Novalis (and which certainly appears in *Elogio de la palabra* by the great Catalonian poet, Joan Maragall), I shall here call "image" the immediate designation (or nomination) of the "object." The word "object" requires a brief comment. On the one hand, the object of the image may be *real* (or commonly accepted as real). In this sense the expressions "the pine tree is green" or "the sea is blue" are images. On the other hand, the image may deal with objects which I shall call "ideal." Thus, Paz creates an image when he states in *Viento entero* "presencia chorro de evidencias."[3]

In a very precise sense, then, the image implies denotation and description, whether of sensed objects, ideal objects, or of both at the same time. Nevertheless, for clarity I shall reserve the word "description" for perceivable analogies and I will employ "image" to designate that which I have called ideal description.

In summary, even when Octavio Paz employs other techniques (for example, the comparison based on the connective "like"), I shall be concerned here primarily with his use of descriptions, metaphors (descriptive or not), and, through metaphors— often thanks to them—images.[4]

The theme of *Viento entero* (1965) is the present; it is also the rupture of the present in order that we might return to the present, to the Presence. In other words, *Viento entero* is a poem which circularly passes from presence to presence through successive ruptures—and successive re-encounters—of the same presence. It is necessary to mention this general scheme of the poem since it is one which has found its way into Paz's most important poems beginning with "Himno entre ruinas" (1949).[5] Let us proceed now to an analysis of some central stanzas of *Viento entero*. We shall see that the poem oscillates between image and description (and metaphor) only to return to the image and stay permanently in the realm of the image.

Viento entero begins with the image which will eventually constitute the leitmotif of the entire poem: "El presente es perpetuo." There follows immediately a serialization in which are combined and intermingled description, image and direct comparison:

Los montes son de hueso y son de nieve
Están aquí desde el principio
El viento acaba de nacer
          Sin edad
Como la luz y como el polvo

The perpetuity of the mountains (*hueso* and *nieve* are metaphorically descriptive) is highlighted in this paradoxical pre-world (*sin edad, acaba de nacer*). We are in a universe of beginnings, of origins. It is a world of purity itself, of innocence, described by an initial image and a subsequent metaphorical series. The lines which follow constitute a denotative and also a metaphorical description of the market of Kabul:

El bazar tornasolea
          Timbres motores radios
El trote pétreo de los asnos opacos
Cantos y quejas enredados
Entre las barbas de los comerciantes
Alto fulgor a martillazos esculpido
En los claros de silencio
             Estallan
Los gritos de los niños
          Príncipes en harapos
A la orilla del río atormentado
Rezan orinan meditan

In this second sub-stanza there is clearly evident a succession of direct descriptions ("timbres motores radios"; "gritos de niños"; "rezan meditan orinan"), descriptive metaphors ("trote pétreo," "asnos opacos," "río atormentado") and somewhat difficult metaphors which tend to approach imagery (principally "alto fulgor a martillazos esculpido" and those extraordinary "claros de silencio"). These latter resemble imagery because after the last descriptive line we return to the theme-image of the poem itself: "El presente es perpetuo."

Through descriptive or descriptive-metaphorical devices, the entire poem approximates an image or, better still, the poem emanates from the image that constitutes its center and axis.

A similar process is found in the third sub-stanza (in actual fact the poem is continuous, devoid of stanzaic divisions):

Se abren las compuertas del año
          Salto el día
     Agata
El pájaro caído
Entre la calle Montalembert y la de Bac
Es una muchacha
        Detenida
Sobre un precipicio de miradas

"Salto el día," the purest of metaphors ("Agata-El pájaro caído"), the passage of time, a description by reference of two Parisian streets, a girl—real, concrete— immediately situated in a metaphorical universe: the girl pauses on a "precipicio" of glances. Little by little, the central image is reborn in love, it is a symbol of union,

121

a cipher of innocence through Eros. The union of the world, love, imagery is achieved in four definitive words which describe an imagined realm: "Presencia chorro de evidencias."

This line might be considered metaphorical; but it involves a metaphor which does not describe tangible, observable, or verifiable reality. Its point of reference is the universe of unity-innocence. In describing that universe, the line becomes an idealized image of an idealized reality which is born of the meeting, the contact, the bringing together of two lovers. Through love we return to the beginning, to the initial pact of unity: "volvimos al día del comienzo."

Again, what follows are lines of precise descriptive reference:

> 21 de Junio
> Hoy comienza el verano . . .
> . . . Tú lees y comes un durazno
> Sobre la colcha roja
> > Desnuda

But this description, as beautiful as it is direct, is subsequently doubly modified: it is modified through comparison ("Desnuda / como el vino en el cántaro de vidrio") and it is further modified to the point of total destruction as a result of the description of those fateful days in Santo Domingo when brutal reality overshadowed love, imagery, the "evidencias." In an almost journalistic fashion, the poem continues: "En Santo Domingo mueren nuestros hermanos / Si hubiera parque no estarían ustedes aquí." This oscillation, this pendular movement between description, metaphor (whether descriptive or not) and image, continues throughout the poem. The fact is that *Viento entero*, primarily a love poem (actually one of the most beautiful erotic poems in the Spanish language), is in addition a poem charged with multiplicity of reversals: soul of the world of matter, matter which is the source, existence which is exile. But the many reversals and ruptures always lead back to a revival of the unity previously disrupted. This return to unity is accomplished through two images: "El presente es perpetuo" and the consummate and conclusive image of the poem aimed at the "presence":[6]

> El mismo día que comienza
> > Gira el espacio
> Arranca sus raíces el mundo
> No pesan más que el alba nuestros cuerpos
> > Tendidos

The poetic techniques employed in *Viento entero* proceed from concrete description to idealized description (the image) which is arrived at through descriptive images, comparisons and metaphors. We know that the poem is built on a single poetic base: presence, love, presence-love-innocence which through imagery is presented to us in an idealized realm which is no less exact, just and precise than the realm of verifiable reality. In this ideal and lucid world "no pesan más que el alba nuestros cuerpos."

In other words *Viento entero* is a circular poem. But a circle implies an axis, a center of the world. What is the meaning of this circular world? Three examples should suffice to answer this question. The first example comes from *Discos visuales*.[7] The fourth visual disk has as its center the double and unified image of trees and lips. If we revolve the disk from right to left we obtain the following successive series:[8] "El agua baja hasta (los árboles)"; "El cielo sube hasta (los labios)"; "el bosque (abajo)"; "arriba (el agua)"; "el viento / por los caminos"; "Quietud desde el (pozo)"; "El cubo el agua es negro es libre"; "el agua baja hasta (los árboles)"; "el cielo sube hasta (los labios)." If we consider the images situated near the center of the disk we obtain the following sequence: trees, below, well, trees, lips. In a splendid attempt at concrete poetry (that is, ideographic and not calligramatic on the order of Apollinaire's poetry), Paz has written a multiple poem based on five image-axes (trees, below, trees, lips) emanating from a single image-center (trees-lips).

Especially interesting—and also especially circular—is "Monumento reversible," a poem based on the movement of the elements:

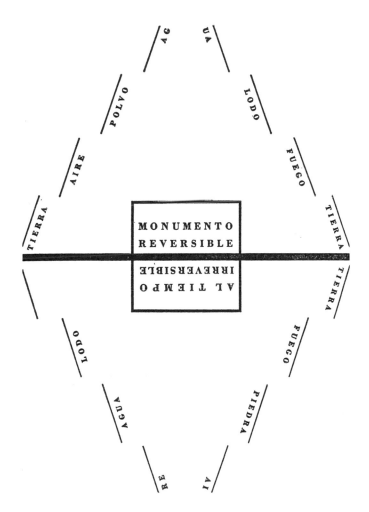

A similar structure can be found in some of the *Topoemas*, for example the one titled "Nagarjuna":

```
        N
        I
        E
        G
        O
   NI        EGO
```

In spite of its playful appearance, this poem shows us that negation (Niego) can be the negation of the ego and that, if so, it becomes by implication the affirmation of another reality, that reality being in this poem an image which is only suggested. Indeed, it is beyond the type of language which ordinarily either denies or affirms. A mirror of contrary and complementary waters, "Monumento reversible" is limited exclusively to naming the elements. Description has been reduced to naming, and the name is the image.

In "Symbolism in the Visual Arts" Aniela Jaffé writes, "The spatial orientation performed by Brahma and Buddha may be regarded as symbolic of the human need for psychic orientation."[9] In effect, both Buddha and Brahma, in similar legends, contemplate the world from a lotus with many leaves and they gaze on the four cardinal points. In this manner, cyclical time is time which spiritualizes and situates us. On the other hand, Mircea Eliade has demonstrated in *The Myth of the Eternal Return* that the cycle of time always revolves around a single center, a single axis of reality (the only motionless reality in that world of circular movement which is the world of Heraclitus). If we apply this double model to the interpretation of one aspect of the poems of Octavio Paz, though not necessarily following to their ultimate consequences the interpretations derived from C. G. Jung, we see that Paz's idea of time is, in part, related to cyclical time; but, in addition, it is also related to linear time (the time of ruptures) and it is above all intimate time, time which converges on us and which confronts us.

I conclude with what amounts to an hypothesis. By virtue of descriptions, metaphors, ruptures and reconstructions, the poetry of Octavio Paz involves vast and complex systems. These systems are clearly seen in such imposing and beautiful poems as "Himno entre ruinas," *Piedra de sol, Salamandra, Viento entero, Blanco,* poems in which the purity of imagery is often dazzling. Nor is it any less brilliant in those brief and concentrated poems of *Discos visuales* or *Topoemas* in which is found pure image almost totally lacking in metaphor and description. In the one or the other, the same final vision persists: "presencia chorro de evidencias."

Colegio de México

Translated from the Spanish
By
Nick D. Mills

[1] Types of language which in fact (and in the work itself) are frequently used interchangeably and do not presuppose exacting delimiting boundaries.

[2] The authors, all from the Study Center of the University of Liège, are J. Dubois, F. Edeline, J. M. Klinkenber, P. Minguet, F. Pire and H. Trianon. The book was published in 1970 by Librairie Larousse, Paris.

[3] When Maragall says that true poetry is embodied in the simple words of that young Pyrenean girl who, gazing at the sky, says "Lis esteles," he is talking about a real and an idealized image at the same time. Something similar occurs with the line by San Juan de la Cruz: "y el ventalle de cedros aire daba."

[4] In part, this conception of imagery (especially that of the idealized image) is similar to the ideas propounded by José Lezama Lima in his essays and poems. Nonetheless, when he speaks of imagery (and analogy), Lezama Lima speaks in poetic-theological terms—for example the man image and the possible resemblance to God. For a discussion of the topic see my *Poesía iberoamericana: Doce ensayos*, Mexico City, SepSetentas, Secretaría de Educación Pública, 1972. Lezama Lima has expressed his theory in *Tratados en Habana, Analecta del reloj*, and *La experiencia americana*.

[5] Two observations: this "mechanism" can be observed in "Himno entre ruinas" as well as in *Piedra de sol* (1958) or *Blanco* (1967). In these poems, just as in *Viento entero*, the mechanism is never rigid, rather it is in continuous movement. On the other hand, the progressions innocence-corruption-innocence, unity-division-unity, do not necessarily constitute the beginning, middle and end of the poem. They occur throughout the poem.

[6] I do not employ the word "presence" capriciously. The present might be transient; the "presence" is enduring and permanent.

[7] The *Discos visuales* (1968), written by Octavio Paz, were designed and sketched by the painter Vicente Rojo.

[8] In the words of Octavio Paz, each visual disk is an "arbol de imágenes." Indeed, each one permits and even demands multiple readings. Thus, a reverse effect would result if we were to read the disk from left to right. Furthermore, a vertical reading would produce brief and beautiful poem-images (for example "El viento por los caminos" and/or "los caminos por el viento"). Or we might focus our attention on a single vibrant image: "el bosque abajo" or "quietud desde el pozo." These poem-images resemble those already referred to by Maragall; they are also similar to the poetic concentration if Matsúo Basho whose work Octavio Paz has translated in collaboration with Eikichi Hayashia.

[9] C. G. Jung, *Man and His Symbols*, London, Aldus Books, 1964, p. 240.

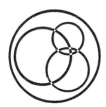

Tributes to Octavio Paz

This homage paid to Octavio Paz at the University of Oklahoma is very timely. The poet himself is there with you. It is a pleasure to confirm that his works are an admirable extension of his person. Poet, critic, essayist; Mexican, European, attracted incessantly by Asian cultures; very sensitive to the most intimate life and very interested in the problems of his time. So many aspects of Octavio Paz are dominated —it is evident—by his poetic nature: creator of the essential word in all its revelatory power. Allow me to join my voice in this homage.

Jorge Guillén

I gladly join you in homage to Octavio Paz: greatest living Mexican writer, great renovator of the Spanish language, great universal poet and essayist.

Carlos Fuentes

At a time when the strict exercise of the critical conscience is about to be reborn in Mexico, I very affectionately salute Octavio Paz, whose technical and theoretical work without doubt will be one of the most characteristic axes around which that new conscience will turn, a conscience to which many writers, here, for the first time will have to accede.

Octavio Paz is the founder of a rigorous and profound criticism of our language, especially in its spoken form, and the attempts to found a poetics based on the results of that criticism have certainly not been fruitless in Paz's own creative work. In fact,

---

These are some of the tributes read at the dinner in honor of the poet held on the second day of the Octavio Paz Conference, 16 October 1971.

one could say that his poetry represents one of the vastest undertakings of that type that has been attempted in a Spanish-speaking country: a freely given patrimony the benefits of which we now retain.

His critical work has valiantly confronted the most generalized and least rigorous suppositions about the values of our modern tradition and even of that paradoxical "tradition of the present" that has so frequently tried to install itself in our intellectual medium.

Therefore, I take this opportunity to wish success to this conference and personal fortune to Octavio Paz.

Salvador Elizondo

Minimum Homage to Octavio Paz

I wonder—once more, now, when everything seems about to go up in flame again—if there is a place for a poem in this uproar, in this confusion of sonorities that surround us like islands everywhere crowding in upon the sea.

Perhaps poetry is another office of darkness, a streaked disc that multiplies, until they come apart, the voices of the great enchanters, dead a century ago at a time when, newly humanized, God buried God and uttered not a see-you-later but a definitive good-bye.

On the other hand I wouldn't want to settle for a perfunctory greeting: I have written many times on him but in doing so I have always restrained myself. I recognize distances, and besides, fervor should be somehow secret or shy.

Nevertheless I open his books again and—through an absolving mirage—the years are as they were: I am again the deplorable adolescent whose only virtue is innocence. And every page becomes a garden and its vegetation is a ferocious star enlightening me.

Appearances are beautiful in their momentary truth. Words are born in the visible center of the earth. Bodies renew their joy. The sun stone lights up streets that do not yet exist. Night dissolves in the sea. Dawn is flooded with birds. Dawn-like, worlds rise over the transparency of space and the shadow of the wind over the water. And suddenly, between stillness and vertigo, *the present is perpetual.*

José Emilio Pacheco

I ask you to accept my enthusiastic support for the homage the University of Oklahoma is paying to the great Mexican poet, Octavio Paz. The undisputed master of the new generation in Latin America, a man of impeccable moral stature, an essayist of a most brilliant and original imagination, Octavio Paz is, above all, a poet whose only parallel can be found among the great inventors of Spanish literature in the 16th century. Therefore I consider the academic recognition you have organized at a North American University appropriate and certainly not the least of those our "miglior fabbro" has received beyond the borders of his own country.

Marco Antonio Montes de Oca

Translated from the Spanish
By
Tom J. Lewis

OLVIDO INOLVIDABLE

By Nathaniel Tarn

for Octavio Paz

The suns of all the galaxies shine suddenly together
the world's blood unfreezes and
runs thru the forest of our veins,
we go with dream-ease thru all our recognitions
she had looked for me a long time between the snows
with the darts of the Arrow-bearer,
I have drunk of her blood at the source
and eaten of her amber load
and washed in the scald of her tears,
she is someone you know and have not seen for a while
you will see her again soon
because her time is wedding to my time
and we move everywhere in step together,
she makes gold in the daytime
and at night she mints silver
under her feet as she comes the dawn grasses grow,
she draws the great bow of our life
the arrow flies straight for the mark and hits heart,
she has found me again after much travail,
the forest is open again, the deer leap,
the hounds belt baying like mad water,
sun and moon wake in each other's arms surprised
and the stars make music together incessantly.

Octavio Paz:
A Biographical Sketch

1914	Born 31 March in Mexico City.
1931–34	First publications in *Barrandal* (1931–32) and *Cuadernos del valle de México* (1933–34).
1937	In Spain (Madrid, Valencia, Andalusia). Sides with Republicans in Civil War.
1938–43	In Mexico. Helps to found journals *Taller* (1938) and *El hijo pródigo* (1943) in which many exiled Spanish writers collaborate.
1944–45	Travels and studies in USA on Guggenheim Fellowship.
1945	Goes to Paris, participates in surrealist movement. Friendship with André Breton and Benjamin Péret.
1946–68	Enters Mexican Foreign Service and serves in various capacities in San Francisco, New York, Paris, Tokyo, Geneva and Delhi.
1952	First visit to India and Japan.
1953–59	Intense literary activity in Mexico. Founds with Leonora Carrington, Juan Soriano and others the group "Poesía en voz alta" (1955). Collaborates closely with *Revista Mexicana de Literatura* whose first editors are Carlos Fuentes and Emmanuel Carballo. Books of poetry and essays. Translates old and modern poets. Presents new poets and painters (Tamayo, Montes de Oca, Coronel, Soriano), defends them against nationalist and "socialist realism" critics. Lectures. Literary and political polemics.
1959	Returns to Paris.
1962–68	Named ambassador to India. Studies of Eastern philosophy, art and literature.
1963	Grand Prix International de Poésie (Knokke-Le Zoute, Belgium).
1964	Marries Marie José Tramini in India.
1968	Resigns as ambassador to protest the repressive measures taken by the Mexican government against demonstrating students shortly before the Olympic games.
1968–70	In Paris. Holds Simon Bolivar Chair in Latin American Studies at Cambridge University. Lectures at University of Texas at Austin, University of

Pittsburgh. First book on Paz: *O.P.: El sentido de la palabra* by Ramón Xirau.

1971   Returns to live in Mexico. Special Paz issue of *Revista Iberoamericana* (January-March, 1971; 297 pages). Several British and American poets translate a representative selection of his recent poems for the bilingual edition *Configurations* published in New York and London. Lectures at University of Oklahoma. Third Oklahoma Conference on Writers of the Hispanic World dedicated to Paz (15–16 October). Edits new literary review *Plural*.

1971–72   Charles Eliot Norton Professor of Poetry at Harvard. *Books Abroad* Paz issue and *The Poetic Modes of Octavio Paz* by Rachel Phillips published.

1973   Regent's Fellow at University of California, San Diego. *The Perpetual Present: The Poetry and Prose of Octavio Paz* published.

Bibliography by and on Octavio Paz

By ALFREDO A. ROGGIANO

I. Works by Octavio Paz

A. Poetry

[Included here are only those poetic works published in book form, presented in chronological order of publication.]

Luna silvestre. Mexico: Fábula, 1933.

¡No pasarán! Mexico: Simbad, 1937.

Bajo tu clara sombra y otros poemas sobre España. Valencia, España: Ediciones Españolas, 1937. Note by Manuel Altolaguirre. [This edition is practically impossible to find today]; 2nd ed.: *Bajo tu clara sombra (1935-37).* Mexico: Tierra Nueva, 9 and 10, no date [1938?, 1941?].

Raíz del hombre. Mexico: Simbad, 1937.

Entre la piedra y la flor. Mexico: Nueva Voz, 1941; 2nd ed., Mexico: Ediciones Asociación Cívica Yucatán, 1956.

A la orilla del mundo y Primer día, Bajo tu clara sombra, Raíz del hombre, Noche de resurrecciones. Mexico: Compañía Editora y Librera ARS, s.a., 1942.

Libertad bajo palabra. Mexico: Tezontle, 1949; 2nd ed.: *Libertad bajo palabra: Obra poética, 1935-1957.* Mexico: Fondo de Cultura Económica, 1960. [Contents: "Bajo tu clara sombra," "Condición de nube," "Puerta condenada," "¿Aguila o sol?," "A la orilla del mundo." The following sections were included in another edition which appeared in 1968 from which forty previously published poems were omitted: "Bajo tu clara sombra," "Calamidades y milagros," "Semillas para un himno," "¿Aguila o sol?," "La estación violenta."]

¿Aguila o sol? Mexico: Tezontle, 1951. [Prose poems on the order of the essay with front cover and illustrations by Rufino Tamayo.]

Semillas para un himno. Mexico: Tezontle, 1954.

Piedra de sol. Mexico: Tezontle, 1957. [The following year this work was included in *La estación violenta.*]

La estación violenta. Mexico: Fondo de Cultura Económica, 1958.

Salamandra (1958-1961). Mexico: Joaquín Mortiz, 1962. [Contents: "Días hábiles,"

"Homenaje y profanaciones," "Salamandra," "Solo a dos voces"]; 2nd ed. [Revised], 1969.

Viento entero. Delhi, 1965.

Blanco. Mexico: Joaquín Mortiz, 1967.

Discos visuales. Mexico: Era, 1968.

Ladera este (1962–1968). Mexico: Joaquín Mortiz, 1969. [Contents: "Ladera este," "Hacia el comienzo," "Blanco."]

La centena (Poemas: 1935–1968). Barcelona: Barral Editores, 1969. [Contents: *Libertad bajo palabra* in abbreviated form, including the following sections: "Calamidades y milagros," "Semillas para un himno," "Piedras sueltas," "¿Aguila o sol?," "La estación violenta," "Salamandra," "Ladera este," "Blanco" and "Topoemas." The last two works had previously been published in the *Revista de la Universidad de México*, Vol. XXII, No. 10, June, 1968.]

Topoemas. Mexico: Era, 1971.

Renga. [In collaboration with Jacques Roubaud, Edoardo Sanguinetti and Charles Tomlinson], Paris: Gallimard, 1971.

B. Prose

El laberinto de la soledad. Mexico: Cuadernos Americanos, 1950. [Copyright date, 1947]; 2nd ed. [Revised and expanded], Mexico: Fondo de Cultura Económica, 1959; 3rd ed., 1963; 4th ed., 1964; 5th ed., 1967; 6th ed., 1968; 7th ed. Revised and expanded, 1969.

El arco y la lira. El poema. La revelación poética. Poesía e historia. Mexico: Fondo de Cultura Económica, 1956; 2nd ed. [Revised and expanded with "Los signos en rotación," an essay published by *Sur*, Buenos Aires, 1965], 1967.

Las peras del olmo. Mexico: Imprenta Universitaria, UNAM, 1957; 2nd ed., 1965.

Cuadrivio. Mexico: Joaquín Mortiz, 1965. [Studies on R. Darío, López Velarde, F. Pessoa, and Cernuda], 2nd ed., 1969.

Puertas al campo. Mexico: Universidad Nacional Autónoma de México, 1966; 2nd ed., 1967.

Claude Lévi-Strauss o El nuevo festín de Esopo. Mexico: Joaquín Mortiz, 1967; 2nd ed., 1969.

Corriente alterna. Mexico: Siglo XXI, 1967; 2nd ed., 1968.

Marcel Duchamp o El castillo de la pureza. Mexico: Era, 1968. [Contents: (1) An essay by Octavio Paz: "Marcel Duchamp o El castillo de la pureza"; (2) Texts by Marcel Duchamp, selected by Octavio Paz and translated by Tomás Segovia; (3) A color insert of the "Large Glass: The Bride Stripped Bare by Her Bachelors, Even"; (4) Three color plates; (5) An envelope with nine ready-made reproductions; (6) A photo album with reproductions of autographed texts, a biographical note by Marcel Duchamp, and a keep-sake portrait.]

México: la última década. The University of Texas. Institute of Latin American Studies. 1969 Hackett Memorial Lecture.

Conjunciones y disyunciones. Mexico: Joaquín Mortiz, 1969.

Posdata. Mexico: Siglo XXI, 1970. 1st ed., February; 2nd ed., April; 3rd ed., June [revised and expanded]; 4th ed., November [expanded again].

Los signos en rotación y otros ensayos. Carlos Fuentes, ed. Madrid: Alianza Editorial, 1971.

Las cosas en su sitio (on twentieth-century Spanish literature). [With Juan Marichal], Mexico: Finisterre, 1971.

Traducción: Literatura y literalidad. Barcelona: Tusquetes, 1971.

Le singe grammairien. Paris: Skira, 1972. Translated from the Spanish by Claude Esteban [Original Spanish version to be published.]

Modern Poetry: A Tradition against Itself. Charles Eliot Norton Lectures. Rachel Phillips, tr. Cambridge, Massachusetts: Harvard University Press, 1973.

C. Theater

La hija de Rappaccini. Mexico, 1956; presented as a part of "Poesía en Alta Voz." *Revista Mexicana de Literatura,* II, 7 (September-October, 1956), pp. 3–26; Maruxa Vilalta, *Primera antología de obras en un acto.* Mexico: Colección Teatro Mexicano, 1959. [I have seen neither this nor the Alvaro Aráoz editions, assuming that they are different editions.] Antonio Magaña Esquivel, ed. *Teatro mexicano del siglo XX.* Mexico: Fondo de Cultura Económica, 1970, pp. 31–56.

D. Editions, Anthologies, Prologues, and Translations

Bashō, Matsúo. *Sendas de Oku.* Translation by Octavio Paz and Eikichi Hayashiya. Mexico: Imprenta Universitaria, UNAM, 1957. 2nd. ed., Barral Editores, 1971. [Eirichi is corrected to Eikichi.]

Deniz, Gerardo. *Adrede.* Mexico: Siglo XXI, 1970. Prologue by Octavio Paz. [Published with the title "Gerardo Deniz, composiciones y descomposiciones," in *La Cultura en México,* supplement to *Siempre!,* No. 899, Sept. 16, 1970, p. XI.]

Gorostiza, José. *Muerte sin fin.* Introduction by Octavio Paz. Mexico: Imprenta Universitaria, UNAM, 1952.

Paz, Octavio, ed. *Anthologie de la poésie Mexicaine.* Translation by Guy Levis Mano, selection, commentary and introduction by Octavio Paz, prologue by Paul Claudel. Paris: Editions Nagel, Collection UNESCO d'Œuvres Représentatives: Série Ibéro-Américaine, 2, 1952. [The introduction, in Spanish, was included in *Las peras del olmo.*]

———, ed. *Anthology of Mexican Poetry.* Translation by Samuel Beckett, preface by C. M. Bowra, introduction and compilation by Octavio Paz. Bloomington, Indiana: Indiana University Press, UNESCO Collection of Representative Works: Latin American Series; published with the cooperation of the Organization of American States, 1958.

———, ed. *Antología poética.* Mexico: Revista Panoramas, 1956.

———, and Pedro Zekelli. *Cuatro poetas contemporáneos de Suecia.* Mexico: Imprenta

Universitaria, UNAM, "Colección Poesía y Ensayo," 1963. [Contains "La línea central," which is the prologue by O. Paz, and translations of poems by Martinson, Lundkvist, Ekelöf and Lindgren.]

——, ed. *Laurel, Antología de la poesía moderna en lengua española*. Mexico: Seneca, 1941. [With E. Prados, X. Villaurrutia and J. Gil-Albert.]

——, ed. *Magia de la risa*. Introductions by Octavio Paz and Alfonso Medellín, photographs by Francisco Beverido. Xalapa, Mexico: Universidad Veracruzana, 1962.

——, ed. *Tamayo en la pintura mexicana*. Mexico: Imprenta Universitaria, UNAM, Colección de Arte, 6, 1959. [See also *Rufino Tamayo 15 reproducciones*. Prologue by O. Paz. Mexico: Instituto Nacional de Bellas Artes, 1967.]

——, ed. *Voces de España (antología)*. Mexico: Letras de Mexico, 1938. Selection and note by Octavio Paz. [There is also an expanded edition.]

Pérez Martínez Héctor. *Cuauhtemoc: La vie et la mort de la culture aztèque*. Translation by Jean Camp, prologue by Octavio Paz. Paris: R. Laffont, 1952.

Pessoa, Fernando. *Antología*. Translation and introduction by Octavio Paz. Mexico: Imprenta Universitaria, UNAM, 1962.

Pizarnik, Alejandra. *Arbol de Diana*. Introduction by O. Paz. Buenos Aires: Sur, 1963.

Poesía en movimiento. Mexico: Siglo XXI, 1966. Prologue by O. Paz. 2nd ed., 1969.

Strand, Mark, ed. *New Poetry of Mexico*. Bilingual edition. Introduction by Octavio Paz. New York: Dutton, 1970.

E. Octavio Paz in Literary Periodicals

The most important periodicals of Europe and America have published articles, poems, translations, interviews, commentaries, et cetera by Octavio Paz. In general, these works have eventually been incorporated into books, at times with modifications which are of special interest from the point of view of providing insight into the poetic and philosophical evolution of the author. A complete listing of these publications in periodicals (certainly a difficult task to carry out) would be doubly interesting, not only in terms of learning more about the evolution of the essayist and poet, but also in terms of learning what Paz has discarded over the years in his constant selective process. We have located hundreds of titles dispersed in newspapers and magazines, and we have confirmed that only a small portion of these has remained unpublished in the books issued with the authorization of Paz himself. Are these articles condemned to be forgotten? Are they being preserved for other books? Whatever the reason, we feel that our decision not to present here a detailed list of these entries is consistent with the desires of the author, even though it may be somewhat inconsistent with the scholarly yearnings of the academician. Besides, those interested in this type of detail may refer to two quite useful sources: Merlin H. Forster, *An Index to Mexican Literary Periodicals* (New York and London: The Scarecrow Press, Inc., 1966, pp. 177–79) and Section E ("Scattered Prose Articles by Octavio Paz") in the doctoral dissertation (1964) by Judith Ann Bernard, pp. 191–94, an important work which can be consulted at the University of Wisconsin. From 1964 to the present Paz has continued to publish in magazines and literary supplements in both Americas and Europe. A few of his books have incorporated part of this material. Among those articles which have yet to be collected in book form, we consider the following to be of great importance: "Presencia y presente. A propósito de Baudelaire" (*Mundo Nuevo*, No. 23, May 1968, pp. 4–10); "¿Poesía latino-americana?" (*Amaru*, No. 8, October-December, 1968, pp. 3–8); "Salvador Elizondo: El placer como crítica de la realidad y el lenguaje" (*L.C. en M.*, No. 819, March 5, 1969, pp. III–V); "*Les poèmes japonais*, de Jacques Roubaud," and "Luz para Octavio Paz" (*Le Monde*, December 11, 1970, pp. 15–16). Paz's latest works have appeared in the magazine *Plural* (October 1971-April 1973), a number of these issues being directed by Octavio Paz himself.

F. Translations of Works by Octavio Paz

[Listed in chronological order of translations.]

Aigle ou soleil? Paris: Ed. Falaize, 1957. Spanish text included. Translation by Jean-Clarence Lambert. [The selection does not coincide with the first Spanish edition of *¿Aguila o sol?*.]

Soleil sans âge. Paris. Falaize, 1959. Translated by Benjamin Péret. Preface by André Breton. [We have not seen it, but it must be a translation of "Piedra de sol."]

Le labyrinthe de la solitude. Paris: Fayard, 1959. Translated from the Spanish by Jean-Clarence Lambert. 2nd ed., Paris: Gallimard, 1972.

La fille de Rappaccini. Paris: N. R. F., 1960. Translated by André Pieyre de Mandiargues. 2nd ed., Paris: Mercure de France, 1972.

Il labirinto della solitudine. Milano: Silva Editore, 1961. Translated from the Spanish by Giuseppe Bellini. Introduction by Ramón Xirau.

The Labyrinth of Solitude: Life and Thought in Mexico. New York: Grove Press, 1962. Translated by Lysander Kemp; 2nd. ed., London: A. Lane. The Penguin Press, 1967.

Pierre de soleil. Paris: Gallimard, 1962. Translated by Benjamin Péret. Bilingual edition. [Fragmentary reprinting by Claude Givaudan Ste.: Paris, 1966.]

Sun Stone. Piedra de sol. London: New Directions, 1962. Translation by Muriel Rukeyser. [Bilingual edition]; 2nd ed., New York: New Directions, 1963.

Sun-Stone. Toronto: Contact Press, 1963. Translation by Peter Miller. [Bilingual edition with explanatory notes.]

Homages et profanations. Paris: Jean Hugues, 1963. Translated by Carmen Figueroa.

Selected Poems by Octavio Paz. Bloomington, Indiana: Indiana University Press, 1963. A bilingual edition with translation by Muriel Rukeyser. [Translations are often either deficient or erroneous.]

Bedouin, Jean Louis. *Anthologie de la poésie surréaliste*. Paris: Pierre Seghers, 1964. [Includes poems by O. Paz translated into French by various translators.]

Libertà sulla parola. Parma: Guanda, 1965. With facing text, introduction and translation by Giuseppe Bellini.

Piedra de sol. Translation into Hungarian by Laszlo Szomogyi [1965?]. [For the translations into this language and into Czech, see the article by E. Volek in No. 74 of *RI*.]

L'arc et la lyre. Paris: Gallimard, 1965. Translated from the Spanish by Roger Munier. Introduction by Roger Munier. [The French text contains omissions and changes and includes, in addition, an epilogue by O. Paz.]

Octavio Paz. By Claire Cea. [Extensive study and poetic selection.] Paris: Pierre Seghers Editeur. Coll. "Poètes d'aujourd'hui," 1965.

Liberté sur parole. Libertad bajo palabra. Paris: Gallimard, 1966. [Bilingual edition.] Poems translated from the Spanish and prefaces by Jean-Clarence Lambert.

Vrindaban. Geneva: Editions C. Givaudan, n.d. [1966, 1969?].

Marcel Duchamp ou Le château de la pureté. Paris: Editions C. Givaudan, 1967. Translated from the Spanish by Monique Fong-Wust.

Marcel Duchamp or the Castle of Purity. London: Goliard, 1970. Translated from the Spanish by Donald Gardner.

Claude Lévi-Strauss: An Introduction. Ithaca, New York: Cornell University Press, 1970. Translated by Jerome S. Bernstein in collaboration with Maxine Bernstein.

Pierres éparsés. Paris: Librairie Nicaise, S. A., 1970. Phonic book-object by Rodolfo Krason, after 22 poems by Octavio Paz translated into French by Jean-Clarence Lambert. Original sound-track by Edgardo Canton.

¿Aguila o sol?—Eagle or Sun? New York: Center for Inter-American Relations, Inc., October House, Inc., n.d. [1970?]. Translated by Eliot Weinberger. [Bilingual edition.]

Das Labyrinth der Einsamkeit. Essays. Aus dem mexikanischen Spanish übertragen und eingeleitet von Carl Heupel. Walter Verlag, Olten und Freiburg, 1970.

Deux transparents: Marcel Duchamp et Claude Lévi-Strauss. Paris: Gallimard. Coll. "Les Essais," 1971. Translated by Monique Fong-Wust and R. Marrast.

Versant est—Ladera este. Paris: Gallimard. Coll. "Poésie du Monde Entier," 1971. [Bilingual texts rendered into French by various translators.]

Configurations. New York: New Directions. London: Jonathan Cape, 1971. [Bilingual edition of selected poems]. Translated by G. Aroul, Paul Blackburn, Lysander Kemp, Denise Levertov, John Frederick Nims, Muriel Rukeyser, J. Swaminathan, Charles Tomlinson, Monique Fong-Wust, and the author.

Conjonctions et disjonctions. Paris: Gallimard, 1972.

Courant alternatif. Paris: Gallimard, 1972.

The Other Mexico: Critique of the Pyramid. New York: Grove Press, 1972. Translated by Lysander Kemp. [Translation of *Posdata*.]

Renga. In collaboration with Jacques Roubaud, Edoardo Sanguinetti, and Charles Tomlinson. Translated into Spanish by Octavio Paz. Mexico City: Mortiz, 1972. [Includes facing text of original and introductory essays by Claude Roy, Octavio Paz, Jacques Roubaud, and Charles Tomlinson.]

Renga. A Chain of Poems. In collaboration with Jacques Roubaud, Edoardo Sanguinetti, and Charles Tomlinson. Translated into English by Charles Tomlinson.

New York: Braziller, 1972. [Includes facing text of original and introductory essays by Claude Roy, Octavio Paz, Jacques Roubaud, and Charles Tomlinson.]

Alternating Current. New York: Viking Press, 1973. Translated by Helen R. Lane. [Translation of *Corriente Alterna*.]

2. Works on Octavio Paz (A Selection)

A

Abreu Gómez, Ermilo, "*Entre la piedra y la flor*, de Octavio Paz," *T. N.*, Nos. 9–10, mayo-agosto 1941, pp. 173–74.

——, *Sala de retratos* (Mexico, 1946), pp. 215–16.

——, "Calificación," *M en la C.*, No. 758, 29 sept. 1963, pp. 1–3.

——, "Inspiración e inteligencia de Octavio Paz," *V.U.*, 13 oct. 1963, p. 7.

Aguilera Malta, Demetrio, "Evocación de cuatro poetas" [On *Cuadrivio*], *G. L.*, No. 177, 14 nov. 1965, p. 4.

Alba, Pedro de, "Trayectoria y horizonte de Octavio Paz," *P.P.*, No. 15, nov. 1943, p. 2.

Alvarez, Alfredo Juan, "Poesía," Supl. de *Siempre*, 1 enero 1969, p. v.

Alvarez, Federico, "Sobre *Cuatro poetas contemporáneos de Suecia*," *L.C.* en *M.*, No. 63, 1 May 1963, p. xx.

A. M. [Antonio Molina], "El presente es perpetuo," *P. de S.A.*, L, 1965, p. 336.

——, "La hora de razonar," [About *Puertas al campo*], *P. de S.A.*, año XII, t. XLV, mayo de 1967, pp. 221–24.

Anonymous [The following is a selection in alphabetical order according to the first letter of the title of the work.]

——, "Assertions and Authenticity" [About *Ladera este* and *Conjunciones y disyunciones*], *T.L.S.*, 9 April 1970, p. 379.

——, "Calendario" [About *Viento entero*], *L.C.* en *M.*, No. 198, 10 dic. 1965, p. XX.

——, "*Cuatro poetas contemporáneos de Suecia*," *T.*, Vol. 43, No. 1104, 1 julio 1963, p. 55.

——, "El mundanal ruido," *D.*, 13 sept. 1963, p. 9.

——, "Gran triunfo de un mexicano," D., 4 julio 1964, p. 3.

——, "Iconoclasts," *T.L.S.*, 5 march 1971. [On *Posdata*, et cetera.]

——, "La flecha en el tiempo. Octavio Paz," *Ins.*, No. 230, enero 1966, p. 2.

——, "La tarea literaria" [on *Salamandra*], *L.C.* en *M.*, No. 45, 26 dic. 1962, p. XVII.

——, "Nota bibliográfica," *A. de la P.M.*, 1962, 1963, p. 102.

——, "Notas bibliográficas. *Piedra de sol*," *Est.*, No. 9, 1958, p. 99.

——, "Octavio Paz figura entre los mayores poetas," *R.S.*, 16 marzo 1964, p. 3.

——, "Octavio Paz, Krasno, Rojo, Junkers, Belkin, Góngora, Zabala . . ." [Comments about *Topoemas* and the act of the signing of the book by Octavio Paz], *Exc.*, 2 sept. 1971, p. 5.

——, "Poesía de Mexico," *M. en la C.*, No. 739, 19 mayo 1963, pp. 3, 9.

——, "*Posdata*, por Octavio Paz," *Nac.*, 16 agosto 1970.

——, "Premio Internacional," *M. en la C.*, No. 758, 29 sept. 1963, p. 1.

———, "Premio Internacional," *C.B.A.*, No. 11, nov. 1963, p. 116.

———, "Publica la UNESCO poemas de O. Paz," *D.*, 15 abril 1965, p. 1.

———, "Cuadripedantical sonnets" [About *Renga*], *T.L.S.*, 30 April 1971, p. 492.

———, "*Salamandra*, de Octavio Paz," *Bull.*, Vol. X, No. 2, Jan. 15, 1963, p. 3.

———, "Su mesa de redacción" [About *Sun Stone*], *D.C.*, 10 marzo 1963, p.2.

———, "Su mesa de redacción" [About *El clía de Udaipur*], *D.C.*, 2 febr. 1964, p. 4.

Ara, Guillermo, "Los signos en rotación," *Dav.* No. 107, 1965, pp. 125–26.

Arana, María Dolores, "Carta de México," *P. de S. A.*, No. 73, abr. 1962. [Contains a critical bibliography on Octavio Paz.]

Arellano, Jesús, "Las rentas de Don Quijote," *N.*, 1, 25 enero 1963, p. 5.

Aridjis, Homero, *Seis poetas latinoamericanos de hoy* (New York: Harcourt, Brace, Jovanovich, Inc., 1972), pp. 145–87.

Arredondo, Ines, "*Cuadrivio*, de Octavio Paz," *R. de B.A.*, No. 5, sept.-oct. 1965, pp. 95–96.

A. S., "Un lúcido ensayista" [About *Corriente alterna*], *Nac.*, 21 abr. 1968.

Aub, Max, *Poesía mexicana,* 1950–1960 (Mexico, 1960), pp. 17–18.

B

Bachelard, Gaston. [According to Jean-Clarence Lambert (See Lambert), the great French thinker wrote a letter to O. Paz in which he says that *Aigle ou soleil?* is always on his work table because in times of stress the reading of this work brings him happiness.]

Balakian, Anna. See *Review 72.*

Bareiro-Saguier, Ruben, "Octavio Paz y Francia," [See No. 74 of *R. I.*]

Bari, Camila, "Octavio Paz: Signos en rotación," *R.L.M.*, No. 7, 1968, pp. 178–79.

Barnatan, Marcos Ricardo, "Octavio Paz: El poderío de una estética renovada," *Ins.*, No. 280, marzo 1970, p. 16.

Batis, Hugo, "*Cuadrivio*, de Octavio Paz," *L.C. en M.*, No. 193, 27 oct. 1965, p. XVI.

———, "*Octavio Paz, par Claire Céa*," *L.C. en M.*, No. 196, 17 nov. 1965, p. XV.

———, "El ensayo literario en 1965," *L.C. en M.*, No. 203, 5 enero 1966, p. 11.

———, "*Puertas al campo*, de Octavio Paz," *E.H.C.*, No. 50, 23 oct. 1966, p. 5.

———, See "Homenaje a Octavio Paz," in section H of this bibliography.

Bellini, Giuseppe, "Studio introduttivo" to *Libertà sulla parola* (Parma, 1965).

———, "Octavio Paz, L'esperienza asiatica nella sua poesia," *Q.I.A.*, No. 34, 1966.

———, *La letteratura ispano-americana* (Milano, 1970), pp. 362–65.

———, *Quevedo en la poesía hispanoamericana del siglo XX: César Vallejo, Jorge Carrera Andrade, Octavio Paz, Pablo Neruda y Jorge Luis Borges* (New York: announced by Eliseo Torres for 1971).

Benedetti, Mario, et al., *Unstill life* (New York: n/d [1970]), pp. 67–69. [Biobibliographical note and translations of poems by Paz.]

Benitez, Fernando, et al., "Nuestra solidaridad con Octavio Paz," *Siempre*, No. 802, Nov. 6, 1968, p. 11.

Benson, Rachel, *Nine Latinamerican Poets* (New York, 1968), pp. 178–209 [Bio-bibliographical note and translations of poems by Paz.]

Bernard, Judith Ann, "Myth and Structure in Octavio Paz's *Piedra de Sol*," *Sym.*, No. 21, 1967, pp. 5–13.

——, "Mexico as Theme, Image, and Contribution to Myth in the Poetry of Octavio Paz" [Doctoral dissertation, University of Wisconsin, 1964.] [See also No. 74 of *R.I.*]

Bly, Robert, "*Configurations*, by Octavio Paz," *N.Y.T.B.R.*, April 18, 1971, Section 7, p. 1.

Bonnefoi, Geneviève, "Le labyrinthe de la solitude, par Octavio Paz," *L.N.*, Vol. VII, No. 29, 22 Nov. 1959, pp. 30–31.

Bosquet, Alain, "Octavio Paz ou le Surréalisme tellurique," *Verbe et vertige. Situation de la poésie* (Paris, n/d), pp. 186–92. [In the same book: "Octavio Paz," pp. 328–29.]

Books Abroad, Vol. 46, Autumn 1972, pp. 541–614, "Symposium on Octavio Paz."

——, "De la magie à la interrogation," *L.M.*, 15 Janv. 1971.

Breton, André, *Entretiens* (Paris, 10e. éd., 1952) [On page 285 he says: ". . . le poète de langue espagnole qui me touche le plus est Octavio Paz . . ."] [Text reproduced from an "Interview by José M. Valverde," published in *Correo Literario*, Madrid, sept. 1950.]

Bross, Jim, "Outstanding Mexican Poet Octavio Paz at O. U.," The *Norman* (Okla.) *Transcript*, Sunday, October 17, 1971, p. 3.

Brushwood, John S., "Pésima traducción de Octavio Paz," *M. en la C.*, No. 769, 15 dic. 1963, p. 5.

——, "Selected poems, by Octavio Paz," *Hisp.*, Vol. XLVII, No. 3, sept. 1964, pp. 652–53.

C

Cadenas, Rafael. [See R. C. in Section R.]

Capistrán, Miguel, "Crítica," Supl. de *Siempre*, No. 810, enero 1, 1969, p. VII.

——, "El ensayo literario," Supl. de *Siempre*, (No. 811?) enero 7, 1970, pp. IX–XI.

——, "El 'Taller' de Octavio Paz," *L.C. en M.*, No. 287, 16 agosto 1967, p. XIII.

Caracciolo-Trejo, E., "*Salamandra*, de Octavio Paz," *Am.*, marzo 1969, pp. 81–83.

——, *The Penguin Book of Latin American Verse*. Edited by E. Caracciolo-Trejo. Introduced by Henry Gifford. (England, U.S.A., Australia, 1971), pp. 275–93.

Carballo, Emmanuel, "*Las peras del olmo*, de Octavio Paz," *M. en la C.*, No. 420, 8 abr. 1957, p. 2.

——, "Octavio Paz. Su poesía convierte en poetas a sus lectores," *M. en la C.*, No. 493, 25 agosto 1958, p. 3 [Interview].

——, "Entre el orden y el caos" [About *El laberinto de la soledad*], *M. en la C.*, No. 553, 18 oct. 1959, p. 4.

——, "La respuesta de Emmanuel Carballo a Octavio Paz," *M. en la C.*, No. 562, 21 dic. 1959, p. 12.

——, "Octavio Paz," *L.C. en M.*, No. 48, 16 enero 1963, p. XIX.

————. "La presencia de Paz en el ensayo," *L.C. en M.*, No. 236, 24 agosto 1966, p. CIII.

Carballido, Emilio, "Sobre *La hija de Rapaccini*." [See No. 74 of *R.I.*]

Carpentier, Hortense and Janet Brof, *Doors and Mirrors. Fiction and Poetry from Spanish America*. Selected and edited by . . . . (New York: Grossman Publishers, 1972), pp. 204–22.

Castro, Rosa, "La libertad del escritor. Una entrevista con Octavio Paz," *M. en la C.*, No. 252, 17 enero 1954, p. 3.

Céa, Claire, *Octavio Paz* (Paris, 1965). [No. 26 of the Col. Poètes d'aujourd'hui, Pierre Seghers éditions. First book on Octavio Paz.]

Cid de Sirgado, Isabel M., "En torno a *El laberinto de la soledad* de Octavio Paz," *Hispan.*, No. 37, sept. 1969, pp. 59–64.

Civrny, Lumír, "Por el mito de la poesía." [In Czech; prologue to the Czech translation of "Piedra de sol" and "A orilla del mundo," Prague, 1966; published in Spanish in *L. C. en M.*, No. 285, 26 julio 1967, pp. II–V. See article by Volek in No. 74, of *R.I.*]

Cohen, J. M., *Poetry of This Age* (London, 1959). In Spanish: *Poesía de nuestro tiempo* (Mexico, 1964), pp. 327–34.

————, "The Eagle and the Serpent," *T.S.R.*, No. 2, Spring 1965, pp. 361–74.

————, *Latin American Writing Today* (Penguin Books, 1967), pp. 87–96. [Translations of Paz's poetry.]

Colinas, Antonio, "A propósito de una lectura de Octavio Paz," *Ins.*, No. 303, febrero 1972, p. 1.

Córdoba Sandoval, Tomás, "Sobre *El laberinto de la soledad*," *C.A.*, Vol. LI, No. 3, mayo-junio 1950, pp. 125–32.

Cortázar, Julio, "Octavio Paz: *Libertad bajo palabra*," *Sur*, No. 182, dic. 1949, pp. 93–95. [See also *Ultimo Round* and No. 74 of *R.I.*]

Covantes, Hugo, "Octavio Paz y la poesía francesa contemporánea, *M. en la C.*, No. 875, 25 dic. 1965, p. 4.

Couffon, Claude, "Entrevista con Octavio Paz," *Cuad.*, XXXVI mayo-junio 1959, pp. 79–82 [Translation of the interview published in *L.N.*, Vol. VII, No. 67, Jan. 1959, pp. 106–11.]

————, "Mexique," in R. M. Albérès et al., *Les littératures contemporaines à travers le monde* (Paris, 1961), pp. 316–19.

————, *Hispanoamérica en su nueva literatura*. Versión castellana de José Corrales Egea (Santander, 1962).

Couturier, Michel, "Entretien avec Octavio Paz: 'La présie occidentale est une'" [propos recueillis par.], *L.Q.L.*, du 1er. au 15 mars. 1971, pp: 14–15.

Crespo de la Cerna, Jorge, J., "Octavio Paz y Michel Charpentier," *D.*, 3 dic. 1965, p. 9.

Cruz, Jorge, "Con Octavio Paz," *Nac.*, 30 marzo 1969.

Cuesta, Jorge, Review of *Raíz del hombre, Letr. de M.*, 1ro. febr. 1937, pp. 3–9. [Collected in *Poemas y ensayos* (Mexico, 1964), pp. 282–84.]

CH

Charry Lara, Fernando, Sobre *Las peras del olmo, D.C.*, 27 oct. 1957, p. 2.

———, "Tres poetas mexicanos: III. Octavio Paz," *U. de M.*, Vol. XI, No. 5, enero 1957, pp. 14–17.

———, "*Cuadrivio y Los signos de* [sic] *rotación* de Octavio Paz," *Eco*, No. 71, marzo 1966, pp. 585–88.

Chumacero, Alí, "*Recinto*, de Octavio Paz," *T.N.*, Vol. II, Nos. 9–10, mayo-agosto 1941, pp. 175–77.

———, "Panorama de los últimos libros. *Entre la piedra y la flor*," *M. en la C.*, No. 399, 11 nov. 1956, p. 2.

———, "Sobre *Piedra de Sol*," *M. en la C.*, No. 459, 29 dic. 1957, p. 2.

———, "Sobre *La estación violenta*," *M. en la C.*, No. 492, 17 agosto 1958, p. 1.

———, "Balance 1962," *L.C. en M.*, No. 46, 2 enero 1963, pp. IV–V.

D

Dallal, Alberto, "Octavio Paz y la poesía en Suecia," *L.C. en M.*, No. 66, 22 mayo 1963, p. XVIII.

Dauster, Frank, *Breve historia de la poesía mexicana* (Mexico, 1956), pp. 173–75.

Diccionario de Escritores Mexicanos. See Ocampo Gómez, Aurora. . . .

Del Campo, Xorge, "Octavio Paz: Valoración múltiple" [On the edition of *Revista Iberoamericana* dedicated to Paz], *U.*, 26 mayo 1971, p. 10.

D'Harnoncourt, Anne. See *Review 72*.

Domenech, Ricardo, Review of *El laberinto de la soledad, Ins.*, Vol. XV, No. 162, mayo 1960, p. 8.

Domingo, Xavier, Review of *Sun Stone*, *R.I.B.*, No. 26, abril-junio 1964, pp. 202–203.

———, "Octavio Paz," *R.S.*, 26 junio 1964, p. 4.

———, "Exito de Octavio Paz. La crítica literaria francesa acoge favorablemente *El arco y la lira*," *D.*, 11 dic. 1965, p. 9.

Droguett Alfaro, Luis, "Poesía de Octavio Paz," *At.*, Vol. 151, No. 401, julio-sept. 1963, pp. 131–46.

Durán, Manuel, "La estética de Octavio Paz," *R.M. de L.*, No. 8, nov.-dic. 1956, pp. 114–36.

———, "Octavio Paz en su libertad," *M. en la C.*, No. 408, 14 enero 1957, p. 2.

———, Review of *La estación violenta, R.H.M.*, Vol. XXV, Nos. 1–2, enero-abril 1959, pp. 101–102.

———, "Libertad y erotismo en la poesía de Octavio Paz," *Sur*, No. 276, mayo-junio 1962, pp. 72–77 [In English: "Liberty and Eroticism in the Poetry of Octavio Paz,"], *B. Abr.*, Vol. 37, 1963, pp. 373–77.

———, Review of *Sun Stone*, *R.I.B.*, No. 26, abr.-junio 1964, pp. 202–203.

———, Review of *La centena, Ladera este, Hacio el comienzo, Blanco, B. Abr.*, Summer 1970, p. 448.

———, Review of *Conjunciones y disyunciones, B. Abr.*, Summer 1970, p. 450 [Also see No. 74 of *R.I.*]

————, "La poesía mexicana de hoy," *R.I.*, Vol. XXXVIII, No. 74, enero-marzo 1971, pp. 741–51.

————, "Presencia de Octavio Paz," *Noc.*, 17 oct. 1971, p. 1.

Durand, José, "Octavio Paz, a Mexican-Poet-Diplomat," *Amer.*, Vol. 15, No. 7, July 1963, pp. 30–33.

————, "Octavio Paz," *M.L.*, Vol. 39, No. 11, nov. 1963, pp. 25–26, 49.

Duvignaud, Jean, "Octavio Paz et la solitude mexicaine," *Preuves*, Vol. IV, No. 122, 1961, pp. 84–85.

————, "Le poéte et l'Amibe," *N.R.F.*, No. 133, Janv. 1964, pp. 118–24.

E

Embeita, María, "Entrevistas: Octavio Paz. Poesía y Metafísica," *Ins.*, Nos. 260–61, julio-agosto 1968, pp. 12–13.

Englekirk, John E., et al., *An Outline History of Spanish American Literature* (New York, 1965), pp. 166–67.

Espinosa Altamirano, Horacio, "Paralelos y discrepancias" [Between Octavio Paz and the Nicaraguan Joaquín Pasos], *B.B.H.*, No. 269, 15 abr. 1963, pp. 14–15.

————, "Octavio Paz o la inteligencia literaria," *R.M. de C.*, No. 971, 7 nov. 1956, pp. 1–2.

Estensoro, Hugo, "*Blanco*, de Octavio Paz," *D.C.*, 31 dic. 1967.

Esteva Fabregat, Claudio, "Octavio Paz, un ritmo existencial en la poesía," *Cuad. Hist.*, Vol. CXII, abr. 1959, pp. 63–65.

————, "El mexicano y su soledad" [Review of *El laberinto de la soledad*], *Cuad. Hisp.* Vol. CXXIV, abr. 1969, pp. 144–47.

F

Fein, John M., "El espejo como imagen y tema en la poesía de Octavio Paz," *U. de M.*, Vol. XII, No. 3, nov. 1957, pp. 8–13.

————, "La estructura de *Piedra de sol*," *R.I.*, Vol. XXXVIII, No. 78, enero-marzo 1972, pp. 73–94.

Fell, Claude, "Au coeur du Mexique et de la littérature," *L.M.*, 15 janv. 1971.

Ferrier, Jean-Louis, "L'ambassadeur et les transparents" [On M. Duchamp and C. Lévi-Strauss], *L'Ex.*, No. 1023, 15–21 febr. 1971, p. 67.

Ferro, Hellen, *Historia de la poesía hispanoamericana* (New York, 1964), pp. 357–58.

Florescano, Enrique, Reseña a *Magia de la risa*, *La P. y el H.*, No. 27, julio-sept. 1963, pp. 511–16.

Florit, Eugenio y José Olivio Jiménez, *La poesía hispanoamericana desde el modernismo* (New York, 1968), pp. 461–68. [Bibliographical note and poems.]

Forrester, Viviane, "La géographie mentale d'Octavio Paz" [*Le labyrinthe de la solitude* and *Le singe grammairien*], *L.Q.L.*, 16 au 30 sept. 1972, pp. 13–14.

Fraire, Isabel, Review of *Salamandra*, *R.M. de L.*, Nos. 7–8, julio-agosto 1963, pp. 56–57.

Franco, Jean, *The Modern Culture of Latin America. Society and the Artist* (New York-London, 1967), pp. 196–98 and 207–208.

————, *An Introduction to Spanish American Literature* (Cambridge, 1969), pp. 290–96. [See also No. 74 of *R.I.*]

Fryd, Norbert, "La magia de las máscaras" [On the chapter entitled "Las máscaras" in *El laberinto de la soledad*], *Sv.L.*, No. 3, 1963, pp. 123–24.

Fuente, Ovidio C., "Teoría poética de Octavio Paz," *C.A.*, 1972, No. 3, pp. 226–42.

Fuentes, Carlos, "Con Octavio Paz en Roma," *L.C. en M.*, No. 216, 6 abr. 1966, p. 11.

————, "El tiempo de Octavio Paz," *Casa con dos puertas* (Mexico, 1970), pp. 151–57. [Fuentes, in addition to Benítez, Monsiváis, and Cuevas, signs a letter (*Siempre*, No. 910) in answer to an allusion to Paz made by the then president of Mexico (*Siempre*, No. 909).]

————, "Seis cartas de Carlos Fuentes a Octavio Paz," *R.I.*, No. 74, enero-mayo 1971, pp. 17–29.

G

G.A., "Octavio Paz, *Corriente alterna*," *R. y F.*, No. 7, mayo-junio 1968, pp. 159–60.

Gally, Hector, "Sobre la crítica invisible" [Comments on *Posdata*], *L.C. en M.*, No. 898, 9 sept. 1970, p. XII.

Gálvez, Ramón, "Octavio Paz, el poeta," *M. en la C.*, No. 51, 22 enero 1950, p. 7.

García Ponce, Juan, Review of *Cuatro poetas . . .*, *U. de M.*, Vol. XVII, No. 12, agosto 1963, pp. 29–30.

————, "El poder de la poesía," *L.C. en M.*, No. 88, 23 oct. 1963, pp. XVI–XVIII.

————, "Pensamiento de poeta" [On *Cuadrivio* and *Los signos en rotación*], *U. de M.*, Vol. XX, No. 3, nov. 1965, p. 32.

————, "La poesía. Libros antiguos, libros nuevos y el milagro renovado de Octavio Paz," *L.C. en M.*, Vol. 654, Supl. No. 203, 5 enero 1966, pp. XIII–XIV.

————, "El otro lado del mundo" [On *Ladera este*], Supl. de *Siempre*, No. 850, 8 oct. 1969, pp. IX–XII.

————, See "Homenaje a Octavio Paz" in letter H of this bibliography.

García Terrés, Jaime, Review of *Libertad bajo palabra*, *U. de M.*, Vol. XVI, No. 1, sept. 1961, p. 31.

Gastelum, Bernardo J., "A propósito de Octavio Paz," *M. en la C.*, 3 sept. 1967, p. 1.

Gil-Albert, Juan. "Octavio Paz" [On *Bajo tu clara sombra*], *H. de E.*, No. VIII, agosto 1937.

————, "America en el recuerdo y la poesía de Octavio Paz," *Letr. de M.*, No. 1, 15 enero 1943, pp. 5–11.

Gimferrer, Pedro, "El testimonio de O. Paz," *Ins.*, No. 239, 1966.

————, "Dos nuevos libros de O. Paz" [On *Puertas al campo* and *Vrindaban*], *Ins.*, Nos. 248–49, 1967.

Goetzinger, Judith. [See Bernard, Judith Ann, and No. 74 of *R.I.*]

Gómez-Gil, Orlando, *Historia crítica de la literatura hispanoamericana* (New York-London-Toronto, 1968), pp. 662–64.

González Casanova, Henrique, "Verdad llena de vida," *G.I.*, No. 6, 5 agosto 1962, p. 2.

González, Eduardo, "Octavio Paz and the critique of the Pyramid," *Diacritics*, Fall 1972, Vol. II, No. 3, pp. 30–34.

González Lanuza, Eduardo, "Octavio Paz: *A la orilla del mundo*," *Sur*, No. 109, nov. 1943, pp. 70–74.

González Noriega, Santiago, "Octavio Paz: *Corriente alterna*" *Cuad. Hisp.*, No. 236, agosto 1969, pp. 516–18.

Grande, Félix, "Un escritor errante para lectores errantes" [On *Ladera este*], *Vis.*, 21 dic. 1969, pp. 112–14.

Guardia, Angel, "Teatro en México. Segundo programa de Poesía en Alta Voz. *La hija de Rappaccini* de O. Paz," *M. en la C.*, No. 386, 12 agosto 1956, p. 5.

Guerra Castellanos, Eduardo, "Octavio Paz: Poeta de la soledad violenta," *Hum.*, No. 7, 1966, pp. 145–53.

Guibert, Rita, "Octavio Paz," *Seven Voices*. Alfred A. Knopf, 1973, pp. 183–275.

H

Hernández, David, "Dos salidas del laberinto de Octavio Paz," *A. y L.*, Año 12, No. 1, marzo 1969, pp. 31–44.

Hernández, Juan José, "Octavio Paz: *El arco y la lira*," *Sur*, No. 252, mayo-julio 1958, pp. 76–78.

Homenaje a Octavio Paz" [J. E. Pacheco, C. Monsiváis, J. V. Rojo, J. García Ponce, G. Zaid, H. Batis, *et al.*], *Siempre*, No. 738 (Supl. 287), 16 agosto 1967, pp. I–XIII.

Huerta, Efraín, Sobre el poema "No pasarán," *T.P.*, No. 3, marzo 1937, p. 45.

I

Iduarte, Andrés, Review of *El laberinto de la soledad*, *R.H.M.*, Vol. XXVII, No. 1, enero 1951, pp. 53–54.

———, "Octavio Paz y el mundo de don Pedro de Alba," *M. en la C.*, No. 759, 6 oct. 1963, p. 1, 9.

I.R.F., "Octavio Paz y su último libro," *M. N.*, Nos. 51–52, sept.-oct. 1970, pp. 120–22.

J

Jiménez, José Olivio, *Antología de la poesía hispanoamericana contemporánea. 1914–1970* (Madrid: Alianza Editorial, 1971), pp. 471–95.

Josef, Bela, *Historia da literatura hispano-americana dos origens à atualidade* (Petró polis: Editora Jozes Lda., 1971), pp. 287–88.

Joset, Jacques, "Des 'Mots de la tribu' a la liberté sous parole. Réflexions sur la parole poétique d'Octavio Paz," *M.R.*, t. XIX, No. 4, 4to. trimestre, 1969, pp. 1–30.

Juin, Hubert, "A la recherche du Mexique," *L.F.*, No. 795, 22–28 oct. 1959, 3.

K

King, Lloyd, "Surrealism and the Sacred in the Aesthetic Credo of Octavio Paz," *H.R.*, Vol. XXXVII, No. 3, July 1969, pp. 383–93.

Kourim, Zdenek, "Marcel Duchamp, visto por Octavio Paz," *C.H.*, Nos. 263–64, (May-June 1972), pp. 520–29.

L

Labastida, Jaime, "Un artículo crítico sobre Octavio Paz," *G.I.*, No. 11, 9 sept. 1962, p. 3.

———, "Conferencia," *V.E.*, No. 5, 15 oct. 1964, p. 13.

Lacôte, René, "Octavio Paz," *L.F.*, 7 julio 1966 [In Spanish: "Octavio Paz y su lenguaje poético," *M. en la C.*, 6 agosto 1967, p. 3.]

Lambert, Jean-Clarence, Prologue to the French translation of *Aigle ou Soleil?*; *F.L.*, 27 Janv. 1969, p. 28.

———, "La obra de Octavio Paz juzgada en Francia," *M. en la C.*, No. 483, 15 junio 1958, p. 3.

Lamothe, Louis, *Los mayores poetas latinoamericanos de 1850 a 1950* (Mexico, 1950).

Larrea, Elba M., "Octavio Paz, poeta de America," *R.N.C.*, Nos. 162–63, enero-abril 1964, pp. 78–88; *At.*, No. 405, julio-sept. 1964, pp. 159–68.

Laus, "Octavio Paz: La crítica de la significación," Interview. *D.C.*, 16 abril 1967, p. 1.

Leal, Luis, "Octavio Paz: *El laberinto de la soledad*," *R.I.*, No. 49, enero-julio 1960, pp. 154–86.

———, "Un poema de Octavio Paz," *Hisp.*, Vol. 48, No. 4, dic. 1965, pp. 841–42.

———, *Breve historia de la literatura hispanoamericana* (New York: Alfred A. Knopf, 1971), pp. 273–76 and 323–25. See also No. 74 of *R.I.*

Leal, Néstor, "Octavio Paz, ensayista," *Im.*, No. 17, 15/30 enero 1968, p. 22. [On *Puertas al campo* and *Corriente alterna*.]

Lefebure, Henri. "La philosophie et le poète," *L.Q.L.*, 16–30 avril 1972, pp. 20–21.

Leiva, Raúl, "La poesía de Octavio Paz," *M. en la C.*, No. 133, 19 agosto 1951, p. 3.

———, Review of *Libertad bajo palabra, Rev. G.*, 2da. epoca, t. I, No. 2, julio-septiembre 1951, pp. 165–69.

———, "Un nuevo libro de Octavio Paz: *Semillas para un himno*,"*M. en la C.*, No. 298, 5 dic. 1954, p. 2.

———, Review of *Puertas al campo*, *M. en la C.*, No. 311, 6 marzo 1955, p. 2.

———, Sobre *El arco y la lira*, *U. de M.*, Vol. X, No. 7, abril 1956, p. 4.

———, También sobre *El arco y la lira*, *M. en la C.*, No. 368, abril 1956, p. 3.

———, Review of *Piedra de sol*, *M. en la C.*, No. 449, 28 oct. 1957, p. 2.

———, *Imagen de la poesía mexicana contemporánea* (Mexico, 1959), pp. 205–26.

———, Review of *Cuatro poetas* . . . , *N.*, No. 5, 25 marzo 1963, p. 3.

———, "El libro [*sic*] hombre de soledad," *G.I.*, No. 55, 14 julio 1963, p. 4.

———, Review of *Cuadrivio*, *M. en la C.*, No. 863, 3 oct. 1965, p. 6.

Lemaître, Monique, "Octavio Paz: *Blanco*," *R.I.*, No. 66, 1968, pp. 380–82.

Lewald, Harald Ernest, *Antología de veinte poetas postmodernistas latinoamericanos* (Buenos Aires, 1967), pp. 109–15 [Bio-bibliographical note and poems.]

López Alvarez, Luis, Review of *El arco y la lira*, *C.*, Vol. XXII, enero-febrero 1957, pp. 118–19.

López Ruiz, Juvenal, "Octavio Paz: *Cuadrivio*," *R.N.C.*, No. 180, abril-mayo-junio 1967, p. 138.

López Urrutia, Margarita, "Blanco Moheno, Octavio Paz," *S.*, No. 914, 30 dic. 1970,

p. 6. [In response to a note by Blanco Moheno which appeared in *Siempre*, No. 911, which, in turn, was related to another note by F. Benítez C. Fuentes, C. Monsiváis, and Cuevas which was published in *Siempre*, No. 910.]

Lorenz, Gunter, W., "Amerikanische Magie, asiatische Mythen. Essays des mexikanischen Lyrikers Octavio Paz," *D.W.*, 15 octubre 1970. [A note on the German translation of *El laberinto de la soledad*.]

Lozano, Rafael, Review of *Libertad bajo palabra*, *I.L.*, 28 febr. 1961, p. 3.

Lunel, Augusto, Antonio, "Octavio Paz, poeta," *L.J.*, Vol. 24, No. 415, nov. 1964, pp. 2–4.

Lunel, Augusto, Review of *Semillas para un himno*, *M. en la C.*, No. 311, 6 marzo 1955, p. 2.

M

Magaña, Enriqueta L., "Octavio Paz: Inteligencia más espíritu claro y agudo," *Siempre*, No. 936, 2 junio 1971, p. 5.

Magaña Esquivel, Antonio, *Medio siglo de teatro mexicano: 1900–1961* (Mexico, 1964), pp. 158–59.

Maliandi, Ricardo, "El pronombre indecible. Multiplicidad y unidad en la obra de Octavio Paz," *Boletín del Instituto de Literatura*, La Plata, Argentina, No. 2, March 1972, pp. 9–29.

Mallán, Lloyd, ed. *A Little Anthology of Mexican Poetry* (New Directions, IX, 1966), pp. 121–39.

Mandiargues. See Pieyre de Mandiargues, André.

Maples Arce, Manuel, *Antología de la poesía mexicana moderna* (Roma, 1940), pp. 417–27 [Bio-bibliographical note and poems.]

Marco, Joaquin, *Nueva literatura en España y en América*. Barcelona: Lumen, 1972.

Martín, María, "Octavio Paz y la literatura de Francia," *D.C.*, 2 agosto 1964, p. 8.

Martínez, José Luis, Review of *Entre la piedra y la flor*, *L. de M.*, Vol. 3, No. 5, 15 mayo 1941, p. 4.

———, *Literatura mexicana siglo XX* (Mexico, 1949–1950), t. I, pp. 130–31; t. II, pp. 93–94.

———, *El ensayo mexicano moderno* (Mexico, 1958), t. II, pp. 302–303.

———, *El trato con los escritores* (Mexico, 1961), pp. 134–35.

M.D.A., "*Salamandra*, de Octavio Paz," *P. de S.A.*, Año *TL*, t. XXXII, No. XLV, pp. 214–16.

Melo, Juan Vicente, "A través de la música," *L.C. en M.*, No. 287, 16 agosto, 1967, p. V.

Meloche, Verna M., "El ciclo de Paz" [On *Piedra de Sol*], *Hispan.*, Año V, No. 13, sept. 1961, pp. 45–51.

Mendoza, María Luisa, "Algunas preguntas a Octavio Paz," *G.I.*, No. 6, 5 agosto 1962, p. 1.

———, "La O por lo redondo" [Review of *Cuadrivio*], *D.*, 29 sept. 1965 p. 2.

Marmall, Thomas, "Octavio Paz: El laberinto de la soledad y el sicoanálisis de la historia," *C.A.*, enero-febrero 1958, pp. 97–114.

——, "Octavio Paz y las máscaras," *C.A.*, Vol. XXXI, No. 1, enero-febrero, 1972, pp. 195–207.

Millán, María del Carmen, "La inteligencia mexicana," *M. en la C.*, No. 728, 3 marzo 1963, p. 7.

Molina, Antonio. See A.M.

Monsiváis, Carlos, *La poesía mexicana del siglo XX* (Mexico, 1966), pp. 55–58; 575 ss.

——, "El escritor vivo" (See "Homenaje a Octavio Paz" in section H of this bibliography).

Monteforte Toledo, Mario, Review of *La estación violenta*, *H.*, Vol. VII, Nos. 50–51, julio-oct. 1958, pp. 133–34.

Mora, Dolores de la, "¿Cómo nace un poeta?", *G.I.*, No. 68, 17 oct. 1963, p. 1.

Müller-Bergh, Klaus. See No. 74 of *R.I.*

Munier, Roger, "Introduction" to *L'arc et la lyre* (Paris, 1966).

Murphy, Robert. See *Review 72*.

N

La Nación [Buenos Aires], Supl. Literario Dominical, 28 dic. 1969. [Issue devoted to "Octavio Paz, poeta." Articles: Enrique Pezzoni, "La pregunta incesante"; Osvaldo Rossler, "La aventura de las palabras," plus a "Poema" by Octavio Paz.]

Nava, Thelma, "Notas de poesía" [Review of "Viento entero"], *D.*, 22 enero 1966, p. 11.

Needleman, Ruth A., "The Poetry of Octavio Paz." [Ph.D. Dissertation, 1970, Harvard University. See also No. 74 of *R.I.*]

Nelken, Zoila E., "Los avatares del tiempo en *Piedra de sol* de Octavio Paz," *Hisp.*, Vol. LI, No. 1, March 1969, pp. 92–94.

Nugent, Robert, "Structure and Meaning in Octavio Paz's *Piedra de Sol*," *K.F.L.Q.*, No. 13, 1966, pp. 138–46.

O

Ocampo Gómez, Aurora and Ernesto Prado Velázquez, *Diccionario de escritores mexicanos* (Mexico: UNAM, 1970), pp. 278–80.

Olcik, Daniel, "Octavio Paz, il poeta ambasciatore," *L.F.L.*, 26 gennaio 1967. [On *Libertá sulla parola*.]

Ortega, Julio, "Notas sobre Octavio Paz," *C.H.*, No. 231, marzo 1969, pp. 1–14.

P

Pacheco, José Emilio, "*Las peras del olmo*, de Octavio Paz," *Est.*, Año II, No. 7, Otoño 1957, pp. 358–60.

——, "Piedra de sol," *Est.*, III, No. 9, Primavera 1958, p. 99. [This is a sonnet signed with the initials J.E.P.]

——, "*La estación violenta*, de Octavio Paz," *Est.*, III, No. 11, Otoño 1958, pp. 334–36.

——, "*Libertad bajo palabra*, de Octavio Paz," *M. en la C.*, No. 624, 26 febrero 1961, p. 3 [See also No. 74 of *R.I.*].

See "Homenaje a Octavio Paz" in section H of this bibliography.

Padilla, Hugo, Review of *Las peras del olmo*, *U. de M.*, Vol. XII, No. 1, sept. 1957, pp. 29–30.

Palau, Josep, Review of *Aigle ou soleil?*, *L.F.*, Vol. LIV, Nov. 1957, pp. 644–45.

Palau de Nemes, Graciela, See No. 74 of *R.I.*

Panico, Marie Joan, "Motifs and Expressions in Octavio Paz: An Explanation of His Spoken Anthology." [Ph.D. Dissertation, 1966, University of Maryland.]

Paramio, Ludolfo, "Paz, Octavio: *Conjunciones y disyunciones*," *Ins.*, No. 290, pp. 8–9.

Paulet Legorreta, Jorge, Letter on Octavio Paz, *Siempre*, mayo 1971.

Peñalosa, Joaquín Antonio, "Octavio Paz: *El arco y la lira*," *Abs.*, Vol. XXXII, No. 2, 1968, pp. 242–43.

———, Peñalosa, Javier, Review of *Cuadrivio*, *N.*, No. 35, 25 nov. 1965, p. 4.

Pezzoni, Enrique. See *La Nación*.

———, "*Blanco*: La respuesta al deseo," *R.I.*, Vol. XXXVIII, No. 78, enero-marzo 1972, pp. 57–72.

Phillips, Rachel, *The Poetic Modes of Octavio Paz* (Oxford: The Clarendon Press, 1972). [See also No. 74 of *R.I.*]

Piatier, Jacqueline, "*L'arc et la lyre*, de Octavio Paz," *L.M.*, 11 Dec. 1965.

Picón-Salas, Mariano, "Mexico en Octavio Paz" [On *El laberinto de la soledad*], *C.*, XLII, mayo 1960, pp. 108–10.

Pieyre de Mandiargues, André, Review of *Aigle ou soleil?*, *N.R.F.*, LVI, Janv. 1958, pp. 325–28. [Included in *Le Belvedere* (Paris, 1958), pp. 103–108.]

———, "Poésie mexicaine," *N.R.F.*, Vol. 19, No. 109, 1962, pp. 103–106.

Pizarnik, Alejandra, "El Premio Internacional de Poesía: *Salamandra*," *M. en la C.*, No. 767, 10 dic. 1963, p. 5.

Poniatowska, Elena, "Octavio Paz, roca solar de la poesía [Translation of the Lambert prologue to the French translation of *Aigle ou soleil?*], *M. en la C.*, No. 450, 3 nov. 1957, p. 3.

———, "Octavio Paz ante el detector de mentiras," *L.C. en M.*, No. 296, 18 oct. 1967, pp. I–V.

R

R. C. [Rafael Cadenas], "Sendas de Oku...," *Papeles*, No. 13, mayo 1971, pp. 167–68.

Ravoni, Marcelo y Antonio Porta, *Poeti ispanoamericani contemporanei* (Milano: Feltrinelli Editore, 1970), pp. 257–75.

Ramírez de Aguilar, Roberto, "Octavio Paz: Poesía y posición," *D.C.*, 24 agosto 1958, p. 1.

Remley Rambo, Ann Marie, "The Presence of Woman in the Poetry of Octavio Paz," *Hisp.*, Vol. LI, No. 2, May 1968, pp. 259–64.

Requena, Julio, "Poética del tiempo en Octavio Paz," *R.U.N.C.*, Vol. 7, No. 13, marzo-agosto 1966, pp. 61–107.

Review 72. Fall. Center for Inter-American Relations, "Focus on Octavio Paz and Severo Sarduy" [Interview by Rita Guibert and articles by Guillermo Sucre, Anna Balakian, Anne d'Harnoncourt, and Robert Murphy].

Revista Iberoamericana, Vol. XXXVII, No. 74, enero-marzo 1971. [Devoted in its entirety to Octavio Paz.]

Reyes Nevares, Salvador, Review of *La estación violenta, M. en la C.*, No. 495, 7 sept. 1958, p. 4.

———, *Panorama das Literaturas das Americas* (Director: Joaquim de Montezuma de Carvalho, Angola, 1963), pp. 2011–15.

Rius, Luis, Review of the anthology of F. Pessoa, *A.L.*, Año II, 1962.

Rivas Sáinz, Arturo, "La poesía de Octavio Paz," *L. de M.*, Vol. I, No. 6, 15 junio 1943, pp. 1–2; 5, 8.

———, "*El arco y la lira*, de Octavio Paz," *Est.*, Vol. I, No. 3, Otoño 1956, pp. 402–404.

Rodman, Selden, *Mexican Journal: The Conquerors Conquered* (New York, 1958). [Memoirs of a trip to Mexico, with interviews of writers, including Octavio Paz.]

Rodríguez Monegal, Emir, "Octavio Paz: Crítica y Poesía," *M.N.*, No. 21, marzo 1968, pp. 55–62. [See also No. 74 of *R.I.*]

Rodríguez Padrón, Jorge, "Octavio Paz: El escritor y la experiencia poética," *C.H.*, No. 243, marzo 1970, pp. 671–78. [Concerning *La centena*.]

Roggiano, Alfredo. See No. 74 of *R.I.*

Rojas Rodríguez, Pedro, Review of *El laberinto de la soledad, F. y L.*, Vol. XL, oct.-dic. 1950, pp. 370–77.

Rojas Rosillo, Isaac, "Los libros. Vigilias de un soñador," *M. en la C.*, No. 40, 6 nov. 1949, p. 7.

Rojo, Vicente. See Benítez, Fernando, *et al.*

Rossler, Osvaldo. See *La Nación*.

Roy, Claude, "Une démocratie poétique [On *Ladera este* and *Renga*], *L.N.O.*, No. 330, du 8 au 14 mars 1971, pp. 47–48.

Rubio y Rubio, Alfonso, "Dos poetas mexicanos contemporáneos," *Tr.*, Año 10, No. 4, julio-agosto 1951, pp. 288–98.

S

Salazar, Alejandro, "*Salamandra*, de Octavio Paz," *E.N.*, 30 dic. 1962.

Salazar Bondy, Sebastian, Review of *El laberinto de la soledad, Sur*, Nos. 195–96. enero-febrero 1951, pp. 64–67.

Sánchez, José G., "Aspects of Surrealism in the Work of Octavio Paz." [Ph.D. Dissertation, 1970, University of Colorado.]

Sánchez, Porfirio, "Imágenes y metafisica en la poesía de Octavio Paz; la negación del tiempo y del espacio," *C.A.*, enero-febrero 1970, pp. 149–59.

Sánchez Barbudo, Antonio, "A la orilla del mundo," *E.H.P.*, Año 1, No. 1, 15 abril 1943, pp. 44–48.

Sarduy, Severo, "Renga," *Libre*, No. 21, dic.-enero-febrero 1971–1972, pp. 140–41.

Seabrook, Roberta, "Octavio Paz. *Viento entero*," *R.H.M.*, XXXIII, julio-oct. 1967, pp. 364ff. [See also No. 74 of *R.I.*]

Segall, Brenda, "Symbolism in Octavio Paz's 'Puerta condenada,'" *Hisp.*, Vol. LIII, May 1970, pp. 212–19.

Segovia, Tomás, "Entre la gratuidad y el compromiso," *R.M. de L.*, VIII, nov.–dic. 1956, pp. 102–13.

———, Review of *Sendas de Oku*, *U. de M.*, Vol. XI, No. 9, mayo 1957, p. 30.

———, "Poesía y un poeta" [On *La estación violenta*], *R.M. de L.* (Second series), I, marzo 1959, pp. 61–64.

———, "Nuevos poemas de Octavio Paz," *R.M. de L.* (Second series), XII–XV, junio–sept. 1960, pp. 82–84.

———, "La obra poetica de Octavio Paz" [On *Libertad bajo palabra*], *R.M. de L.* (Second series), XVI–XVIII, oct.–dic. 1960, pp. 73–75.

———, "Una obra maestra de Octavio Paz. *Piedra de Sol*," *L.C. en M.*, No. 189, 29 sept. 1965, p. XIII.

Selva, Mauricio de la, "Octavio Paz," *D.C.*, 14 abril 1957, p. 2.

———, Review of *La estación violenta*, *C.A.*, t. CI, 6 nov.–dic. 1958, pp. 284–85.

———, "Asteriscos" [Review of *Salamandra*], *D.C.*, 23 dic. 1962, p. 4.

———, "Octavio Paz: Búsquedas infructuosas," *C. de B.A.*, Año IV, No. 7, julio 1963, pp. 17–25.

———, "Asteriscos" [Review of *Magia de la risa*], *D.C.*, 24 marzo 1963, p. 3.

———, Review of *Cuatro poetas . . .* , *C.A.*, julio-agosto 1963, pp. 279–80.

Siempre, No. 738 (Supl. L.C. en M., No. 287), 16 agosto 1967. [Devoted in its entirety to Octavio Paz.]

Silva Villalobos, A., Review of *Semillas para un himno*, *M.*, No. 2, mayo-junio 1955, pp. 37–38.

———, Review of *Las peras del olmo*, *M.*, No. 15, julio-agosto 1957, pp. 40–41.

Solana, Rafael, "Política literaria," *P.*, 13 nov. 1938, pp. 5–6.

Sologurén, Javier, "Octavio Paz, la India, la visión poetica," *Am.*, No. 11, dic. 1969, pp. 92–93.

Somlyó, György, "Octavio Paz y *Piedra de Sol*," *Dial.*, No. 5, julio-agosto 1966, pp. 8–12.

Souza, Raymond D., "The World, Symbol and Synthesis in Octavio Paz," *Hisp.*, XLVII, 1 March 1964, pp. 60–65.

Stierlin, Henri, "El mexicano Octavio Paz, un gran poeta de nuestro tiempo," *T. de G.* [1958?].

Suárez, Luis, "Octavio Paz habla desde París," *M. en la C.*, No. 560, 7 dic. 1959, p. 2.

Sucre, Guillermo, Note on *La estación violenta*, Supl. Lit. de *El Nacional*, Caracas, LXVI, oct. 1958, pp. 105–105.

———, "Lo que se piensa en el extranjero de la poesía de Octavio Paz," *U. de M.*, Vol. XIII, No. 3, nov. 1958, pp. 28–29. [A reprinting of the previously mentioned note in *El Nacional*.]

———, "El poema: Un archipiélago de signos," *Im.*, No. 24, 1/15 mayo 1968, p. 24. [Reprinted with the title "Blanco: Un archipielago de signos" in *Siempre*, No. 790, 4 agosto 1968, p. VII.]

———, "Poesía y crítica en movimiento" [On *Discos visuales* and *Marcel Duchamp*], *Im.*, No. 45, 15/31 marzo 1969, pp. 4–5. [Reprinted with the title "Las síntesis, las visiones y las correspondencias de Octavio Paz" in *Siempre*, No. 840, 30 julio 1969, pp. VI–VIII. See also No. 74 of *R.I.*]

Szyzlo, Fernando de, "Creación y silencio en Marcel Duchamp," *Am.*, marzo 1969, pp. 83–85.

T

Tentori, Francesco, *Poesia Ispano-Americana del 900* (Parma: Guanda, 1957), pp. 382–91 and 470–71.

U

Usigli, Rodolfo, "Poeta en libertad," *C.A.*, Vol. XLIX, No. 1, enero-febrero 1950, pp. 293–300.

V

Valdivieso, Mercedes, "Entre el tlatoani y el caudillo. Octavio Paz: post data a *Posdata*," *L.C. en M.*, No. 876, 8 abril 1970, pp. II–IV.

Varios: "El premio a Octavio Paz es un triunfo y un honor para las letras nacionales," *D.*, 11 sept. 1963, p. 3. [Testimonials by Carlos Pellicer, Alí Chumacero, Salvador Novo, José Gorostiza, and Andrés Henestrosa.]

Veiravé, Alfredo, "Octavio Paz: *Discos visuales*," *Sur*, No. 318, mayo-junio 1969, pp. 82–84.

Venegas, Roberto, "Poetas mexicanos. Octavio Paz," *D.C.*, 30 agosto 1964, pp. 3, 7.

Vernengo, Roberto, "Una entrevista con Octavio Paz," *Sur*, No. 227, marzo-abril 1954, pp. 61–64. [The same article also appears in *U. de M.*, Vol. VIII, No. 6, febrero 1954, p. 24.]

Villela, Víctor, "Octavio Paz. Rubén Bonifaz Nuño," *E.H.C.*, No. 34, 3 julio 1966, p. 2.

Vitier, Cintio, "Prólogo a una antología," *R.M. de L.*, IV, marzo-abril 1956, pp. 388–95.

———, "Octavio Paz, *La estación violenta*," *N.R.C.*, Vol. I, No. 1, abril-junio 1959, pp. 144–46.

Volek, Emil. See No. 74 of *R.I.*

W

Wilson, J. "The Poetry of Octavio Paz." [M.Ph. Thesis, University of London, 1968.]

Wing, George Gordon, "Octavio Paz: Poetry, Politics, and the Myth of the Mexicano." [Ph.D. Dissertation, University of California, Berkeley, 1960.]

X

Xirau, Ramón, "La poesía de Octavio Paz," *C.A.*, Vol. LVIII, No. 4, julio-agosto 1951, pp. 288–98.

———, *Tres poetas de la soledad* [Gorostiza, Villaurrutia, Paz] (Mexico, 1955), pp. 39–70. [On *Libertad bajo palabra*, *El laberinto de la soledad*, and *Himno entre ruinas* with the title "La dialéctica de la soledad."]

———, Review of *Semillas para un himno*, *U. de M.*, Vol. IX, Nos. 5–6, enero-febrero 1955, p. 28.

————, Review of *Las peras del olmo, R.M. de L.*, XI, mayo-junio 1957, pp. 81–84.

————, "La poesía," *M. en la C.*, No. 500, 13 oct. 1958.

————, "Notas a *Piedra de sol*," *U. de M.*, Vol. XII, No. 6, febrero 1958, pp. 15–16.

————, "Laberintos en torno a laberintos," *R.M. de L.*, (New period), IV, oct. 1959, pp. 27–28. [Reprinted in Vol. II of *U. de M.: Nuestra década*, pp. 648–53.]

————, Introduction to the Italian translation of *El laberinto de la soledad* (Milano: Silva, 1961).

————, "Tres calas en la reflexión poética" [On Sor Juana, Gorostiza, and Paz], *L.P. y el H.*, No. 17, enero-marzo 1961, pp. 69–85.

————, *Poesía hispanoamericana y española* (Mexico, 1961), pp. 45–55.

————, *Poetas de México y España* (Mexico, 1961), pp. 45–55.

————, "Nota a Octavio Paz," *Ins.*, No. 184, marzo 1962, p. 3.

————, "The Poetry of Octavio Paz," *M.Q.R.*, Año 1, No. 1, Winter 1962, pp. 26–28.

————, Los hechos y la cultura" [On *Salamandra*], N. (Second period), No. II, 25 febrero 1963, p. 12.

————, "Dos libros de Octavio Paz: *Cuadrivio y Los signos en rotación*," *Dial.*, nov.-dic. 1965, pp. 39–40.

————, Review of *Viento entero, Dial.*, enero-febrero 1966, p. 42.

————, "*Blanco*, de Octavio Paz," *Dial.*, No. 20 marzo-abril 1968, p. 29.

————, *Octavio Paz: El sentido de la palabra* (Mexico, 1970). [See also No. 74 of *R.I.*]

————, " 'Trivio' de Octavio Paz," *Poesía iberoamericana contemporánea* (Mexico: Secretaria de Educación Pública, 1972), pp. 113–37.

————, "El mono gramático," *Plural*, No. 13 (October 1972), p. 36.

————, See No. 74 of *R.I.*

Y

Young, Howard T., Review of *La estación violenta, B. Abr.*, XXXIII, 4, Autumn 1959, pp. 415–16.

Yurkievich, Saul, "La topoética de Octavio Paz," *Car.*, No. 12, 1969, pp. 183–89. [See also No. 74 of R.I.].

Z

Zabludovsky, Jacobo, "La hora de Octavio Paz," *S.*, No. 535, 25 sept. 1963, pp. 12 and 69.

Zaid, Gabriel, "Notas convergentes sobre Octavio Paz," Supl. to *Siempre*, No. 735, 26 julio 1967, p. V.

————, "Dos notas sobre Octavio Paz," Supl. to *Siempre,* No. 850, 8 oct. 1969, pp. VI–VIII.

————, "La poesía," Supl. to *Siempre*, No. 706, 4 enero 1967, p. V.

————, See also "Homenaje a Octavio Paz" in section H of this bibliography.

Zimmerman, Rachel. See Phillips, Rachel.

ABBREVIATIONS

Abs. Abside. Mexico.

A. de la P. M. Anuario de la poesía mexicana. INBA, Mexico.

A. L. Anuario de Letras. Fac. de F y Letras, Universidad Nac. Aut. de México.

Am. Amaru. Lima, Peru.

Amer. Américas, Washington, USA.

At. Atenea, Concepción, Chile.

A. y L. Armas y Letras. Universidad de Nuevo León, Mexico.

B. Abr. Books Abroad. University of Oklahoma, USA.

B. B. H. Boletín Bibliográfico de la Secretaría de Hacienda . . . Mexico.

Bull. Bulletin of the Centro Mexicano de Escritores.

C. Cuadernos. Paris.

C. A. Cuadernos Americanos. Mexico.

Car. Caravelle. Université de Toulouse. France.

C. de B. A. Cuadernos de Bellas Artes. INBA. Mexico.

C. H. Cuadernos Hispanoamericanos. Madrid.

D. Diario *El Día.* Mexico.

Dav. Davar. Buenos Aires.

D. C. Diorama de la Cultura, Supl. literario del diario *Excelsior.* Mexico.

Dial. Dialogos. Mexico.

D. W. Die Welt. Hamburg. Germany.

Eco. Revista *Eco.* Bogotá. Colombia.

E. H. C. El Heraldo Cultural. Supl. literario de *El Heraldo de México.*

E. H. P. El Hijo Pródigo. Mexico.

E. N. Diario *El Nacional.* Caracas. Venezuela.

Est. Estaciones. Mexico.

Exc. Diario. *Excelsior.* Mexico.

F. y L. Filosofía y Letras. Mexico.

G. I. El Gallo Ilustrado. Supl. dominical del diario *El Día.* Mexico.

G. L. Guión Literario. Supl. literario del diario *El Día.* Mexico.

H. Humanismo. Mexico.

H. de E. Hora de España.

Hisp. Hispania. USA.

Hispan. Hispanófila. USA.
H. R. Hispanic Review. University of Philadelphia. USA.
Hum. Humanitas. Universidad de Nuevo León. Mexico.

I. L. Indice Literario. Supl. literario de *El Universal.* Caracas.
Im. Imagen. Caracas.
Ins. Insula. Madrid.

K. F. L. Q. Kentucky Foreign Languages Quarterly. University of Kentucky. USA.

Libre. Revista *Libre.* Paris.
L. C. en M. La Cultura en México. Supl. literario de *Siempre.* Mexico.
L. de M. Letras de México. Mexico.
L'Ex. L'Express. Paris.
L. F. Les Lettres Françaises. Paris.
L. F. L. La Fiera Letteraria. Rome.
L. J. La Justicia. Mexico.
L. M. Le Monde des Livres. Paris.
L. N. Les Lettres Nouvelles (Nouvelle Série). Paris.
L. N. O. Le Nouvel Observateur. Paris.
L. P. y el H. La Palabra y el Hombre. Universidad Veracruzana. Mexico.
L. Q. L. La Quinzaine Littéraire. Paris.

M. Metáfora. Mexico.
M. en la C. México en la Cultura. Supl. literario del diario *Novedades.* Mexico.
M. L. Mexican Life. Mexico.
M. N. Mundo Nuevo. Paris-Buenos Aires.
M. R. Marche Romane. Université de Liège. Belgium.
M. Q. R. The Mexico Quarterly Review. Mexico City College. Mexico.

N. Nivel. Mexico.
Nac. Diario *La Nación.* Buenos Aires.
N. R. C. Nueva Revista Cubana. Habana. Cuba.
N. R. F. La Nouvelle Revue Française. Paris.
N. Y. T. B. R. Supplement of *The New York Times.* New York.

P. Diario *El Popular.* Mexico.
Papeles. Revista *Papeles.* Caracas. Venezuela.
P. de S. A. Papeles de San Armadans. Palma de Mallorca. Spain.
P. P. Papel de Poesía. Saltillo. Mexico.
Preuves. Revista *Preuves.* Paris.

Q. I. A. Quaderni Iberi-Americani. Florence. Italy.

R. de B. A. Revista de Bellas Artes. INBA. Mexico.
R. G. Revista de Guatemala. Guatemala.
R. H. M. Revista Hispánica Moderna. Columbia University. USA.
R. I. Revista Iberoamericana. Mexico-Pittsburgh.
R. I. B. Revista Interamericana de Bibliografía. Washington. USA.
R. L. M. Revista de Literaturas Modernas. Mendoza. Argentina.
R. M. de L. Revista Mexicana de Literatura. Mexico.
R. N. C. Revista Nacional de Cultura Caracas.
R. S. Revista de la Semana. Supl. literario de *El Universal.* Mexico.
R. U. N. C. Revista de la Universidad Nacional de Córdoba. Argentina.
R. y F. Razón y Fábula. Bogotá. Colombia.

Siempre. Semanario *Siempre.* Mexico, in which is included the literary supplement *La cultura en México.* The numbering of the supplement is distinct from that of the periodical in which it is found. At times we cite *Siempre,* other times we cite *L. C. en M.*
Sur. Revista *Sur.* Argentina.
Sv. L. Svetova Literatura. Prague. Czechoslovakia.
Sym. Symposium. University of Syracuse. USA.

T. Tiempo. Mexico.
T. de G. Tribune de Genève. Geneva. Switzerland.
T. N. Tierra Nueva. Mexico.
T. P. Taller Poético. Mexico.
Tr. Trivium. Monterrey. Mexico.
T. L. S. The Times Literary Supplement. London.
T. S. R. The Southern Review. USA.

U. Diario *El Universal.* Mexico.
U. de M. Revista de la Universidad de México.

V. E. Vida Escolástica. Universidad de Hidalgo. Mexico.
Vis. Visión. Mexico.
V. U. Vida Universitaria. Monterrey. Mexico.

University of Pittsburgh

Octavio Paz in *Books Abroad* 1951-1973

1. *Libertad bajo palabra* (Mexico, Tezontle, 1949), reviewed by Donato Internoscia in *BA* 25:2, p. 160.
2. *El laberinto de la soledad* (Mexico, Cuadernos Americanos, new ed. 1950), reviewed by Muna Lee in *BA* 33:4, pp. 415–16.
3. *La estación violenta* (Mexico, Fondo de Cultura Económica, 1958), reviewed by Howard T. Young in *BA* 33:4, pp. 415–16.
4. *An Anthology of Mexican Poetry*, Octavio Paz ed., Samuel Beckett tr. (Bloomington, Ind., Indiana University Press, 1958), reviewed by George G. Wing in *BA* 33:4, p. 465.
5. *Las peras del olmo* (Mexico, Imprenta Universitaria, 1957), reviewed by Manuel H. Guerra in *BA* 34:1, p. 65.
6. *El laberinto de la soledad* (Mexico, Fondo de Cultura Económica, 2nd ed., 1959) reviewed by Kurt L. Levy in *BA* 35:1, p. 76.
7. José Vázquez-Amaral, "Tradition and Innovation in the Occidental Lyric of the Last Decade: IV. Present-Day Hispanic Lyric," in *BA* 35:3, pp. 212–13.
8. *Libertad bajo palabra: Obra poética (1935–1957)* (Mexico, Fondo de Cultura Económica, 1960), reviewed by Dorothy Clotelle Clarke in *BA* 36:2, p. 185.
9. *Sun-Stone*, Peter Miller, tr. (Toronto, Contact Press, 1963), reviewed by Manuel Durán in *BA* 37:3, p. 367.
10. Manuel Durán, "Liberty and Eroticism in the Poetry of Octavio Paz," in *BA* 37:4, pp. 373–77.
11. In coll. with Alfonso Medellín, *Magia de la risa* (Xalapa, Universidad Veracruzana, 1962), reviewed by Johannes A. Gaertner in *BA* 38:4, p. 418.
12. *Cuadrivio* (Mexico, Mortiz, 1965), reviewed by Lawrence H. Klibbe in *BA* 41:1, pp. 79–80.
13. "Cochin" (poem), Lysander Kemp, tr., in *BA* 44:1, p. 51.
14. *Libertad bajo palabra* (Mexico, Fondo de Cultura Económica, new ed. 1968), reviewed by Klaus Müller-Bergh in *BA* 44:1, p. 88.
15. *La centena* (Barcelona, Barral, 1969) and *Ladera este* (Mexico, Mortiz, 1969), reviewed by Manuel Durán in *BA* 44:3, p. 448.

16. *Conjunciones y disyunciones* (Mexico, Mortiz, 1969), reviewed by Manuel Durán in *BA* 44:3, pp. 450–51.

17. Ramón Xirau, *Octavio Paz: el sentido de la palabra* (Mexico, Mortiz, 1970), reviewed by Manuel Durán in *BA* 44:4, p. 634.

18. *Posdata* (Mexico, Siglo XXI, 1970) reviewed by Manuel Durán in *BA* 45:2, p. 285.

19. *¿Aguila o sol? Eagle or Sun?*, Eliot Weinberger, tr. (New York, October House, 1970), reviewed by Gordon Brotherston in *BA* 45:4, p. 672.

20. "Symposium on Octavio Paz," in *BA* 46:4, pp. 541–614.

21. In coll. with Jacques Roubaud, Edoardo Sanguinetti, Charles Tomlinson, *Renga*, Octavio Paz, tr. (Mexico City, Mortiz, 1972), reviewed by Tom J. Lewis in *BA* 46:4, pp. 636–37.

22. George Gordon Wing, "Octavio Paz, or the Revolution in Search of an Actor," in *BA* 47:1, pp, 41–48.

The paper on which this book is printed bears the watermark of the University of Oklahoma Press and has an effective life of at least three hundred years.